The Belligerent Pr

The Belligerent Prelate:
An Alliance between Archbishop Daniel Mannix
and Eamon de Valera

By

Patrick Mannix

CAMBRIDGE
SCHOLARS
PUBLISHING

The Belligerent Prelate:
An Alliance between Archbishop Daniel Mannix and Eamon de Valera,
by Patrick Mannix

This book first published 2012. The present binding first published 2013.

Cambridge Scholars Publishing

12 Back Chapman Street, Newcastle upon Tyne, NE6 2XX, UK

British Library Cataloguing in Publication Data
A catalogue record for this book is available from the British Library

ISBN (10): 1-4438-4618-X, ISBN (13): 978-1-4438-4618-9

I dedicate this book to my family & friends who have provided the hours of countless support that made this dream become a reality.

Omnia Omnibus – All Things to All Men

—Archbishop Daniel Mannix's Episcopal Motto

TABLE OF CONTENTS

LIST OF ILLUSTRATIONS

Front Cover: President of The Irish Republic Eamon De Valera & Archbishop Daniel Mannix of Melbourne, Australia during their visit to Boys Town, Omaha, Nebraska – June 1920

FOREWORD

De Valera and Mannix: two leaders, one vision?

More than any other figure Eamon de Valera can be considered the architect of modern Ireland. A role at the forefront of revolutionary politics in the early Twentieth Century entailed direct engagement in several key stages of Ireland's emergence from the United Kingdom and British Empire. American citizenship and good fortune enabled de Valera to survive the bloody aftermath of the 1916 Rising when all other leaders of his stature were executed by the British military. By no means merely the last man standing, he steered the reorganization of militant Irish republicanism with skill, vision and determination and helped achieve the landslide democratic endorsement of the project in the 1918 General Election. Victory paved the way for the creation of the first Dáil, which, although unrecognized by Westminster, comprised the most democratic and sovereign authority in Irish history. Britain's repudiation of the will of the Irish electorate set the stage for the War of Independence and the dispiriting Civil War which ensued.

By then de Valera's path had already crossed that of the ascendant Daniel Mannix, who from 1917 served as Archbishop of Melbourne, a stronghold of Irish-Australian power and influence. Mannix shared de Valera's Munster origins, devout Catholicism and dynamic ambition. Physical detachment did not prevent the causes of Irish sovereignty and national identity providing common ground for two of the main voices on Ireland's destiny in the 1910s into the 1960s. The robust leadership of Mannix drove Australia's ethnic Irish and Catholic communities into the political centre of a new nation enjoying the benefits of 'home rule' from 1900. Achieving comparable advances in his native country was a life long goal which he addressed primarily through support for de Valera.

The personal bond between the two leaders was all the more striking for spanning the globe and multiple decades. Contexts inevitably shifted over time yet the common ground remained and this rare sense of international joint interest matured. Concurrent involvement in major campaigns against conscription in 1918 in both Ireland and Australia evidenced an early manifestation of this phenomenon. At the same time that de Valera became globally prominent as the public face of Sinn Fein, Mannix consolidated his position with the Catholic church in Australasia and used his growing religious constituency and temporal authority to bolster Ireland's nascent republican democracy.

A characteristically bold attempt at personal intervention was only prevented in August 1920 when British authorities seized Mannix in order to prevent him landing in Ireland during the War of Independence. The archbishop, however, could not be silenced and maintained his firm and open identification with the agenda of de Valera's clique. Both men experienced detention for their political activities, weathered the challenges of negotiating their ideological objectives with determined opponents and survived the general travails of occupying high office in restive times. De Valera, although defeated in a Civil War which claimed the lives of many close associates, rose to the office of President of Ireland and a leading position in the League of Nations. Mannix, perpetually controversial in Australian society, was unquestionably the country's most pre-eminent churchman when he died in office in Melbourne in 1963.

Patrick Mannix explores the origins of an unusual and complicated relationship in this compelling, detailed and nuanced new account. He draws on many new strands of analysis and information to provide a highly readable yet authoritative study of leadership, comradeship and power in the Irish world.

Dr. Ruan O'Donnell
University of Limerick
May 2012

PREFACE

This book is an examination and evaluation from a historical perspective of the alliance that was established and forged between the former taoiseach and President of Ireland, Eamon de Valera and the former president of Maynooth and archbishop of Melbourne, Australia, Dr Daniel Mannix.

Both men played a significant role, through their intervention in both the political and clerical fields, in the most formative years of Ireland's fight for independence and subsequent goal to stabilise the new state during the years 1916 to 1948. As relating to this period this book will examine how de Valera often turned to Mannix as a sort of fatherly figure for advice on a number of issues relating to Ireland's push for independence. These issues included the influence of the Irish diaspora, the taking of the oath of allegiance and the future of partition in Ireland. The vast Irish diaspora worldwide including Dr Mannix, through their support, both financially and physically, and through demonstrations held for Ireland, helped keep the push for autonomy alive.

Having examined the role the archbishop played through his relationship with de Valera and the clergy the book will appraise how Dr Mannix, so revered at one stage in Irish society, later became such an isolated and neglected figure in Irish history. This historical analysis will be grounded in research of both primary and secondary sources including previously undocumented oral evidence, archival papers, written public and private correspondence between the two characters and a range of visual sources.

ACKNOWLEDGEMENTS

This book originated during my Leaving Certificate year in the Intermediate School Killorglin. Therefore, my first debt is to my then history teacher Mr Shane O'Shea who first informed me of the connection between Archbishop Mannix and Eamon de Valera. This book would not have come to fruition; however, had it not been for the considerable support, guidance and perceptive criticism received from my supervisor Dr Ruan O'Donnell over the past number of years. I would also like to thank the staff and members of the History Department at the University of Limerick, especially Dr Bernadette Whelan, Dr John O'Callaghan, Dr Mícheál Ó hAodha and Paul Hayes for their help and support. I would also like to thank Dr John Logan and Dr Mary Harris for their constructive roles as examiners during my research masters degree.

In the process of researching and writing this book, I have greatly benefited from the kind and generous assistance of many people and institutions. Firstly, to Mr Jeremiah O'Callaghan who so kindly allowed me to use some of his own personal resources to help with the final fruition of this book. Sincere thanks also to Fr Brian Murphy for the numerous occasions he offered advice to me and pointed me in the right direction. I am extremely grateful to the Sisters of Mercy in Charleville for all their help, support and advice particularly Sr Mary Lyons and Sr Mary Coleman. To Brenda Niall for her advice, help and direction following on from her recent excellent research on Fr Hackett along with Danny Cusack for his help with sourcing material. To Val Noone & Rachel Naughton in Australia for providing me with useful information from the Australian perspective along with Jim and Helga Griffin for their warm support and advice. To the staff and my friends in the Houses of the Oireachtas – Committees and Library & Research sections who were always very supportive and helpful over the years with my numerous queries, especially Art, Eileen, Mary, Anna and Seamus.

Thanks to the exceptionally helpful staff of the University College Dublin Archives especially Mrs Kate Manning and Mr Seamus Helferty; the Director of the National Archives of Ireland and the staff especially Elizabeth McEvoy and Aideen Ireland; the staff of the National Archives of England, Kew; Archbishop Diarmuid Martin and Noelle Dowling at the Dublin Diocesan Archives for their help and permission; Penny Woods and Susan Durack at the Russell Library and Collections Library in Maynooth; the Central Catholic Library especially Mrs Teresa Whitington; Limerick County Library, Limerick Local Library in Dooradoyle and the staff at Limerick City Museum especially Brian Hodkinson. My thanks also to Ken Bergin of the Special Collections Department of the Glucksman Library at the University of Limerick; the staff and Director at the National Library of Ireland. My gratitude to Vicky Moran and John Glendon of RTÉ Library & Archives for their endless perseverance. The staff at Trinity College Dublin Library particularly Trevor Peare for allowing me to use Patrick Murray's theses. ABC Australia, in particular, Amy Donald.

Thanks to Mrs Margaret Pigott of Killarney Town Council for her kind assistance in acquiring the Killarney Urban District Council Minutes for me. The staff at Killarney town library especially Mrs Mary Murray as well as the staff at Kerry Local Studies & Archives in Tralee.

Sincere thanks to the Columban Fathers in the USA for sending me the account of their former Regional Director Fr McCarthy. My gratitude also to the Provincial Minister of the Order of Friars Minor Capuchin, Ireland as well as archivist Dr Brian Kirby. I am very grateful to the co-operation of Mr Henry Scannell of the Boston Public Library's Microtext Department and Mrs Anne Butler of U.L's Glucksman library for sourcing de Valera's speech at Fenway Park in 1919. A very special heartfelt thanks to Mr Martin Fagan and the Rector of the Irish College in Rome. Joe Fanning in particular at Getty Images for his patience and help during the publication process. Mr Tony Grieve for his information on the Archbishop Mannix foundation. To Karan Oberoi, Sarah Callanan, Pádraig Ó Mairtín, Barry Finnegan, Anthony Cawley and anyone else I have forgotten to mention. Thanks to all these friendly, helpful and courteous people, this piece of historical research was able to come to fruition.

During the many draftings of the final text, I have had the benefit of constructive criticism from many people, but I would especially like to thank Mrs Mary Guerin and Fr Tom Looney for their detailed and helpful comments.

I would especially like to thank my publishers, Cambridge Scholars Publishing and the very helpful, friendly and patient staff including Soucin Yip-Sou, Amanda Millar and Carol Koulikourdi. Thank you all.

To the extended surviving family of Archbishop Mannix especially Mrs Patricia Wallis-McCombe and Mr McCombe for welcoming me into their home and being so kind and generous throughout my research, my heartfelt thanks. Also to Mrs Winifred Cross and Mrs Mary Ellen McCarthy in America for sending me excellent material and providing useful links to Dr Mannix's past. To Jim Leo for his time and assistance in unlocking aspects of the Archbishop's childhood. Thank you all sincerely.

Finally to my family and my girlfriend for their support, love, and ability to tolerate the trials and tribulations that come with undertaking such a book – my girlfriend Anna, my brother John Paul, my brother-in-law Chris, my sisters Norita and Helen, my niece Molly Lucia and most importantly my parents John and Christina. This book is dedicated to them.

Patrick J. Mannix, April 2012

Permissions

I am grateful to the publishers, archivists and editors who granted permission to reproduce here material that originally appeared in their scholarly journals, collections or other publications. These include the National Library of Ireland, National Archives of Ireland, National Archives of England, RTÉ Library & Archives, Limerick City Museum, ABC Australia, Oxford University Press, Cork University Press, The Orion Publishing Group, Continuum International Publishing Company, Transaction Publishers, Taylor & Francis Ltd. (www.tandfonline.com), Sage Publications, Edinburgh University Press (www.euppublishing.com), HarperCollins Publishers Ltd., Random House Group Ltd., Order of Friars Minor Capuchin, Ireland, Cambridge University Press and Irish American Cultural Institute, UCD School of History & Archives, Dublin Diocesan Archives and the Maynooth College Archives. Milo Spillane of Crom Abú, Tom O'Donovan of the Old Limerick Journal, Philip O'Connell of the Charleville and district historical journal and finally the Irish National Association of Australasia.

T. M. Healy, *Letters and Leaders of My Day*; John, O'Sheehan, *Archbishop Mannix: A Sketch of His Life and Work*; Cearbhall O'Briain, *Dr. Mannix in Australia*; Dr. Daniel Mannix, *Speeches of His Grace* are courtesy of the National Library of Ireland. The quotation from the Turbulent Priest is courtesy of RTÉ Library & Archives. Archbishop Mannix on the campaign against the oath is courtesy of Limerick City Museum. "The Riddle of Father Hackett", *Late Night Live*; Archbishop Mannix during an interview with Gerald Lyons are reproduced by permission of the Australian Broadcasting Corporation and ABC Online. (c) (2009) ABC. All rights reserved. B.A., Santamaria, *Santamaria: A Memoir* is reproduced by permission of Oxford University Press Australia

& New Zealand. © Oxford University Press. Whyte, J. H., 'The Influence of the Catholic Clergy...' is reproduced by permission of Oxford University Press. Dermot Keogh, *Ireland and the Vatican*; Senia Paseta, *Before the Revolution*; Patrick O'Farrell, *The Irish in Australia*; Corkery, Daniel, *Synge and Anglo-Irish Literature*; John A. Murphy, 'The Achievement of de Valera'; Printed with the kind permission of Cork University Press, Youngline Industrial Estate, Pouladuff, Togher, Cork. Elias Canetti, *Crowds and Power* is printed with permission from Weidenfeld & Nicolson, an imprint of The Orion Publishing Group, London. Moirin Chavasse, *Terence MacSwiney* and Davis, Graham, 'The Historiography of the Irish Famine' are printed with permission from the Continuum International Publishing Company. Sidney Hook, *The Hero in History* Copyright © 2012 by Transaction Publishers. Reprinted by permission of the publisher. *British Journal of Ethnomusicology* publisher (Taylor & Francis Ltd, www.tandfonline.com) Reprinted by kind permission of the publisher. *Journal of Contemporary History* and Duck, Steve, *Human Relationships* publisher Sage Publications. Reprinted by kind permission of the publisher. *Irish University Review* publisher (Edinburgh University Publishing, www.euppublishing.com). *Collins English dictionary* reprinted by permission of HarperCollins Ltd. © (1991).

Eamon de Valera by Thomas O'Neill and the Earl of Longford; *De Valera: Long Fellow, Long Shadow* by Tim Pat Coogan, published by Hutchinson. Reprinted by permission of The Random House Group Limited. *Inventing Ireland: The Literature of a Modern Nation* by Declan Kiberd published by Vintage Books. Reprinted by permission of The Random House Group Limited. The Capuchin Annual © Capuchin Provincial Archives, Dublin, Ireland. *Placing Friendship in Context* reprinted by kind permission of Cambridge University Press. Rev. Ebsworth, *Archbishop Mannix*; James Murtagh, *Australia: The Catholic Chapter; Footprints: Quarterly Journal of the Melbourne Historical Commission* reprinted by kind permission of the Catholic Archdiocese of Melbourne ©. In the absence of clear copyright ownership, the publishers, the Catholic Archdiocese of Melbourne have given permission to use Frank Murphy, *Daniel Mannix*. *Éire Ireland* reprinted by kind permission of the Irish American Cultural Institute. *The Irish Uprising, 1914-1921* Contains public sector information licensed under the Open Government License v1.0. www.nationalarchives.gov.uk/doc/open-government-license/

ABBREVIATIONS

GAA	Gaelic Athletic Association
GPO	General Post Office
FOIF	Friends of Irish Freedom
ICA	Irish Citizens Army
INA	Irish National Association
IPP	Irish Parliamentary Party
IRA	Irish Republican Army
IRB	Irish Republican Brotherhood
IRPDF	Irish Republican Prisoners Dependant Fund
UVF	Ulster Volunteer Force

INTRODUCTION

Historian Joe Broderick first highlighted a "special" relationship that existed between Eamon de Valera and Archbishop Daniel Mannix in 1994, fourteen years after de Valera's death. Broderick wrote how:

> Nowadays Daniel Mannix merits no more than a footnote – often a misleading one – in texts on the War of Independence and its aftermath. Yet his performance had considerable bearing on the course of events. And for a moment at least, in 1921, he played a starring role on the stage of Irish history.[1]

Broderick recast Archbishop Daniel Mannix of Melbourne, who had been a vital player in the War of Independence, back into the central pages of Irish history. Archbishop Mannix's relationship with de Valera is a significant component of modern Irish history that needs to be investigated in depth, due to its historical importance and that is what this book will aim to achieve. The alliance de Valera had with Mannix is a significant connection that historians have often overlooked in their analysis of the Irish independence movement. This book will assess and analyse that alliance for its importance and relevance to Ireland's fight for freedom and for the subsequent effect it had on both men's distinguished careers.

This book will be able to offer an analysis of key events that took place in Ireland during the years 1920 to 1925, through the medium of de Valera and Mannix's special relationship. Although de Valera is one of the two protagonists of this book, the investigation into their alliance will not be symmetrical. The book will rather consider the forgotten character of Archbishop Mannix and portray how his relationship with de Valera helped influence Irish affairs during the years 1920 to 1925. These years generate the core argument of the book, as the alliance between the two men was most active during this period. The primary evidence for this period of the alliance is also more abundant than for the latter period of their friendship, the years 1925 to 1963.

---

[1] Joe Broderick, 'De Valera and Archbishop Daniel Mannix' in *History Ireland*, 2 (3)1994, p. 37.

Why should their relationship be deemed as special? This book will suggest different reasons for this historical debate. Having been the first to acknowledge a special relationship, Broderick's work will be built on in detail. The discussion will offer an analysis of the impact the alliance between Eamon de Valera and Archbishop Mannix had on Irish national aspirations. One particular example why their relationship may be deemed special and merits further historical investigation, is that Mannix was the only member of the Irish clerical hierarchy, at home or abroad, who supported de Valera both during and after the Civil War, even though he received fierce criticism for doing so.[2] The primary objective of this book is to pick Mannix from the footnotes of history and replay the role his character had in the history of Ireland's fight for independence and allow the reader rediscover just how influential both he and de Valera were in their respective callings. This was largely due to each other.

Both men have had many critics and devotees over the years. Therefore, both have had two very different epitaphs written for them in the annals of Irish history. De Valera is a not-too-distant figure in the memory of the Celtic Tiger generation. He has drawn numerous publications on all aspects of his political career. The most recent, by Diarmuid Ferriter and John J. Turi, and the publicity that they generated, show just how controversial a character de Valera remains for Irish historians.[3] De Valera kept a colossal archive of his life, now housed at University College Dublin and open to scrutiny and interpretation. Mannix, in stark contrast, has been kept within a Vatican-like sealed box, particularly the matter of his relationship with the Roman Catholic Church in Ireland and his role during the War of Independence. Mannix's part in the war has largely been consigned to certain biographies especially those of his close friend de Valera. Some of de Valera's key biographers, including the Earl of Longford and Thomas P. O'Neill, T. R. Dwyer, Tim Pat Coogan and most recently Diarmuid Ferriter, make only fleeting mention of any relationship between de Valera and Mannix.[4] Only Longford and Coogan mention a connection between the two characters,

---

[2] ibid, p. 38.

[3] Diarmuid Ferriter, *Judging Dev* (Dublin: Royal Irish Academy, 2007) and John J. Turi, *England's greatest spy: Eamon de Valera* (London: Stacey International, 2009).

[4] T. R., Dwyer, *Eamon de Valera: The Man & the Myths* (Dublin: Paperview/Irish Independent, 2006) *and* T. P. Coogan, *De Valera: long fellow, long shadow* (London: Hutchinson, 1993) and The Earl of Longford and Thomas P. O'Neill, *Eamon de Valera* (London: Hutchinson, 1970) and Ferriter, *Judging Dev*.

both describe Mannix as an "old friend" of de Valera.[5] In other works such as Dermot Keogh, *Ireland and the Vatican*, Mannix is described as "a strong supporter of Eamon de Valera".[6] The alliance that existed between the men is a chapter of Irish history, which needs to be written, and that is what will be achieved here as both men contributed immensely to the historical legacy of Ireland and, in Mannix's case Irish Australia.

De Valera's prominent position at the centre of Ireland's fight for independence has been subjected to extensive analysis. Mannix for his part has largely been forgotten by Irish historians, but on the other hand, his legacy has been celebrated by the vast majority of Australian historians. Irish literature on de Valera views him either as the main catalyst behind the schism in Irish politics or, as the great leader of a revived Catholic Gaelic Ireland. Mannix is also seen as a divisive figure by some, particularly during his early years in Australia where some judge him of fomenting tension between the pro-Commonwealth Protestants and the anti-empire Catholics, primarily the ethnic Irish. Mannix, like de Valera, has had numerous biographies. However, the main difference between the two is that while de Valera's papers survive, Mannix's have been lost, because of his order to have them destroyed after his death. For this reason, the historian is now faced with a more difficult task of deconstructing a caricature. Historian T. P. Boland has correctly argued that 'Mannix is responsible for the caricatures of himself that pass as history. He has left no one the wherewithal to correct the distortions of his character that are currently accepted.'[7]

The most extensive study of Mannix's life was undertaken by Rev. Walter Ebsworth.[8] His book provides the result of extensive research into every detail of his life. However, while it is extensive in detail it lacks analytical discussion and instead leaves that to others. The biographies by Frank Murphy, Colm Kiernan, B. A Santamaria and Michael Gilchrist all

---

[5] Earl of Longford & O'Neill, op. cit., p. 204 and Coogan, op. cit., p. 639.

[6] Dermot Keogh, *Ireland and the Vatican: the politics and diplomacy of church-state relations 1922-1960* (Cork: Cork University Press, 1995), p. 16.

[7] T. P Boland, *The ascent of Tabor: writing the life of Archbishop Duhig* (Queensland: Aquinas Library, 1986). Aquanius Memorial Lecture, p. 5. http://library.acu.edu.au/other_collections_and_catalogues/aquinas_memorial_lectures/?a=49310
Date accessed 1 September 2010.

[8] Rev. Walter Ebsworth, *Archbishop Mannix,* (Armadale, Vic.: H. H. Stephenson, 1977).

offer the analytical discussion that Ebsworth lacks.[9] Santamaria's books on Mannix are written in a hagiographic style. A reason for this is that Santamaria was very much influenced by Mannix during his political life in Australia, as leader of the Democratic Labor Party. However, no work focuses on Mannix's relationship with de Valera as thoroughly as Kiernan does. In his *Daniel Mannix and Ireland*, he argues, "no one was more important than Mannix in promoting de Valera's cause and in its eventual triumph".[10] Although outlining the key meetings between the two men and providing analysis of these it does not seek to develop further on the alliance that existed between de Valera and Mannix. He does argue however, "de Valera did what he could to develop his friendship with Mannix and to exploit it".[11] Kiernan was the son of former Irish ambassador to Australia, Mr T.J. Kiernan and would have been well placed to comment on Mannix's life due to his father's regular interaction with Mannix. Santamaria however, would also claim this right as he would later become the lay protégé of Mannix and, as will be argued later, became closer to Mannix as Mannix's relationship with de Valera became more distant and cordial. Santamaria's book, *Daniel Mannix: the Quality of Leadership*, maintains the respect and esteem that Santamaria held for Mannix during their friendship and finds it hard to offer a conflicting viewpoint on his former confidant. An objective middle ground will thus be sought through a range of sources, instead of through the medium of hyperbolic biographies of Mannix, alone, in order to offer the reader a more rounded insight into how their partnership developed.

This will be achieved firstly through surviving correspondence between the two men. The primary source that is most valuable is the "Mannix file" within the "Eamon de Valera Papers" at University College Dublin.[12] This collection provides this book with the best material for the alliance. However, the collection also has its limitations as only cordial handwritten letters from Mannix exist after 1932 suggesting the key correspondence between 1920 and 1932 has been lost forever. To compensate for the lack of correspondence with de Valera during the key

---

[9] Frank Murphy, *Daniel Mannix: Archbishop of Melbourne 1917-1963* (Melbourne: Advocate Press, 1948) and Colm Kiernan, *Daniel Mannix and Ireland* (Morwell, Victoria: Alella Books, 1984) and B. A. Santamaria, *Archbishop Mannix: his contribution to the art of public leadership in Australia* (Melbourne: Melbourne University Publishing, 1978) and Michael Gilchrist, *Daniel Mannix: wit and wisdom* (Melbourne: Ihs Press, 2nd ed., 2005).

[10] Kiernan, op. cit., p. 223.

[11] ibid, p. 187.

[12] UCD Archives: De Valera papers, P150.

period, 1920 to 1925, The Monsignor John Hagan papers stored at the Irish College in Rome play a valuable role.[13] These papers highlight Mannix's significance in the talks that took place in Rome in 1924, paving the way for the formation of Fianna Fáil and its entry into Dáil Éireann. Historian Richard J. Evans acknowledged effectively the essential role that such letters and correspondence play in historical research by commenting:

> A text is always written for a readership and framed according to the writer's expectations of how the intended readers will take it. Similarly, the reader is always mindful of the purposes and intentions of the writer during the act of reading. All this remains true even when people read a document not addressed to them – people like historians, in fact.[14]

Other key archives used to indicate Mannix's influence on Irish affairs from 1920 to 1925 include files on Mannix at the National Archives of Ireland.[15] These files provide us with key views from the former Taoiseach, William T. Cosgrave and shed light on the reaction of other bishops in the antipodes to political developments in Ireland. The National Archives of the UK at Kew, London also house files on Mannix relating to the views and worries of the British Foreign Office on key incidents involving Mannix between the years 1920 to 1925.[16] Other key deposits, including those of Archbishop William Walsh in the Dublin Diocesan Archives, throw light on the kind of president Mannix was at Maynooth.[17] Some primary sources relating to the archbishop are contained here. The Maynooth College Archives have a file relating to Mannix but unfortunately, it does not contain any new primary accounts relating to his alliance with de Valera.[18]

This book will offer an analysis of how the alliance between these two men was formed. Two main themes will also dominate this book, church-state relations in the late nineteenth and early twentieth century Ireland and the relationship between the fledgling Irish state and its wider Irish diaspora. The book will use the two men as "markers" for their respective fields to highlight the dominant themes. Mannix will be viewed as a symbol of the Irish diaspora particularly in Irish Australia along with the

---

[13] Irish College Rome: Msgr. Hagan papers, HAG1.

[14] Richard J. Evans, *In defence of history* (London: Granta Books, 1997), pp 106-107.

[15] National Archives of Ireland/NAI, D/Taoiseach, S1369.

[16] National Archives of the UK, CO537/1144.

[17] Dublin Diocesan Archives, AB6/336 (uncatalogued)

[18] Maynooth College Archives, 20-7-16.

Roman Catholic Church in Ireland. De Valera will be used as the symbol
of the Irish State particularly once he was elected to power in 1932.

The theme of church-state relations has always played a part in Irish
society but from the early nineteenth century, as Whyte argues, the church:

> ... no longer felt that political action was necessarily and in all
> circumstances wrong; and as the main issue in Irish affairs at this period
> was one which clearly concerned them – Catholic emancipation – it was
> likely to be only a matter of time before they began to intervene in
> politics.[19]

In the early part of the nineteenth century, church-state relations moved
from the clergy taking a laissez-faire attitude to politics, to taking a more
pro-active interest in events, particularly those relating to religious
matters. Although the famine did untold damage to the congregation of the
church through death and emigration, the church from the 1850s onwards,
with Cardinal Paul Cullen leading from the front, would once again rise to
the question of political involvement of the clergy. Cullen would become
one of the most influential men of the Roman Catholic Church in Ireland
in the second half of the nineteenth century. Dermot Keogh argues that,
"no other cleric in the nineteenth century did more to reform and
Romanise the Irish Church."[20] As the church moved into the twentieth
century, others such as Cardinal D'alton and Logue and Archbishops
Croke and Walsh took up the mantle of Cullen. However, with the rise of
the Irish parliamentary party under Parnell, the church's influence began
to decline. The church threw whatever weight it had left behind the anti-
Parnellite party and as Whyte suggests:

> ... the violence with which so many clergy threw themselves into the
> struggle against the Parnellites can at least partly be ascribed to a feeling
> that this was their last chance to restore their now rapidly waning authority
> in political matters.[21]

The Irish church was peculiar in its relationship with the state at this
period compared to other European countries. As Miller argues:

---

[19] J. H Whyte, 'The influence of the Catholic clergy on elections in nineteenth
century Ireland' in *The English Historical Review*, 75 (295) 1960, p. 240.
[20] Dermot Keogh, *Ireland and the Vatican: the politics and diplomacy of church-
state Relations 1922-1960* (Cork: Cork University Press, 1995), p. 3.
[21] Whyte, op. cit., p. 257.

... the fact that the Irish Church had not enjoyed a privileged position under the State in the centuries prior to the appearance of the Nation as a meaningful political force both strengthened her positive moral influence over the people and partially shielded her from the kind of attacks which several continental States were making upon the Church at this time.[22]

In the period when Mannix and de Valera were born, towards the latter half of the nineteenth century, the dominant trends in church-state relations were that the:

... state would respect the Church's vested interests, especially in the area of publicly financed education, and that the Church would use her very considerable influence to curb direct challenges to the State's monopoly of physical force.[23]

This position would change with the formation of the Irish Free State when Mannix and de Valera's capacity to influence Irish national affairs was most dominant.

The characters' relationship also provides valuable insight into the relationship between Ireland and its diaspora. In emphasising the role of the Irish diaspora with particular focus on the Irish-Australian community, Mannix is an important example of the diaspora's influence and contribution to Irish affairs, even from countries as far away as Australia and the U.S.A. The relationship will highlight the part, which the diaspora played in Irish affairs during the struggle for independence. Australia will play a big part in this book as the adopted home of the main character Archbishop Mannix. Not alone would it become his home, but it would also become home for many Irish who had emigrated there from the early nineteenth century onwards. As Oliver MacDonagh notes, "in no other region of settlement did the proportion of Irish among the immigrants equal – or nearly equal – Australia's during this century and a quarter".[24] The Irish would gain a foothold much more easily in Australia than in any other country. Historian David Fitzpatrick argues that, "the Irish had the advantage of being in on the act first, and never let the English or Scots

---

[22] David W. Miller, *Church, state and nation in Ireland, 1898-1921* (Dublin: Gill & Macmillan, 1973), p. 3.

[23] ibid, p. 4.

[24] Oliver MacDonagh, 'The Irish in Australia: a general view' in Oliver MacDonagh & W.F. Mandle (eds.) *Ireland and Irish-Australia: studies in cultural and political history* (London: Croom Helm, 1986), p. 159.

secure a monopoly of economic or political power".[25] This Irish community, however, lacked social and political direction and Archbishop Mannix's arrival gave the Irish-Australians this direction, as O'Farrell argues: "Mannix amounted to an Irish delegation that would not go away as the other had done, a permanent outside force that made Irish issues unavoidable".[26] He kept alive support of the Irish cause with the diaspora in Australia and elsewhere even though, as MacDonagh suggests, considering the distance involved, the feelings were that "the separation was permanent and the disruption irreversible".[27] This claim is re-enforced by prominent Irish-Australian historian Patrick O'Farrell who claims that by the time of the 1948 anti-partition tour, Irish-Australians interest in Irish national affairs had diminished. The 1948 anti-partition tour would be undertaken by de Valera to secure worldwide support for an end to partition in Ireland. O'Farrell argues that, "de Valera's language was not the language of Australian politics, and by 1948 very few Irish Australians believed that Australia had anything to learn from Ireland".[28]

President Mary Robinson in her speech to a special joint sitting of the Houses of the Oireachtas, in 1995, gave an accurate summary of the story of the diaspora: "Emigration is not just a chronicle of sorrow and regret. It is also a powerful story of contribution and adaptation."[29] The total figure the president gave for people with Irish descendants was seventy million.[30] However, back at the beginning of the twentieth century, "good authorities have estimated that between 1901 and 1921, at least eight million Irish men, women and children left Ireland".[31] Australia, America and Britain became the key destinations for Irish emigrants and would hence become solid bases for Irish national support in the years ahead. Mannix, like so

---

[25] David Fitzpatrick, 'The settlers: immigration from Ireland in the nineteenth Century' in Colm Kiernan (ed.) *Ireland and Australia* (Cork: The Mercier Press Ltd., 1984), p. 27.
[26] Patrick O'Farrell, *The Irish in Australia* (Kensington NSW: New South Wales University Press, 1987), p. 261.
[27] MacDonagh, op. cit., p. 162.
[28] Patrick O'Farrell, *The Irish in Australia: 1788 to the present* (Cork: Cork University Press, 2001), p. 304.
[29] Mary Robinson, 'Address by Uachtarán na hÉireann Mary Robinson to joint sitting of the Houses of the Oireachtas, 2 February 1995, http://www.oireachtas.ie/viewdoc.asp?fn=/documents/addresses/2Feb1995.htm Date accessed 30 August 2010.
[30] Michael O'Sullivan, *Mary Robinson: the life and times of an Irish Liberal* (Dublin: Blackwater Press, 1993), p. 213.
[31] Donald Harman Akenson, *The Irish diaspora: A primer* (Belfast: The Institute of Irish Studies, 1993), p. 15.

many before him, would set out on a voyage into the geographical unknown, for him, to Melbourne, Australia. Victoria's capital city would become the centre of Daniel Mannix's life for the next fifty years. In Melbourne, he would become the beacon of hope for Irish Australians. Mannix would articulate the views of the Irish diaspora and keep alive their interest in Irish national affairs.

The key tool of the Irish nationalist has always been rhetoric particularly, when aimed at garnering international support. Both Mannix and de Valera realised this at a very early stage, most notably during the American tour of 1920. The discourse used by both men in various public speeches and statements offer the historian a portal into a wide range of issues such as conscription, religion and independence. Both men focused on the most pertinent political and social questions of their day and were never afraid to challenge the accepted norm.

What this book will offer, and which differs from previous literature, is an exploration of the development of their alliance. It will show how through their correspondence and interaction they influenced each other's actions from the years 1920 to 1925. It will also examine how they influenced one another's respective opinions on the Irish cause and the diaspora. The examination of these two characters may lead to problems, as discussed previously by historians Boyce and O'Day when they commented; "revising national history is perilous, especially if cherished legends are debunked or heroes pushed off their pedestals".[32] However, this book is not a revisionist examination of church-state relations but an analysis, ground in the present understandings of opinion on church-state structures and national acceptance of the Irish diaspora.

Church-state relations have changed dramatically in the period since the dawn of the Celtic Tiger economy in the late twentieth century, right up to the revelations in the Murphy Report in 2010.[33] Archbishop Mannix's life can be used to exemplify how the role of the prelate has changed in modern society with particular regard to church-state relations. The role of the state has also changed to an all-embracing attitude by the Irish government in its relationship with the wider diaspora, exemplified most effectively in the call for its expertise at the Global Irish Economic

---

[32] D George Boyce & Alan O'Day, "'Revisionism and the "revisionist controversy"'" in D. George Boyce and Alan O'Day (eds.) *The making of modern Irish history.* (London: Routledge, 1996).

[33] Judge Yvonne Murphy, 'Report by Commission of Investigation into Catholic Archdiocese of Dublin', July 2009, http://www.justice.ie/en/JELR/Pages/PB09000504, Date accessed 1 March 2010.

Forum at Farmleigh in 2009.[34] Using the vehicle of both public and political change in attitudes towards the diaspora and in church-state relations, this book will attempt like, "a generation of historians before it", and in the words of T.W. Moody, "to interrogate the Irish past and, if necessary, the current public misunderstanding of it".[35] The book will aim to draw a conclusion that should offer the reader a window into the past as objectively as possible and reconstruct the stage that allowed both actors to be so influential. The object of this analysis is to open up historical discussion on a chapter of Irish history that has largely been forgotten.

Historian Ian McBride believes that "in Ireland, as is well known, the interpretation of the past has always been at the heart of national conflict. Indeed the time-warped character of Irish mindsets has become a cliché of scholarly and unscholarly writing".[36] This book will contribute to the understanding of the influence certain foreign prelates held over Irish affairs, men who were sometimes almost renegades battling against the church's hierarchy. The Catholic Church in Ireland held significant influence over its clergy and their actions in the early twentieth century. Its authoritarian and disciplinarian manner had an influence not alone on Archbishop Mannix, but also on the ultra-Catholic de Valera. When they failed to accept the church's early line on Irish national affairs and began to speak out, they threatened the accepted social doctrine and risked isolation. Keogh would argue that "it was through both their rhetoric and actions that this isolation manifested itself and quite possibly drove the two men closer together".[37] Previous literature including works by Broderick and Keogh has touched on how Mannix brought high-profile clerical backing to de Valera during the Civil War. However, this discussion will focus on the relevance of Mannix's support and whether it

---

[34] *The Irish Times*, 'Martin hails ideas forum input', 19 September 2009, http://www.irishtimes.com/newspaper/breaking/2009/0919/breaking6.html, date accessed 01 March 2010.
[35] T. W. Moody quoted in Declan Kiberd, 'The elephant of revolutionary forgetfulness' in Máirín Ní Dhonnchadha and Theo Dorgan (eds.) *Revising the Rising*. (Derry: Field Day, 1991), p. 6.
[36] Ian McBride, 'Memory and identity in modern Ireland' in Ian McBride (ed.) *History and memory in modern Ireland*. (Cambridge: Cambridge University Press, 2001), p. 1.
[37] Dermot Keogh, 'Mannix, De Valera and Irish nationalism', in John B. O'Brien and Pauric Travers (eds.) *The Irish emigrant experience in Australia* (Dublin: Poolbeg, 1991), p. 221.

actually had the impact attributed to it.[38] The priest in twentieth century Ireland was seen by the congregation as the leader of the flock, the voice of the people. The hierarchy tried their best to act in accordance with both the wishes of their flock and clergy on the ground should they wish to remain a dominant force in Irish society. By going against the Roman Catholic Church during the Civil War, both de Valera and Mannix threatened its dominance in Irish society.

This book will follow a chronological path. Chapter One will set the scene by looking at the early lives of both characters, offering tentative reasons for the development of their nationalist views. Chapter Two will look at the early careers of both men and evaluate the reasons for Mannix's departure from Maynooth to Melbourne in 1912. This book will also focus on key events outside this timeline, but the core period of 1920 to 1925 was when Archbishop Daniel Mannix and Eamon de Valera's alliance was at its peak historically. Chapter Three will look at the progression of both men's careers between the years 1913-1919. Chapter four will focus on the tour of America in 1920 where both men's relationship was cemented. Following on from this Chapter Five will examine the role played by Mannix in supporting de Valera during the Civil War period and after. Finally Chapter Six will analyse the final phase of their alliance with their last meeting on de Valera's anti-partition tour in 1948 central to this. The conclusion will offer an evaluation on their alliance and how it has been overlooked in Irish history. It will also aim to resurrect the historical profile of Archbishop Mannix, who has largely been forgotten in the study of modern Irish history. This period of Irish history is the subject of some of the most detailed and vividly written accounts of Ireland's fight for independence and the subsequent Civil War. It is by analysing and detailing the largely "sidelined" case of Mannix and de Valera's alliance that this book will offer the reader a nexus to analyse church-state relations in the early Free State.

Both Mannix and de Valera were unique leaders and inherited the strong leadership traditions of notable predecessors. Ireland had been robbed of strong political leadership and religious direction following the deaths of Charles Stewart Parnell and Cardinal Cullen. This political and social vacuum had to be filled and:

> ... with the lack of political initiative on the part of the Catholic professional classes, the constant vigilance against proselytism in its

---

[38] Broderick, op. cit., p. 37 and Keogh, 'Mannix' in *The Irish emigrant*, op. cit., p. 220.

various forms – this all helped to clear for the political power and social influence of the priests after the famine.[39]

Mannix as president of Maynooth College from 1903 to 1912 was well placed to influence the next generation of Irish prelates. After the Rising of 1916, de Valera also grew in prominence and began to relish his public role. These two men, through their action and public displays of national fervour, offered the receptive Irish and Irish-Australian publics a locus for their national aspirations. For those categorised under the vast catch-all phrase of the Irish diaspora and those within the episcopal arena, Mannix was a strong leader willing to confront any challenge. De Valera too, for many in Ireland, embodied the resurgent nationalist struggle through his involvement in the Rising and his subsequent activities in Sinn Féin. Through strong and determined leadership, both men would lead from the front in the fight for Irish independence. Not alone this, but they were also able to appeal to both the religious and political elements of society, Mannix through his politically charged statements and de Valera through his interactions with the church. As Sidney Hook laments:

> The basic fact that provides the material for interest in heroes is the indispensability of leadership in all social life, and in every major form of social organisation. The controls over leadership, whether open or hidden, differ from society to society, but leaders are always at hand not merely as conspicuous symbols of state, but as centres of responsibility, decision and action.[40]

This book will examine how these "heroes", by their leadership, shaped and moulded key junctures in Irish and Australian history. They had the uncanny knack of grabbing the public's imagination and creating an aura around themselves and their ideals. In many ways, all the great agitators stole the limelight from other great leaders of their day, such as Pádraig Pearse from Arthur Griffith and the same can be said of de Valera with respect to Mannix. Through their fight for Irish independence, "they both gave the impression that they were engaged on a work to which they were

---

[39] John A. Murphy, 'Priests and People in Modern Irish History' in *Christus Rex: Journal of Sociology*, 23 (1969), p. 252.
[40] Sidney Hook, *The hero in history: A Study in Limitation and Possibility* (New York: Transaction Publishers, 1943), pp 3-4.

driven by some inner compulsion ... they gave the impression that they were obeying some call and that personal choice had little to do with it".[41]

Both men did not foresee their future involvement in the Irish independence movement. At an early stage of their lives, both men had choices that would ultimately lead to their paths crossing. Just as Mannix had a choice to enter the priesthood he also had a choice not to partake in politically charged statements and give public displays of republican fervour. De Valera, similarly, had a choice not to enter the priesthood, but also had a decision to make on whether or not to take the oath of allegiance and enter democratic politics through Fianna Fáil in 1926. The question this book will investigate is just how much influence their alliance had on the taking of these critical decisions. It may require a divergence into the sociological perspective on friendship and relationships, but this will allow the historian a wider perspective. Sociologist Graham Allan describes how, "the solidarity of the friends, based solely on their personal and voluntary commitment to each other, is taken to be unfettered by any selfish or instrumental concerns. Each gives what the other needs, without thought to cost or reward, simply because of the fact of their friendship."[42]

Just as Mannix and de Valera complimented each other both in their rhetoric and action, history also has to provide a balanced narrative leading to objective conclusions. James Joyce saw history for the Irish as a nightmare from which they were trying to awake, evoking Marx's decisive observation "that the past always seemed to weigh like a nightmare upon the brains of the living".[43] Depending on which side of the historical fence the reader finds himself or herself perched on, this topic will no doubt bring criticism and praise for its traditional, revisionist and post-revisionist approaches, but the overall aim is to allow the topic to be brought to light through historical debate and argument. The Irish diaspora remains uncertain territory for Irish historians. Using the case of Archbishop Mannix, the leitmotif of the Irish diaspora will be carried through the discussion. It will offer an analysis of how influential the diaspora was on Irish affairs. Patrick O'Farrell, writing on the Irish in Australia, notes that the, "catholic Irish operated like a loyal opposition and as a constructive irritant in that general polity, questioning the consensus on values that

---

[41] Joan Towey Mitchell, 'Yeats, Pearse and Cuchulain' in *Éire-Ireland*, 11 (4) 1976, p. 52.

[42] Graham Allan, *Friendship: developing a sociological perspective* (Hemel Hempstead: Westview Press, 1989), p. 13.

[43] James Joyce quoted in Kiberd, op. cit., p. 5.

characterised the other (Protestant) groups from the British Isles."[44] The diaspora had bonded on such issues as conscription and state sponsored education so that, they were well positioned to influence Irish national issues with Mannix at the helm as the all powerful godfather.

This book will endeavour to open other avenues of research. In garnering enough evidence, the necessary objectivity of this debate must be maintained throughout as Richard Evans warns:

> When we call a historian objective, we mean two things. First of all, we mean that he has a capacity to rise above the limited vision of his own situation in society and in history … Secondly, we mean that he has the capacity to project his vision into the future in such a way as to give him a more profound and more lasting insight into the past than can be attained by those historians whose outlook is entirely bounded by their own immediate situation.[45]

Sufficient time has lapsed for greater objectivity to be achieved and this is so with so many historical topics. Nostalgia and sentimentality for these two historical characters has certainly diminished substantially and for the next generation of Irish, the so-called "Celtic Tiger" generation, Mannix and de Valera's contribution will be re-assessed in this book. Their friendship could be seen as the beginning of a succession of close working relationships between members of the Irish Catholic hierarchy and government leaders since the formation of the state. Just as the church had so much influence over the state, the reverse is also true. In many friendships as Wiseman points out there is:

> … a voluntary contract of friendship which involves us tacitly agreeing to support our friends in time of need, to offer them help even if it is personally inconvenient, to take time away from our own business in order to attend to *their* business, and to engage with their demands upon our psychological and physical resources.[46]

Therefore, as Wiseman urges, it will be argued if there was indeed a "voluntary contract" between de Valera and Mannix and whether it had certain moral and political clauses attached. The church was instrumental, no-doubt, in covertly converting along with other methods de Valera to constitutionalism, but was de Valera also covertly converting Mannix to

---

[44] Patrick O'Farrell quoted in Donald Harmon Akenson, *The Irish diaspora: a primer* (Belfast: The Institute of Irish Studies, 1993), pp 113-114.
[45] Richard J. Evans, *In defence of history* (London: Granta Books, 1997), p. 225.
[46] Steve Duck, *Human relationships* (London: Sage Publications, 1998), p. 129.

his cause? Whatever the case may be, this book will aim to show that both men had undoubted love and affection for their country and in Mannix's case, his adopted country.[47] As Terry de Valera lamented in his father's case, "try as his detractors may, nothing can diminish his integrity, his sincerity, his courage and his unselfish devotion to his beloved country. All this has been demonstrated clearly throughout his long life."[48] Tim Pat Coogan; however, noted that "de Valera did little that was useful and much that was harmful".[49] Whether one agrees with Coogan or not, this discussion of the alliance will help remind the public of the importance that this bond had on modern Irish history.

> They who in ignorance calumniate you today, will tomorrow be forced to do you honour.[50]

---

[47] Keogh, 'Mannix, De Valera and Irish nationalism', op. cit., pp 203-204.
[48] Terry de Valera, *A memoir*, (Dublin: Currach Press, 2004), p. 308.
[49] Coogan, op. cit., p. 693.
[50] ibid, p. 140.

CHAPTER ONE

COMMUNITY POLITICS (1845-1882)

The themes of land and national independence were the dominant issues affecting Irish society in the latter half of the nineteenth century. The insecurity of the remaining population after the famine did not quell the spirit of rebellion. T.W. Moody reinforces this argument when he suggests "the revolutionary tradition was represented by the sporadic violence of agrarian secret societies, by the Young Ireland rising of 1848, and above all by the Fenian movement of the sixties."[1] This persistence of the revolutionary mindset, later coupled with the struggle for ownership of the land, would eventually lead to a strong united front between both the constitutional and militant nationalists under Charles Stewart Parnell.

Daniel Mannix was born in Charleville, Co. Cork in 1864. During his adolescence, he would have been well in tune with both the constitutional and militant traditions in Irish society in the latter half of the nineteenth century. De Valera was born in 1882 and would not have been old enough to realise the split in the traditions that Daniel Mannix had grown accustomed to in his youth. Eamon de Valera would have only been nine years old by the time of Parnell's political fall in 1890. Irish society was looking for a new leader to fill the vacuum left by Parnell and influence the young de Valera and the next generation of Irish people. The aim of this chapter is to establish, how the changing and evolving Ireland of the late nineteenth century would mould them into the leaders they were to become.

Ireland was always viewed as an agricultural entity, easily able to provide the vastly expanding British Empire with a rich, accessible supply of food. The famine had a devastating effect on Ireland not just alone in terms of immigration and souls lost, but also upon the country's agricultural sector. As Ireland had largely been ignored by the Industrial Revolution, with the exception of Belfast, agriculture was the prime sector

---

[1] T.W. Moody, 'Fenianism, Home Rule and the Land War: 1850-91' in T. W. Moody and F.X Martin (eds.) *The course of Irish history* (Dublin: The Mercier Press Ltd., 2001), p. 228.

for economic growth and change after the famine. As historian J. J. Lee
points out, there was a radical shift from tillage to livestock farming,
eventually leaving the livestock sector contributing to three-quarters of the
total value of the agricultural sector by 1914. Lee contends that this shift
towards livestock farming eventually left:

> ... the Irish farmer behaving as a rational economic man, and after the wave
> of famine evictions ebbed, it was he, not the landlord, who drove his
> children and the labourers off the land.[2]

After the famine, the land question had become the most pertinent issue to
the ordinary Irish citizen. Farms tended to be subdivided and emigration
was a likely option for most young men. The radical reversal of substantial
population growth to mass emigration jolted the land question into the
public mindset. McCaffrey emphasises this by outlining how, "tenant
security had been an issue in the O'Connell and Young Ireland versions of
Irish nationalism, but the famine and emigration made it the number one
consideration." [3] The immediate future for the general population,
including the Mannixes of Charleville, after 1848 left a lot to be desired,
especially after yet another failed rebellion under the Young Irelanders.
This new generation of revolutionaries were inspired by widespread
change in Europe towards the second half of the nineteenth century. The
famine was yet another indictment of British rule according to the
revolutionaries. Mitchel was one of the first to document the consequences
of the famine and his account, as Davis suggests, "transformed the events
of the Famine for eternity into a terrible indictment of English 'colonial'
rule", subsequently harnessing it "to the bandwagon of Irish nationalism".[4]

At a later stage, it will be argued that both de Valera and Mannix were
swept away on this bandwagon of nationalism, but the political
developments during their youth clearly influenced their future. The
origins of young Daniel Mannix's revolutionary ideals are explained
differently in the literature on Mannix. B. A. Santamaria believes that
Mannix's first relationship to the national question began in Maynooth,

---

[2] Joseph Lee, *The modernisation of Irish society 1848-1918* (Dublin: Gill &
Macmillan, 2008), p. 10.
[3] Lawrence J. McCaffrey, 'Components of Irish nationalism' in Thomas E. Hachey
and Lawrence J. McCaffrey (eds.) *Perspectives on Irish nationalism* (Kentucky:
University Press of Kentucky, 1989), p.11.
[4] Graham Davis, 'The historiography of the Irish Famine' in Patrick O'Sullivan
(ed.) *The Irish worldwide: history, heritage, identity, Volume Six: The meaning of
the Famine* (Leicester: Leicester University Press, 1997), p. 16.

where he was exposed to the trials and tribulations of other young Irishmen of his generation:

> ... it was only as adolescence merged into manhood that he became conscious of the Ireland of reality at the level of practicality through his association with fellow seminarians coming from harsher and therefore inevitably more nationalistic environments.[5]

Colm Kiernan had a different opinion on the origins of Mannix's staunch nationalism. He claims that Mannix's "firm commitment to Irish nationalism was one which he had inherited." Kiernan reinforces this by outlining the activities of the male side of the family; Daniel's father Timothy "was secretary of the Land League in the area. Four of Timothy Mannix's brothers were actively involved in the Land League movement, which young Daniel always supported."[6] For young Daniel, the old Irish saying of "briseann an dúchais trí shúile an chait" – "Nature will break out through the eyes of a cat" was very relevant.

Kiernan argues the Land League seemed to sow the seed of public involvement for the young Daniel Mannix. The Land League was the nuts and bolts of the Land War machine, which by 1909, would see nearly all of its substantial aims met with the introduction of the Birrell Act. Although there had been a history of uprising in Ireland, both before and during Mannix's formative days, the psyche of the Irish people dictated survival through the ownership of the land. The Mannix family, like many others in the countryside, was unwilling to risk their comparatively sizable land holding for revolutionary action that had a record of failure. In 1891, the Mannix property was "described as consisting of just over 135 acres, with forty cows, twelve calves and two horses".[7] It would take an issue closely related to the land that warranted national cohesion, for Timothy and his brothers to risk their holdings and this duly arrived in the late 1870s.

> ... wet summers and autumns were catastrophic; wet winters also meant flooding, loss of livestock and impossible foddering. The bad years of 1859-64, the worldwide depression and bad weather contributing to the

---

[5] B. A Santamaria, *Daniel Mannix: A biography* (Melbourne: Melbourne University Publishing, 1984), p. 3.

[6] Colm Kiernan, 'Appréciation Archbishop Daniel Mannix of Melbourne, 1864-1963' in *Éire-Ireland*, 19 (3) 1984, p.122.

[7] Rev Walter Ebsworth, *Archbishop Mannix* (Armadale: Victoria: H.H. Stephenson, 1977), p. 11.

political crisis of 1879-81, the droughts in the mid-1880s leading to collapse of prices for dairy produce, all represented considerable hardship.[8]

The consequence of these conditions was a spiralling of evictions along with social discontent. It was time for new leadership to tackle the stranglehold of landlordism and assume the mantle of spokesperson for the tenant farmer. James Donnelly suggests that an organised agrarian body would have to maintain the fight for land ownership on a continuous basis and not just during periods of crop uncertainty, when agrarian unrest began:

> ... widespread, organised agrarian discontent was admittedly discontinuous, with a pronounced tendency to rise and fall in accordance with economic fluctuations, particularly in prices and crop yields. But even during the intervals between outbreaks of agrarian unrest, nationalist chieftains could still feel the heat of the land question.[9]

This agrarian led organisation would arrive in the form of the Land League.

The Fenians under John Devoy realised by backing ex-IRB member, Michael Davitt, and his land agitation movement that they would not be left behind, in the sense of public representation and subsequent action. The militant element of their organisation waited for an opportunity to start another rebellion whilst the moderate constitutionalists led from the front. However, as prominent Fenian John O'Leary commented, the militant component never relinquished their goal of a rebellion:

> I saw little chance of the satisfactory settlement of the land question, or, indeed, of any question; and to shake, if not to shatter, that rule, was then, as it is still, the great aim, or, if you will, dream of my life.[10]

This coming together of various elements, including the militant and constitutional nationalists, with the land question looming gave Parnell the opportunity to achieve the realistic ambition of Home Rule for Ireland. This was certainly a "New Departure" in Irish politics. However, Parnell

---

[8] Caitriona Clear, *Social change and everyday life in Ireland, 1850-1922* (Manchester: Manchester University Press, 2007), p. 18.

[9] James S. Donnelly Jr., 'The Land Question in Nationalist Politics' in Thomas E. Hachey & Lawrence J. McCaffrey (eds.) *Perspectives on Irish nationalism* (Kentucky: University Press of Kentucky, 1989), p. 79.

[10] John O'Leary, *Recollections of Fenians and Fenianism Volume I* (Shannon: Irish University Press, 1968), p. 38.

was only taking up the mantle Isaac Butt had left behind. Butt had laid the foundations for constitutional nationalism through the Home Rule Party. Although Butt had drawn the political roadmap of constitutional nationalism for Ireland, it would take a pragmatic and charismatic Parnell to build upon his legacy. Parnell was the perceptive, cunning politician and knew how to work this "New Departure" to his own ends as a possible future leader of a Home Rule Parliament in Ireland. Like Butt before him, Parnell:

> ... forged to the front of Home Rule and made it popular by combining the demand for an Irish Parliament with a war on landlordism. Still, he did not abandon the inclusive ideology of Irish nationalism. He said that Ireland needed the talents of all classes and creeds.[11]

It is easy to see how the Mannixes were actively involved in the Land League, as it was a strong agrarian led organisation against British landlordism. Timothy Mannix's involvement as secretary to the local Land League showed the Mannix family's involvement in the movement. Previous Fenian revolts did not have the mandate of the ordinary Irish rural farmer. The dominant mantras of the Land League were "Ireland for the Irish" and "The land for the people", which sounded vaguely similar to the mantras that would be used almost three decades later by Mannix when in Australia.[12]

Having discussed the development of Irish politics during the formative years of Daniel Mannix the book will now focus on the other main protagonist. De Valera's childhood was strikingly different to Mannix's, not alone due to the development of Irish society during de Valera's youth in Bruree, but also in his family's structure. Much has been written of his birth in America in 1882 and his relationship with his mother that would follow him all through his political life. The family was at the centre of the Irish community in the late nineteenth century and the de Valeras were no different. At the heart of this family was the mother, "without whom the entire family enterprise was inconceivable and would have collapsed", as Santamaria contends.[13] Kate de Valera, his mother, could not afford to care for young Eamon in America after her husband Vivion's death. Therefore, she sent him back to Bruree, Co. Limerick into

---

[11] McCaffrey, op. cit., p. 8.

[12] Mark Tierney, *Ireland Since 1870* (Dublin: CJ Fallon, 1988), p. 39.

[13] Santamaria, op. cit., p. 16.

the care of his grandmother, uncle and aunt.[14] Whereas the young Mannix had strong family foundations during his youth, de Valera largely relied on the only male in his household for political influence, his Uncle Pat. De Valera's official biographers contend how, "uncle Pat's politics spread beyond the national issues to other problems. He would become a member of the Land and Labour League also", which shows the popularity of the land question in both the Mannix and De Valera households.[15] However, young de Valera seemed to have little time for matters in Irish politics.

Whether Mannix or de Valera, nominally or willingly, took an active interest in politics mattered little, as no person could avoid contact with the national machine that the Land League had become. Politics, particularly central politics in Westminster, mattered little to the Irish farmer of the mid nineteenth century, but the land agitation movement changed all this. "The land agitation achieved the largest participation of any movement in Irish history, mobilising sectors of the population and areas of the country just beginning to become politicised."[16] Successive militant and constitutional attempts to improve standards for Irish citizens had failed to provide sustained effort through the rifle or ballot box, but the Land League under Davitt, Devoy and most importantly, Parnell, would put in motion the wheels of Irish independence culminating in a new generation of forced action through the I.R.B in 1916. Three years before Mannix was to enter the politically isolated institution of Maynooth, the well-known Irish language advocate Fr Peter O'Leary brought the fifteen-year-old Mannix and his classmates from Kilfinane classical school to attend the first meeting of the Land League in Charleville town.[17] It seems that the organisation, as advocated by the "New Departure", appealed not just to the ordinary farmer, but also to all branches of society.

For any organisation with hopes of national recognition and acceptance to survive, that strong pillar of Irish society, the Catholic Church, had to support it and bless its objectives. The Catholic Church was not governing from Dublin like the central British administration, but instead it had its clergy located in every townland and community in Ireland, wearing the cloth of religious governance. The Catholic Church attempted to gain influence in Irish society through its dioceses and parishes especially since its confidence was at a high due to its victory in the Emancipation

---

[14] The Earl of Longford and Thomas P. O'Neill, *Eamon de Valera* (London: Hutchinson, 1970), p. 2.

[15] ibid, p. 4.

[16] Lee, op. cit., p. 96.

[17] Santamaria, op. cit., p. 18.

struggle. Historian John A. Murphy supports this argument suggesting, "the political power of the Irish priest may be traced back to his whole-hearted involvement in the final stages of the Emancipation struggle."[18] This new mode of political organisation in Irish politics, symbolised by the Land League, also heralded a new generation within clerical circles in Ireland. Cardinal Paul Cullen had a strong distrust for all revolutionary organisations during his lifetime, particularly the Fenians. However, this new clerical renaissance spearheaded by Michael Logue and William Walsh, "had none of Cullen's hatred of revolution, his suspicions about where nationalism ultimately led or his contempt for popularity".[19] These two prelates would be important characters much later in the life of Daniel Mannix. Following their promotion to the fore of the church hierarchy, they allowed the new political ideology of the Land League to flow freely among the various parishes in Ireland, sometimes even partaking in the activities themselves. Archbishop Walsh's first speech in June 1885, following his appointment to Dublin, gave firm support to the work of the League. He focused on how Ireland had the right, "to have her own laws made upon Irish soil and by the legally and constitutionally chosen representatives of the Irish people".[20]

The first connection between these two future leaders of the Irish, both at home and abroad, comes in the form of their education. Their first direct link arrives through their education at the Christian Brothers School in Charleville, Co. Cork. The Christian Brothers had a distinguished role in the education of generations of young Irish men with many of their students going on to achieving global fame. Both Mannix and de Valera would go on to represent Ireland at a high level and it can be argued that both carried that strong Christian Brothers ethos with them throughout their lives. Even later, in 1911, Mannix would as president of Maynooth, introduce the Christian Brothers' *Manual of Etiquette and Good Manners* in an attempt to solve student disciplinary problems within the college.[21] The education of the two characters contained strong religious teaching, but also incorporated favourable nationalistic sentiment. For the young de Valera, the discipline and lessons learned during his years in Charleville would indubitably stand him in good stead through a long, rough and mentally demanding public life. The mental steeliness that both teenagers

---

[18] John A. Murphy, 'Priests and People in Modern Irish History' in *Christus Rex: Journal of Sociology*, 23 (1969), p. 248.

[19] Marcus Tanner, *Irelands holy wars: the struggle for a nation's soul 1500-2000* (New Haven, London: Yale University Press, 2003), p. 252.

[20] ibid.

[21] Ebsworth, op. cit., p. 53.

developed was very similar. This, along with their bravery in the face of public adversity, became the reason for their public's adulation. De Valera's son Terry, in later years would comment how, "fundamentally his father was far too brave, both morally and physically to allow himself to become overcome or lose control, most particularly in a grave situation."[22] The education of Ireland's young Catholics lay in the hands of the various religious organisations around the country, and some harboured and portrayed strong nationalistic tendencies, including the Christian Brothers. This vice-like grip on education by the Catholic Church also fostered an opportunity to push for new recruits and the two young intellectually gifted students would be ideal future recruits.

Although de Valera's education was as strongly grounded in religion as Mannix's, he decided after careful deliberation against the idea of entering the priesthood. Historian T. Dwyer writes how, "for a time de Valera seriously considered entering the priesthood with the Holy Ghost Fathers."[23] Mannix was set however, to illuminate the ranks of the church, strongly influenced by his admiration of the strongly nationalistic clerics William Croke, future Archbishop of Cashel and the archbishop's uncle, Thomas William Croke of the same name. Thomas William Croke who was parish priest of Charleville would baptise Mannix as a baby.[24] Mannix would later claim that it was from Archbishop Walsh, "whom he learnt that the priest is not to remain hidden and isolated in the sanctuary, but should go out among his people to guide them in the whole of their lives, socially, culturally and even politically".[25] Indeed the church had long intertwined itself with every strand of Irish society as Archbishop Croke had. The Catholic Church would play an important role in the two characters' futures. It would also play a key role in Irish life particularly when it came to national issues. At the forefront of the church's public image were the shepherds on the ground including Dr Mannix leading their flocks, many being closer to the parish then to Rome. A strong, influential and, more often than not, united body was something the nationalists needed on their side particularly after Catholic Emancipation in 1829 allowing Sean Ó Faoláin to comment how, "that terrible bogy-man of the nineteenth century all over Europe, 'the priest in politics', had arrived".[26] Although the Land Wars and the subsequent push for Home

---

[22] De Valera, *A memoir*, p. 164.

[23] Dwyer, *Eamon de Valera: The Man & the Myths* (Dublin: Paperview/Irish Independent, 2006), p. 13.

[24] Ebsworth, op. cit., p. 28.

[25] ibid, p. 29.

[26] Murphy, op. cit., pp 249-250.

Rule under John Redmond dominated the political landscape as Ireland entered the twentieth century, there was a counter-movement stirring that would eventually be led by de Valera. This counter-movement would lead to a new organisation challenging the church's position on Irish independence. In 1889, a talented journalist named Arthur Griffith became founder-editor of the paper the *United Irishman*. Although fiercely separatist in tone, the paper did not condone military action.[27] A young seventeen-year-old de Valera would have begun to read the ideas preached by Griffith and others. It would take two long decades, however before Griffith's political party of Sinn Féin in the 1918 general election, with de Valera as a candidate, would begin to challenge England's view of Ireland's right to self-governance.

As the church's status grew, it also gradually led to its encroachment into areas outside of the educational sphere into areas of "general social concern" namely the national question.[28] The Irish Parliamentary Party under John Redmond would provide leadership on the national question as Ireland entered the twentieth century, but the church was also effective in this regard. Whyte suggests that "before the opinions of the people could be made effective, they needed leadership; and that leadership was provided by the clergy."[29]

With Home Rule dominating Irish politics at the start of the twentieth century, the Church did not want to find its position in society once again under threat from the politics of nationalism. The Church always sought to establish and maintain a dominant position in Irish society and became very insecure with regard nationalist issues. J. H. Whyte, in his book *Church and State in Modern Ireland 1923-1970,* argues that, "three episodes in particular can be mentioned in the sixty years before 1923, in which Catholics simply defied the rulings of the Church."[30] The first two events, the 1867 Fenian Rising that had no church support and secondly, the 1890 fall of Parnell due to his affair with Mrs Kitty O'Shea had left the church in a precarious position with regards to Irish nationalism. However, most ironically it was at the third juncture of church interference in nationalist issues, following its condemnation of the anti-treaty forces

---

[27] Declan Kiberd, *Inventing Ireland: the literature of the modern nation* (London: Vintage Books, 1995), p. 191.

[28] Patrick Corish, *The Irish Catholic experience: a historical survey* (Dublin: Gill & Macmillan, 1985), p. 226.

[29] J. H Whyte, 'The influence of the Catholic clergy on elections in nineteenth century Ireland' in *The English Historical Review*, 75 (295) 1960, p. 249.

[30] J. H. Whyte, *Church & state in modern Ireland: 1923-70* (Dublin: Gill & Macmillan, 1971), p. 9.

during the Civil War, that eventually cemented both Mannix's and de
Valera's relationship with each other. The church's reaction to anti-treaty
violence during the Civil War effectively meant that the Catholic Church
would lose favour with the hard-line nationalists by 1923. It would also
lose both Mannix's and de Valera's loyalty on these issues. By 1923 they
would become central religious and political leaders respectively. The
people began to lose faith in the church. In later years, Mannix would turn
against this idea and would consistently decide to intervene in the political
arena in both Ireland and Australia.

The history of Ireland during both men's youth is of conflict between
militant and constitutional nationalism. The Roman Catholic Church was
the constant variable, keeping the fabrics of society interwoven, with the
two variant nationalisms either being in the ascendant or descendant. The
Catholic Church in Ireland could not alone claim ownership of Ireland's
past although previously they had tried. Under Cardinal Cullen, the
Catholic Church had warned the Fenians and other organisations away
from ownership of Ireland's national and social history. Cullen "repeatedly
reminded the Fenians that they held neither a monopoly in patriotism nor
ownership of the Irish past".[31] The Catholic Church at the turn of the
nineteenth century bore all the hallmarks of an establishment and acted
accordingly.[32] Daniel Mannix would become a part of this establishment
in 1882 and would subdue his political ideas to gain greater accreditation
within the Roman Catholic Church. De Valera having become a member
of Conradh na Gaeilge in 1908 would develop a love for all things Irish,
but particularly the language. That organisation was part of another branch
of society seeking to gain ownership of Ireland's past through a revival of
the Irish language. At this juncture in Irish history, the various strands and
organisations were each looking for their own interpretation of an "Irish
Nation" and how they might accomplish it separately.

The so-called Irish-Ireland movement deemed that the Irish people
should eliminate all that was English from Irish life and take control of
their own destinies. This revival had its roots in Gaelic ethnicity and
organisations such as the Gaelic Athletic Association, the Literary Revival
and the Gaelic League, aimed to re-unite Irish people with their own
special Celtic past.[33] The revival's ideals began to spread into every aspect
of Irish society and the Catholic Church was no exception. There was a lot
of cross membership, but no one body had enough popular support to push

---

[31] Kevin Collins, *Catholic churchmen and the Celtic revival in Ireland 1848-1916*
(Dublin: Four Courts Press, 2002), p. 16.
[32] Corish, op. cit., p. 226.
[33] Tierney, op. cit., pp 108-109.

for outright British withdrawal from Irish life. The changing and evolving nature of Irish society in the late nineteenth century had a profound influence on members of the public and Mannix, and de Valera were not exceptions. As discussed, the Land League and subsequent Land Wars had moulded Mannix's political outlook before he entered the priesthood. The book will later show how in Maynooth, Mannix still held a key interest in the Land question. De Valera, although not as politically involved as Mannix at an early age, could not ignore the efforts made by the Irish Parliamentary Party towards Home Rule. However, as Ryle Dwyer comments, "when the British suspended the Home Rule Bill, which was due to become law in 1914, he began to have doubts about the policy of the IPP."[34] The land question had effectively ended with better rights for the landowners secured in 1909 with the Birrell Land Act. The way was open for a new actor to enter the scene of Irish nationalism. The historical narrative had changed and it was time for the story to be re-written with a fresh beginning and new characters as Ireland entered the twentieth century. The seeds of their political education had been sown in our two protagonists. Each was planted within the evolving Irish political arena of the late nineteenth century. It would not be long before the paths of the two characters would begin to come into view and cross each other on the final road to Irish Independence. Just as Pearse retorted at his court-martial that he and his men had "kept faith with the past, and handed a tradition to the future", it was now time for Mannix and de Valera to carry the mantle of Irish republicanism well into the twentieth century like those before them.[35]

"Ireland would live when other countries are remembered only in
history".[36]
—Archbishop Daniel Mannix – 27 March 1921

---

[34] T Ryle Dwyer, *Eamon de Valera (Gill's Irish Lives)* (Dublin: Gill & Macmillan, 1991) p. 7.

[35] Sidney Hook, *The hero in history: A Study in Limitation and Possibility* (New York: Transaction Publishers, 1943), p. 63.

[36] Handwritten account by [...] of a meeting at the Irish College welcoming Archbishop Mannix, 27 March 1921 (Irish College in Rome, Msgr. Hagan papers, HAG1 1921-174-0002).

CHAPTER TWO

MAYNOOTH, A GAELIC INSTITUTION?
(1882-1913)

The catholic priest in late nineteenth and early twentieth century Ireland played a key role at the centre of parish and diocesan affairs. A culture of reverence and respect for religion accompanied the position that the priesthood established in society. As John A. Murphy points out, "every generation has venerated the priest who seemed to be making a stand for liberty against political or social oppression".[1] In the eyes of the Irish Catholic Church, Maynooth was seen as being just as important as Downpatrick due to its role in educating young men for the priesthood. In 1882, Daniel Mannix would enter Maynooth and would eventually become part of the Irish Catholic establishment. Mannix, or in Irish – Ó Mainchín, which translates as "little monk",[2] may have entered as an eighteen-year-old farmer's son, but by the time he would leave it thirty-one years later a significant metamorphosis would have taken place. As he began life there in his adolescence, he probably never could have envisaged that he would be leaving the college as president.[3] As the Irish Catholic Church's prime recruitment agency of young educated males, Maynooth would continue as a powerbroker in Irish society. This chapter will focus on the early career of Mannix. It will focus on Mannix's term as president of Maynooth College and how his first connections with de Valera were established during this period.

As Mannix was progressing with his studies, Charles Stewart Parnell was propelling himself to the fore of Ireland's push for Home Rule. The Irish Catholic Church also had some cunning politicians of its own, most notably Archbishop William Walsh. As president of Maynooth, Walsh

---

[1] John A. Murphy, 'Priests and People in Modern Irish History' in *Christus Rex: Journal of Sociology*, 23 (1969), p. 258.
[2] Edward MacLysaght, *The surnames of Ireland* (Dublin: Irish Academic Press Ltd., 1973), pp 207-208.
[3] B. A Santamaria, *Daniel Mannix: A biography* (Melbourne: Melbourne University Publishing, 1984), p. 2.

was in control of the next generation of clerical graduates, which would help stem the tide of anti-clericalism that had swept across Europe in the later part of the nineteenth century. His standing as a "considerable academic with specialist knowledge in the fields of theology, law, economics and the natural sciences" made him the ideal candidate to promote loyalty in the young, rejuvenated, clerical ranks at Maynooth.[4] The loyalty that Walsh encouraged was exemplified in the academic performance of the young Mannix. To say he was an outstanding student would be an understatement. It is evident that the young native of Deerpark impressed the clerical ranks of Maynooth through his consistently high standard of achievement. As Bishop of Goulburn would later express, "he set a standard of merit which became traditional. All students since his time have been measured by that standard".[5] The standard of study at Maynooth was consistently high and this would have been maintained under Walsh's stewardship. De Wiel suggests that one of the reasons for this was that Walsh "as a teacher did not seem to have much patience for weak pupils".[6] After his ordination in 1889, Mannix decided to undertake a further year of study in the Dunboyne Establishment with a view to a future role in professorship.

Daniel Mannix entered the priesthood on Sunday, 8 June 1890 at the age of twenty-seven and gained the privilege of being the first student to be ordained in the recently opened college chapel, by Archbishop Walsh.[7] As Mannix was exiting Maynooth, Parnell was at the peak of his political career. Under Parnell's stewardship, the Irish Parliamentary Party was seeking to establish a Home Rule Parliament for Ireland in Dublin. If Home Rule were granted to the Irish people, it would signify a considerable step towards overall democratic independence from Britain. For Mannix, de Valera and so many generations of Irish, this would be a significant milestone in the history of their nation. Aspirations of gaining Home Rule were dealt a substantial blow when a split would occur in the I.P.P. due to Parnell's implication in the O'Shea's divorce case. Parnell would not live to witness the achievement of Home Rule. The Irish Catholic Church is often considered as being the catalyst behind his demise because of its response to his involvement in a divorce case. J. J.

---

[4] Dermot Keogh, *The Vatican, the bishops and Irish politics 1919-1939* (Cambridge: Cambridge University Press, 1986), p. 8.
[5] Rev Walter Ebsworth, *Archbishop Mannix* (Armadale: Victoria: H.H. Stephenson, 1977), p. 43.
[6] Jerome Aan de Wiel, *Catholic Church in Ireland 1914-1918: war and politics* (Dublin: Irish Academic Press, 2003), p. 54.
[7] Ebsworth, op. cit., pp 44-45.

Lee, however, vindicates the church with regard to this position by acknowledging that, "it was not Ireland, but the nonconformist wing of the Liberal Party in England that set the wheels in motion to bring down Parnell."[8]

Parnell had tried before his death to use the dominant issues in nineteenth century Ireland to push for a united effort to achieve Home Rule. Canon Sheehan, like Mannix, another product of the Maynooth system, identified these themes throughout his works of literature. In novels such as *The Graves at Kilmorna*, the leitmotifs of "nationality, land and religion" dominated the lives of Sheehan's characters. Fleischmann, developing further upon the ideas of Daniel Corkery[9], sees Sheehan's works being dominated with "the moving forces of Irish history" and sees Sheehan's key issues "as the central themes of Irish literature".[10] The themes in Sheehan's novels were also represented in the lives of Mannix and de Valera. During his adolescence, Mannix was exposed to the workings of the Land League before moving onto the priesthood. His first entry into the political arena would be in his opposition to the conscription issue in Australia. De Valera's life, it could be said, also followed Sheehan's leitmotifs, but in a different order to Mannix. These began with de Valera's consideration of joining the priesthood, to pushing for Ireland's case for independence, to his eventual role as Taoiseach and his attempts at Irish reunification.

By the time of Parnell's death in October 1891, Mannix had progressed well up the long slope towards the peak of his public renown. Aged thirty-five, he had already occupied the Chair of Moral Theology at Maynooth for four years and would continue to do so for another five years.[11] Had he not opted for the academic route a vacant position in the Irish hierarchy might have been offered to him. His intellectual prowess and capacity as a determined and focused prelate began to garner attention, not just from the Irish Catholic hierarchy, but also from abroad. During his time in Maynooth, Mannix would become secretary to the newly formed Maynooth Union. The union was a body that celebrated Maynooth college through gatherings of its former students and teachers. As secretary,

---

[8] Joseph Lee, *The modernisation of Irish society 1848-1918* (Dublin: Gill & Macmillan, 2008), p. 118.

[9] Daniel Corkery, *Synge and Anglo-Irish literature: A Study* (Cork: Cork University Press, 1931).

[10] Ruth Fleischmann, *Catholic nationalism in the Irish revival: a study of Canon Sheehan, 1852-1913*, (New York: St. Martin's Press, 1997), p. x.

[11] B. A. Santamaria, *Santamaria: a memoir* (Melbourne: Oxford University Press, 1997), p. 16.

Mannix invited his future superior, Archbishop Carr, to address the union on Carr's work at improving education standards for Catholics in Victoria, Australia. Fr Michael O'Hickey D.D., Professor of Gaelic at Maynooth, opened that particular meeting.[12] Both Hickey and Carr played large parts in the succession of events, which culminated in Dr Mannix leaving for the distant shores of Melbourne, Australia.

While Mannix's career was progressing, young de Valera was also making a name for himself in education circles. He won a small scholarship enabling him to attend Blackrock College. His special aptitude for mathematics earmarked him as a future teacher like Mannix, leaving behind his vocation for the religious life.[13] What is strikingly similar about both men is their academic ingenuity and how both were yet young as they made an impression in their respective fields. The year 1903 was a significant year in both men's early careers. De Valera, aged 21, qualified as a maths teacher that year. He later accepted a position at Rockwell College, Co. Tipperary.[14] Dr Mannix became president of Maynooth and led the college through the early years of the twentieth century.

The political climate in Ireland at the start of the twentieth century showed no signs of unrest. Fitzgibbon points out that, "the comparative and indeed unusual, placidity of Irish political life was, at the time, briefly and irrelevantly interrupted by the Boer War (1899-1902)."[15] This war saw the might of the British Empire pitted against Dutch small farmers in South Africa. Irishmen fought on both sides. The war had untold consequences for people like John MacBride and Arthur Griffith. Having fought in the war on the side of the Boers, MacBride would later return to take part in the 1916 Rising. After witnessing the Boer War in South Africa, journalist Griffith later returned to Ireland and would form the Sinn Féin party. His party, of which de Valera later became president, was the dominant nationalist party by 1918. While the political undercurrents of militant and constitutional nationalism remained dormant to an extent during the opening years of the twentieth century, a nascent nationalism was beginning to sweep across Ireland. New organisations began to spawn countrywide most notably the Gaelic Athletic Association (1884)[16], the Gaelic League (1893)[17] and the Abbey Theatre (1904).[18] The collective

---

[12] Ebsworth, op. cit., pp 50-51.
[13] Constantine Fitzgibbon & George Morrison, *The life and times of Eamon De Valera* (Dublin: Gill & Macmillan, 1973), p. 25.
[14] ibid
[15] ibid, p. 26.
[16] The G.A.A was founded on 1 November 1884.
[17] The Gaelic League was founded on 31 July 1893.

aim of these new organisations was to promote and revive the idea of a Gaelic Ireland. The dominant mantra of this movement was "Ireland for the Irish"; through the promotion of the Irish language, literature and sport, they aimed to generate a separate autonomous Irish identity. In many respects, it was the cultural equivalent of the Land League. All political classes and creeds in Ireland became involved in this Gaelic revival. The diverse membership heightened the movement's popularity and success at the onset of the twentieth century. It was unusual for the time that women were involved in such movements. Hannah Sheehy Skeffington states that, "women who were interested in politics usually joined the Gaelic League or Sinn Féin."[19]

The Catholic Church also became part of this Gaelic revival and Maynooth was to the forefront as an institution of Catholic, Gaelic ethnicity. Kevin Collins contends that, "the Roman Catholic Church took upon itself the role of 'keepers of Ireland's historical identity' by placing early Christian Ireland at the centre of its historical perspective."[20] The Irish language was a much more powerful weapon against British Imperialism than sport or Gaelic traditions. The language pushed the Gaelic League to the forefront of the Gaelic revival in the search for a Gaelic Ireland. W.B. Yeats often evoked this vision of an Irish Ireland in his works through the character of Cathleen Ní Houlihan. Pádraig Pearse later expressed the view that:

> ... the Gaelic League will be recognised in history as the most revolutionary influence that has ever come into Ireland. The Irish Revolution really began when the seven Proto Gaelic Leaguers met in O'Connell Street.[21]

By the turn of the twentieth century, the Gaelic League had already gathered significant support within the ranks of the Irish Catholic clergy, even including members of the hierarchy. This is demonstrated in a letter dated 12 March 1902, from the editor of the Gaelic League's newspaper An Claidheamh Solais, from Pádraig Pearse to the then archbishop of Dublin. In the letter, Pearse thanked Archbishop Walsh for his subscription

---

[18] The Abbey Theatre first opened its doors on 27 December 1904.

[19] Senia Paseta, Before the revolution: nationalism, social change and Ireland's Catholic elite, 1879-1922 (Cork: Cork University Press, 1999), p. 64.

[20] , Kevin Collins, Catholic churchmen and the Celtic revival in Ireland 1848-1916 (Dublin: Four Courts Press, 2002), pp 29-30.

[21] Pádraig Pearse quoted in Terry de Valera, A memoir (Dublin: Currach Press, 2004), p. 99.

to the language fund. Walsh's subscription indicates sympathy on the part of a leading member of the Catholic hierarchy for the aims and objectives of the League.[22] Led by Douglas Hyde, a Protestant from Roscommon, the Gaelic League began to expand rapidly. It set about achieving the aim of putting the Irish language at the forefront of national and cultural aspirations. Hyde lamented that "the continuity of Irish life" would be finally broken unless the trend of language decline since after the famine was reversed.[23] The church provided a stable pillar upon which the public could lean upon during the famine, periods of emigration and rebellion. The Catholic Church, eager to continue its dominance in Irish society sought to be at the forefront of this Gaelic Ireland movement. The movement was non-denominational. The promotion and revival of the Irish language captured the imagination of the Irish public; therefore, it was evident that conflict would emerge over the "ownership" of the language question as an issue of socio-political dominance. The Catholic Church, although happy with the work of the League, tried to use it to augment its position within Irish society. The Gaelic revival would fuel a new strain of cultural nationalism in Ireland that would dominate the political landscape during the opening decade of the twentieth century.

Dr Mannix's presidency of Maynooth coincided with this movement. Two issues would largely be associated with his presidency. The first was the college's recognition by the National University of Ireland. Secondly and most controversially, however, was the issue of Irish language use within the college. Mannix often stood between the wishes of his hierarchical superiors and fellow clerical colleagues on various issues, but the Irish language question would prove to be the greatest source of conflict. In a way, as Frank Biletz states,

> ... this was paradoxical, because the cultural revival tended to strengthen the identification of the catholic faith with Irish nationality. Most priests, moreover, considered themselves sympathetic to the national cause in general and many actively participated in the Gaelic League and other organisations of the new nationalism.[24]

---

[22] Pádraig Pearse letter to Archbishop William Walsh, 12 March 1902, (Dublin Diocesan Archives/AB6/376/2-4).

[23] Lee, op. cit., p. 142.

[24] Frank A. Biletz, 'The Irish peasant and the conflict between Irish Ireland and the Catholic bishops 1903-1910' in Stewart J. Brown & David W. Miller (eds.) *Piety and power in Ireland , 1760-1960 : essays in honour of Emmet Larkin* (Belfast: The Institute of Irish Studies, 2000), p. 108.

Maynooth had a strained relationship with the Irish language. Firstly, it was not recognised in the college, as Ebsworth points out, "as a vernacular language". Having had a chair of Irish from 1802, the college discontinued the chair in 1878 due to the lack of students opting to study it.[25] To native speakers of the language this must have seemed like an outstanding surrender of national culture and traditions by the Irish Catholic Church however, the famine had done extensive damage to its base throughout the countryside. Some scholars like Donald Akenson, argued that Irish was in decline well before the famine and that it only accelerated the death of a language. Akenson estimates that "by roughly the year 1800, English was in the ascendant. Among young people, knowledge of English was more common than among their elders and it was the younger people who most often chose to emigrate".[26] There were three root causes to the decline of the language. Two of them have already been highlighted: the famine and emigration. The third, economic progress, is not as readily obvious, but it is just as significant. English was the language of the bustling British Empire; it became the language of trade and commerce. Irish became associated with rural marginalisation and poverty in the west of Ireland, and a life of economic stagnation. Many native Irish speakers were forced to relinquish the language of their youth if they hoped to succeed in the limited market economy that was Ireland. Many of Ireland's youngest and brightest including the great Daniel O'Connell suddenly became enemies in the eyes other native Irish speakers, for relinquishing the language. This did not as Kevin Collins contends, "prevent O'Connell from, raising his two eldest sons as Irish-speaking".[27] The decline of the language had long since set in and "Irish linguistic nationalism was developing, if belatedly in comparison with other contemporary nationalisms during O'Connell's time."[28]

Irish linguistic nationalism slowly began to find its way into the corridors of Maynooth. The return of the language to the forefront of Maynooth's push for inclusion in the broad-sweeping cultural movement of the twentieth century can be largely accredited to one man, Fr Eugene O'Growney. Ordained in 1888, he was afforded the new Chair of Gaelic in 1891 and succeeded in making Irish a "compulsory subject in Humanity and Rhetoric classes."[29] O'Growney became a rock for the linguistic

---

[25] Ebsworth, op. cit., pp 76-77.
[26] Donald Harmon Akenson, *The Irish diaspora: a primer* (Belfast: The Institute of Irish Studies, 1993), pp 40-41.
[27] Collins, op. cit., p. 12.
[28] ibid.
[29] ibid.

revival and gave vast encouragement to organisations such as the Gaelic League. Most importantly, he sowed the seed for the language in people like Canon Sheehan, Fr Peter O'Leary, but most significantly in Mannix's case, Fr Michael O'Hickey, successor to O'Growney and the new professor of Irish at Maynooth.[30]

Maynooth in a historical sense would become one of the last strongholds and institutions of hope for Irish. Although the language had long been in decline, "the proportion of clerical speakers of Irish at Maynooth in 1851 was almost twice as high as the percentage for the population as a whole".[31] According to Gaelic enthusiasts such as Fr Michael O'Hickey, Mannix, due to his position as head of this institution, should have played a substantial part in the promotion of the language. This student of O'Growney felt that priests in Maynooth should be at the heart of this prominent Gaelic revival, if not leading from the front. The education of priests with a view to their future role on the missions was more important to Dr Mannix, than those interests promulgated by the priesthood in Ireland.[32] The Irish language was largely irrelevant for those priests who would take up positions abroad. The Catholic clergy encouraged by the hierarchy's endorsement of the organisation became members of the Gaelic League as they were. Although cultural nationalism bloomed as a multi- denominational, cross-class initiative, a metamorphosis was taking place with the inclusion of many Catholic priests in its swelling ranks. The approval of Fr O'Hickey, as vice-president of the organisation, confirmed the Catholic hierarchy's acceptance of the Irish language movement. O'Hickey lectured to an audience in Liverpool in 1902 that, "Gaelic was the mind, the soul, the great bulwark of the Irish nationality. The mission of the Gaelic League is to minister to the soul of the nation".[33] The hierarchy supported the Gaelic League as it allowed it another avenue by which it could attach itself to the Irish public. It was also very pleasing for the primate Cardinal Logue and Archbishop Walsh to see the priests heavily involved in this cultural revolution. However, this cultural renaissance also had hints of militancy in its membership and it became more politicised.

A public confrontation was about to take place and the spark that ignited this was the National University debate in 1908. The debate entailed the argument concerning whether Irish should be a compulsory

---

[30] Ebsworth, op. cit., p. 82.

[31] Collins, op. cit., p. 49.

[32] Santamaria, op. cit., pp 24-25.

[33] Marcus Tanner, *Irelands holy wars: the struggle for a nation's soul 1500-2000* (New Haven, London: Yale University Press, 2003), pp 269-270.

subject for students wishing to matriculate. The key protagonists behind this disagreement were Fr O'Hickey and Mannix. The hierarchy of the Irish Catholic Church was represented through Mannix's presidency at the college. The bishops collectively opposed the argument for compulsory Irish, fearing it would drive unqualified candidates into Trinity College. O'Hickey argued strongly and vocally against this. He had come from a strong nationalist background in Waterford and viewed Irish as the cornerstone on which Ireland's national resurgence would be laid. As president the guidance and safeguarding of the interests of a future diasporic clergy was more important to Mannix than those interests appropriated to the priesthood in Ireland.[34] Mannix was not known to have ever spoken Irish and would later accredit this to the prominent Gaelic scholar, Fr O'Leary. In 1912, after receiving the freedom of Dublin City, Fr O'Leary was invited along with Kuno Meyer, a distinguished scholar of Celtic philology and literature, to spend the night at the college as guests of the president. In conversation with his guests that evening, the president related to them that O'Leary his former teacher, had indeed, "never taught Mannix a word of Irish". Ebsworth, however, argues in Canon Leary's defence, who was also a prominent Irish literary scholar, that "strangely, Gaelic was not a subject at the president's school in Charleville".[35] The president's lack of association with the Irish language as a boy was not unusual to Irish society in the 1860s and 70s. The revival of the Irish language by the Gaelic League would certainly prove to be a monumental task.

Mannix's lack of education in the Irish language would not help his case, especially when pressure was placed on him by Irish language enthusiasts to have Irish made compulsory for admission to Maynooth. In hindsight, Mannix's pragmatic approach in his capacity as president ensured the success of an important function for the college, the ordination of priests for the missions. James Griffin, acknowledges Mannix's success by outlining how, "in 1903 only 11 of 80 Maynooth entrants had qualified for matriculation studies, all priests now met degree requirements", due to his stance against compulsory Irish.[36] Mannix was able to make his case not only through his role as president, but also in his capacity as a member of the N.U.I. senate. The Senate became the object of derision for language enthusiasts such as Pearse, Hyde and O'Hickey. Here, Mannix, supported by other who opposed the language requirement, objected on

---

[34] Gerry Macardle, 'Turbulent priest' (RTÉ drama documentary, 1989) Disc 1.
[35] Ebsworth, op. cit., p. 28.
[36] James Griffin, 'Archbishop Daniel Mannix' in *The Old Limerick Journal*, 27 (1990), p. 28

the issue "on the grounds that most Irish students could not speak the
language, so that they would be ineligible for admission to the university if
Irish were a prerequisite".[37] Mannix's strength and independence during
this period would impress many but also gain him numerous enemies.
Historians have largely neglected Mannix's contribution to both Irish
church and Maynooth college's history. Historian John B. O'Brien lauds
Mannix's achievements, in his primary role as president of Maynooth,

> ... when he was appointed President only a small proportion of entrants to
> Maynooth had matriculated or even aspired to matriculate but within four
> years he reported that, all the students of the Rhetoric and Logic classes
> have entered for the First and Second University examinations
> respectively.[38]

In a strange irony of history, the father of modern Irish nationalism,
Pádraig Pearse began the assault on Mannix, in his capacity as editor of *An
Claidheamh Solais*. To the present day reader, the following quote by
Pearse seems almost surreal, considering Mannix's future republican role.
However, between 1907 and 1916 Mannix became for the Irish nationalists
the epitome of a "Castle Catholic". Pearse accused Mannix of treason in
light of his views on the Irish language question by asking, "Can it be that
where Irish Ireland hoped to find a friend she has found an enemy who is
in a position to do her untold harm"?[39]

Archbishop Walsh's backing was pivotal in determining the outcome
of this argument. He feared that this argument could prove detrimental to
the credibility of the Irish Catholic Church in the eyes of the cultural
nationalists. At the onset of this prolonged affair, Walsh was firmly
committed to Mannix's cause. He even threatened to end his approval of
the work of the Gaelic League because of Pearse's denunciation of
Mannix. Agnes O'Farrelly would later appeal to Walsh for his continued
support. In a letter to the archbishop, she wrote:

> I need hardly say that I regret extremely that Your Grace disapproves of
> any action of the Gaelic League and that the organisation is in danger of
> losing your sympathy and friendly help.[40]

---

[37] ibid.

[38] John B. O'Brien, *Daniel Mannix: builder of the Australian church* (Dublin:
Veritas, 1988), pp 10-11.

[39] Ruth Dudley Edwards, *Patrick Pearse: the triumph of failure* (Dublin: Irish
Academic Press Ltd., 2006), p. 74.

[40] ibid, p.75.

Similarly, through the publication of his booklet entitled *An Irish University – Or Else!* in 1909, Fr O'Hickey began to question Archbishop Walsh's loyalties. The archbishop thus resolved to give O'Hickey his support, thereby turning his back on Mannix. O'Brien suggests that the reasoning behind this was that Walsh was "a long standing friend of O'Hickey and was also a Gaelic enthusiast".[41]

Mannix's strength of character and resolve were put to the test over the next four years. O'Hickey seemed to have a liking for provocative, intemperate language that certainly garnered attention, but not always the unequivocal support that he could have had. In his booklet, he launched a verbal tirade against the opponents of Irish, most notably, Mannix. He preached to his readers to:

> ... let us not ourselves to be cajoled ... by a section of the Irish population, who, though Catholics, are un-Irish, when not anti-Irish, in every fibre of their being, even in the innermost marrow of their bones.[42]

The fiery clash had become public through the writings of Pearse and others in such newspapers as *An Claidheamh Solais* and the controversy put Mannix's presidency to the test.

Mannix proved his mettle by recommending O'Hickey's dismissal to the Irish bishops, who were the Board of Trustees at Maynooth. He knew he had to defend his corner or risk a substantial challenge to his presidency. It was also possible that it might lead to Mannix being overlooked for a future episcopal nomination in Ireland. He outlined to the trustees how O'Hickey's contempt for his decision and even his slandering of the president was, "giving the worst possible example to the students whom he was bound to train in obedience and respect for authority".[43] Mannix succeeded in securing O'Hickey's dismissal and set out to assert his presidential authority in the college. Showing no reluctance, he followed O'Hickey's dismissal with the closure of the Dunboyne postgraduate institute for a year. He also had "five of its students who had signed a telegram to a militant League meeting in Dublin – 'Uncompromisingly we stand for immediate compulsory Irish' – given their marching orders".[44] The worst thing from Mannix's perspective

---

[41] O'Brien, op. cit., p. 11.
[42] Collins, op. cit., p. 53.
[43] Dermot Keogh, 'Mannix, de Valera and Irish nationalism', in John B. O'Brien and Pauric Travers (eds.), *The Irish emigrant experience in Australia* (Dublin: Poolbeg, 1991), p. 197.
[44] Ebsworth, op. cit., p. 85.

about this series of events is that it did not end there. O'Hickey, backed strongly by prominent Irish historical figures including Eoin MacNeill, Sir Roger Casement and Thomas MacDonagh, sought to appeal his case. His supporters set up a fund "for O'Hickey to allow him bring his case all the way to Rome".[45] Not only was the pressure of prominent Irish language nationalists upon Mannix to reverse his decision, but he ran the risk of losing discipline in the college and the support of the senate and Cardinal Logue if he did not act accordingly. Mannix had some staunch support of his own, most notably Archbishop Healy of Tuam. In a letter to Monsignor O'Riordan of the Irish College in Rome, he agreed with Mannix's dismissal of O'Hickey, explaining that, "in his judgement, such a man is wholly unfit to take any part in the training of ecclesiastical students".[46] Even though Mannix's presidency had support, its very foundation had suffered a seismic shift. He knew that O'Hickey's decision to take the case to Rome did not sit well with the Irish hierarchy and, "while initially he received the support of the College trustees, the hierarchy and the University Senate, he was convinced that their concurrence was reserved".[47]

The idea of Mannix being a lone renegade within the hierarchy of the Irish Catholic Church was something that was to become accepted norm in later years by de Valera and the anti-treatyites. Mannix, feeling isolated by Walsh and the Trustees pulled no punches in his retort to Pearse and the League. Reminding the Irish nationalists of his successes at Maynooth, Mannix suggested:

> ... it would be a day of joy and of hope for the friends of the national language when the Gaelic League, in its great work throughout the country, begins to follow the example and to rival the success of Maynooth. The Irish language would then be safe.[48]

The O'Hickey case demonstrates distinctly how Mannix reacted and managed potentially delicate situations. This would stand him in good stead later in life in his numerous public confrontations. There are many views on who was the real winner of the O'Hickey case and one must cast an eye on the book of Mannix's one time mentor, Dr Walter McDonald, or "Watty" McDonald as his peers referred to him. *Reminiscences of a*

---

[45] Colm Kiernan, 'Appréciation Archbishop Daniel Mannix of Melbourne, 1864-1963' in *Éire-Ireland*, 19 (3) 1984, p. 123.
[46] Ebsworth, op. cit., pp 85-86.
[47] O'Brien, op. cit., p. 11.
[48] Edwards, op. cit., p. 75.

Maynooth Professor gives a detailed account from the viewpoint of McDonald. His opinion on the course of events have been challenged by people such as B.A. Santamaria, who sees McDonald's account as a "strong propagandist version of O'Hickey's case", which contained a "long personal attack on the President of the College".[49] Walter Ebsworth, on the other hand, sees McDonald's contribution and attitude towards the case as, "dictated by neither spite nor jealousy; he was far above that".[50] McDonald's evaluation should be treated with caution in light of his own involvement and later events. After the decision was taken to dismiss O'Hickey, McDonald rebelled against Mannix, as he felt aggrieved over O'Hickey's dismissal. We note the occasion where McDonald published *The Irish Theological Quarterly*, without consent of the trustees and the president, knowing that by doing so he had violated a college statue. This is outlined in personal correspondence between McDonald and the President published in *Reminiscences*.[51] McDonald was willing to test the trustee's faith in Mannix's presidency and his presidency duly survived. Watty outlined how:

> ... the Trustees, did not meet till June 1909, when they had Dr. Hickey before them. They thought, I suppose, that one such culprit was enough at a time; and so, I fancy, I owe to Dr. O'Hickey my escape from censure on that occasion.[52]

It is evident from *Reminiscences of a Maynooth Professor* that McDonald took the side of O'Hickey in his argument with Mannix. The last word on the affair comes from two distinguished historians and specialists in Irish Church and Irish language history. Patrick Corish sees McDonald's account as being "widely known", but also "very partial", and believes that the best-balanced assessment comes from Leon Ó Broin.[53] In his summary, Ó Broin outlines how, "in the absence of all the relevant papers a final judgement is not possible". He adds that "McDonald planned O'Hickey's strategy and fed fuel to his discontent from his own sense of grievance". As for Mannix, it is easy to see his sense of unhappiness with the hierarchy and his superiors. Ó Broin observes "from

---

[49] Santamaria, *Daniel Mannix*, op. cit., pp 34-35.

[50] Ebsworth, op. cit., pp 86-87.

[51] Dr. Walter McDonald, *Reminiscences of a Maynooth professor* (Cork: The Mercier Press Ltd., 1967), pp 322-323.

[52] ibid, p. 339.

[53] Patrick Corish, *The Irish Catholic experience: a historical survey* (Dublin: Gill & Macmillan, 1985), p. 240.

the other side, there has been silence. But that silence is perhaps justified because the Bishops do not seem to have anything to answer".[54]

The Roman Rota struck out the "O'Hickey Case" after six years, in favour of Mannix. Mannix may have won the battle, but he had made many enemies including prominent Fenian rebel John Devoy. Much later in 1926, Devoy wrote how he felt Fr O'Hickey had "died of a broken heart". Devoy saw Mannix as the guilty party and vowed "if Archbishop Mannix lives a hundred years and did penance in sackcloth and ashes for his crimes against Ireland, he ought never to be forgiven".[55] Mannix's role as president had become untenable due to the O'Hickey case. His role in the whole affair "was increasingly portrayed as tyrannical. This was obviously embarrassing for the hierarchy who could not short-circuit the appeal process therefore, Mannix became indispensible".[56]

It has been important to highlight the role of Mannix during the O'Hickey case as it showed the contempt he was viewed with by some prominent members of the language movement. This would be in stark contrast to his expected triumphant homecoming in 1920 where he was hailed as a national hero.

This metamorphosis in nationalist opinion would take place in the decade before Mannix would become properly acquainted with de Valera. De Valera may well have been distant from the clerical politics of Maynooth, but Mannix's experience with the hierarchy would no doubt be useful to him in his capacity as leader of an independent Ireland. De Valera had been making a name for himself in education circles during Mannix's turbulent years in Maynooth. He had since relocated to Dublin and was assuming part-time teaching all across the city including the Royal University, Loreto College, Clonliffe and Catholic University, St Stephen's Green among others.[57] Though a lover of the Irish language and a member of the Gaelic League, his true love was maths and it is through maths that both Mannix and de Valera would first meet.

De Valera had not yet entered the public sphere and Mannix may not have wished to, but in 1903, with his ascension to the vice-presidency at Maynooth, he was thrust into the limelight. Mannix pre-1916 is seen as "a royalist" in many quarters not because of the O'Hickey case and his opposition to the Irish language in Maynooth, but also due to his role in

---

[54] Leon Ó Broin, 'The Gaelic League and the Chair of Irish in Maynooth' in *Studies: An Irish Quarterly Review*, 52 (208) 1963, p. 360.

[55] Seán Ó Lúing, *John Devoy* (Báile Átha Cliath: Cló Morainn, 1961), p. 186.

[56] O'Brien, op. cit., p. 12.

[57] Earl of Longford Frank Pakenham & Thomas P. O'Neill, *Eamon de Valera* (London: Hutchinson, 1970), pp 13-14.

the two royal visits of 1903 and 1911. On 23 June 1903, as the newly appointed Vice-President of the college, it was his duty, (due to the illness of the president, whom he would replace later that year) to prepare for the first visit of British royalty since James II. No Union Jack was flown, but instead Mannix opted for alongside the royal standard, the King's racing gonfalon.[58] Although Mannix may not have been enthusiastic about hosting a royal visit, due to the political tensions of the time, he had little choice in the matter. The college was royally funded and he also had to follow the wishes of his superiors including Cardinal Logue, who Biletz claims "enjoyed waiting upon royalty, delighted in entertaining British dignitaries with champagne and oysters".[59] The resurgence of hotbed nationalism through the medium of the cultural movement meant Mannix needed to make a careful judgement regarding the upcoming proceedings. In an astute and diplomatic move, Mannix pulled a masterstroke through his welcoming speech. As Santamaria comments, "his speech lacked nothing in courtesy. However, while warmly welcoming the royal couple, he took great care never once to mention the word 'loyalty'".[60] Mannix also entertained a second royal visit in 1911. After the public debate over the "O'Hickey Case" lingered long after his dismissal in 1909, the second royal visit provided another opportunity for the Irish nationalists to attack Mannix and his presidency. Mannix counteracted this once again. With his presidency in the balance and the language enthusiasts angered by such royal visits, Mannix was under immense public pressure.

Mannix envisaged that if what he called "the castle bishops" had their way, the Church would be visibly absent from the zeitgeist, the nationalist struggle for an independent Ireland.[61] Rather than promoting the display of the Union Jack, Mannix opted for the display of the King's colours, which delighted not only Archbishop Walsh, but also Cardinal Logue. The Cardinal later described the decision as "inspiring as it kept the ruling powers happy and the nationalists could not take offence".[62] Historically speaking there is the nationalist perspective and "West Brit" slur. However, most accurate is the viewpoint taken by Dermot Keogh who outlines how, "unfair it is to juxtapose Mannix 'the royalist' of 1911 with Mannix 'the rebel' of 1921".[63] Keogh's argument is indeed very strong but it is still evident that Mannix was not a royalist. He rather kept his

---

[58] Ebsworth, op. cit., pp 58-59.
[59] Biletz, op. cit., p. 125.
[60] Santamaria, *Daniel Mannix*, op. cit., p. 24.
[61] Santamaria, *A memoir*, op. cit., pp 18-19.
[62] Macardle, Turbulent priest, op. cit.
[63] Keogh, 'Mannix, de Valera and Irish nationalism' op. cit., p. 198.

opinions rightly reserved until later. Mannix's cousin, Sister Carmela puts forward evidence of this reservation. She tells of a conversation she had with Mannix in which he said "people think I am pro-British, but little do they dream what a rebel I am at heart". Mannix also indicated to her "that if the Bishops knew his inner feelings they would never have appointed him President of Maynooth."[64] Although surviving O'Hickey's attack the prolongation of the affair with Rome meant Mannix had become expendable in the eyes of the Irish hierarchy.

The first four years of his presidency were where Mannix visibly left his distinctive stamp. However, the second half of his presidency would become the historical legacy of his term in office, and superseded the good work that he had achieved during his first four years. His good work as president has largely been overshadowed by his dealings with the political undercurrents of the time, both lay and clerical. In fact, Mannix's administration and management of Maynooth is hugely important in light of his future role in Melbourne. As previously argued, his most notable and important achievement academically was the recognition of Maynooth by the new National University of Ireland. He became heavily involved in not just political issues, through the language debate, but also in social issues. As Daniel Murphy suggests, he "encouraged his fellow clerics to join the cooperative movement, founded to alleviate rural deprivation, and urged them to campaign for the provision of housing for the poor, the provision of hospital care services and other such reforms". [65] His particular focus on social as well as educational issues would be the benchmark he would set for his future episcopal role.

While undoubtedly his presidency was unpopular with the Gaelic revival movement, it was at times also unpopular with the students, even though he had their best interests at heart. Before his presidency commenced and even during his long stint as a student, Mannix would have seen first-hand conditions of life in the seminary, which left a lot to be desired. The main areas of discontent focused around student living conditions, food, health and general indiscipline. As Jeremiah Newman writes in 1884, "a 'butter-taster' had to be brought in to examine some supplies received; a loaf of bread, taken at random by the president from the bread-room, was sent for analysis, while the medical officer in the town reported that the college sewage system was a danger to the health of

---

[64] Ebsworth, op. cit., p.62.
[65] Daniel J. Murphy, *A history of Irish emigrant and missionary education* (Dublin: Four Courts Press, 2000), p. 388.

the people living there".[66] Indeed, Mannix's term as president is often seen as being authoritarian and dismissive of opinion. However, this was not always the case. Upon the recommendations of C.J. Nixon and Patrick Canning in their medical report for the year ending 1907, Mannix pushed for improvements in the senior infirmary. He outlined to Archbishop Walsh in his presidential report for that year that "improvements could be effected in the heating and sanitary arrangements of the Senior Infirmary at a very moderate cost" continuing that "the suggestions in the Medical Report could be examined and dealt with in the ordinary course by the Financial Council".[67] Mannix realised quickly that a firm hand was needed to return order to the college, lest the students lose their discipline. MacDonald agreed with what Newman had written on the lack of discipline amongst the students arguing in *Reminiscences* of his student days that:

> ... the one great cause was that discipline was slack; not on the students' part alone, but on the part of the officials, who were careless in doing their work and paid little heed to the student's complaints, which, however, did not justify the measures which these took to make their complaints effective.[68]

Maynooth, under Mannix, would return to the forefront of missionary vocation due to its education of priests for the missions. The leadership he showed at Maynooth was etched into the memory of any cleric who served under him. One of his many biographers, Niall Sheridan commented on Dr Mannix as being "not at all approachable, but in spite of his severity, there were clear indications of a gentleness of character, which in later years, others were to see and enjoy the benefit of", most notably Fr William Hackett.[69] Hackett would later become a close friend of Mannix's in Melbourne. Although Mannix had his subsequent encounter with the Irish nationalists, he still believed he needed to restore Maynooth to its position as the true institution of the Irish Catholic Church and Roman Catholicism in Ireland. Sidney Hook viewed this initiative of Mannix to preserve the calibre of the institution as an embodiment of his leadership qualities.

---

[66] Jeremiah Newman, *Maynooth and Victorian Ireland*, (Galway: Kenny's Books, 1983), p. 246.

[67] Letter from president of Maynooth Dr. Mannix to Archbishop Walsh, 13 June 1907, Report of the president for the year 1906-1907 (Dublin Diocesan Archives/AB6/336 (uncatalogued).

[68] McDonald, op. cit., p. 81.

[69] Ted O'Riordan, 'Great men we have given to history' in *Charleville and district Historical Journal*, 2 (1987), p. 61.

Hook believes that "you cannot keep the idea of a nation alive where there are no national institutions to reverence, no national success to admire, without a model of it in the mind of the people".[70] Mannix's refusal to accept the demands of the Irish language enthusiasts and bow to the pressure of nationalists such as Pearse and Devoy during his presidency was an indication of his strength of character and belief in his role at the head of Ireland's great Catholic institution. History has left many detractors of his tenure at Maynooth. However, Mannix always tried to do his best and would later profess:

> as President of Maynooth I always tried to do my duty, whether it brought popularity or whether it did not, if you court popularity and if you do things which are not right, because they seem to be popular for the moment, you can achieve a fleeting popularity, but time will probably reveal your insincerity, and you will feel always you should have acted otherwise.[71]

This assessment of his tenure at Maynooth offers an overall summary of the man; however, he will be remembered more as Dr Mannix, archbishop of Melbourne rather than president of St Patrick's College, Maynooth.

Mannix accurately predicted that he would not win popularity in clerical circles for his stand against Dr O'Hickey. His popularity, if any, with the nationalist section ground to a halt before it could take off, but as James Griffin rightly contends, "however liberal he may have wanted to be, he was compelled, if he wished to join the hierarchy, to satisfy his narrow Episcopal trustees".[72] By 1912, Mannix had spent thirty-one years rising through the ranks of the institution where he eventually became president. Therefore, it was with great sadness that he learnt he was to be transferred by the hierarchy for the foreign shores of Melbourne, Australia. With the prolongation of the Irish language question continuing in Rome, J.B. O'Brien argues that "the request by Archbishop Carr of Melbourne for a coadjutor was indeed fortuitous for the Irish hierarchy".[73] It offered the hierarchy a viable escape route whilst offering, what seemed to be, a satisfactory conclusion to events. Mannix had little option but to accept the new appointment, but it left a bitter taste in his mouth as he journeyed across the sea for Australia. Reminiscing later on the conclusion reached

---

[70] Sidney Hook, *The hero in history: A Study in Limitation and Possibility* (New York: Transaction Publishers, 1943), p. 57.

[71] O'Brien, op. cit., p. 9.

[72] Griffin, op. cit., p. 28.

[73] O'Brien, op. cit., p. 12.

he lamented that leaving Maynooth "was a great wrench" and "he left Ireland and Maynooth with regret". What was most upsetting for Mannix, as O'Brien suggests, was that "unlike Dr Croke of Cashel and Emly, who was originally appointed to Auckland, Dr Mannix was not to return to an Irish bishopric".[74] Mannix had fulfilled all the criteria for an episcopal vacancy, but he was being cast aside. It made the decision of the hierarchy even more disappointing for Mannix when we consider Michael O'Flanagan's views on episcopal succession in Ireland:

> ... once in every twenty or thirty years any given diocese produces this boy prodigy. He gets a chair at the end of his course, and there his glory is embalmed for twenty years until his native diocese becomes vacant and then the men who have grown up in the Maynooth atmosphere vote him in as bishop.[75]

As a leading member of the Gaelic League, de Valera had been well aware of the "O'Hickey Case", but instead of holding a sense of loathing for Mannix, he had much to be thankful to him for. On a professional level, De Valera could not find the professorship role he craved. Mannix sent a letter to de Valera in 1912 inviting him to apply for a part-time lectureship in Mathematics at Maynooth. The first formal meeting of these two men was about to take place albeit in a professional capacity. It was one of Mannix's last acts in his official capacity as president and was indeed one, which would prove very fortuitous, in establishing links between the hierarchy and the members of the nationalist movement. De Valera would acknowledge many years later in a television interview that "one of my treasured possessions for many years has been a letter written by His Grace inviting me to apply for the lectureship".[76]

After showing much loyalty to both the hierarchy in Ireland and by guiding Maynooth through a turbulent period Mannix was now being transferred to Melbourne. He was banished "as an exile to Australia not only in space and distance but also from his own class and from the establishment that he had so assiduously cultivated in the past".[77] Mannix was no longer a product of the institution, but instead a lonesome idealist

---

[74] ibid, pp 12-13.
[75] Michael O'Flanagan quoted in Ronan Fanning, 'Patrick Corish's "Maynooth"' in *The Furrow*, 46 (12), p. 705.
[76] *The Standard Newspaper*, 'Treasured possessions', a Standard reporter, unknown date.
[77] John B. O'Brien, 'The British Government and Archbishop Daniel Mannix' in *Journal of the Cork Historical & Archaeological Society*, 93 (1988), p. 56.

who would now be viewed as a "radical" and become a heretic to the flock he often preached to. All his grievances aside, he still loved Ireland and like so many before him set out upon the waves of uncertainty to new beginnings with new institutions.

CHAPTER THREE

BUILDING A NEW LIFE IN IRELAND
AND AUSTRALIA (1913-1919)

The Irish Catholic Church and state maintained a very close working relationship in the early twentieth century. Mannix, during his presidency of Maynooth, operated under similar circumstances when it came to the upper echelons of the Irish Catholic Church's hierarchy. This working relationship would end by the time of his appointment to Melbourne in 1912. The president and his role in the O'Hickey case had become a problem for Archbishop Walsh and the Irish Catholic hierarchy. Walsh, the cunning ecclesiastical politician, would use Roman Catholic Church politics to oust Dr Mannix from his position at Maynooth and eventually shift him overseas. Joe Broderick argues that, "Mannix would have been the obvious man to step into Walsh's shoes but Walsh was a firm supporter and a good friend of O'Hickey". Broderick contends that "though recognising Mannix's ability, he would probably not have chosen him as his successor".[1] This hypothetical view matters little as Mannix was far removed from Irish episcopal positions by the time of Archbishop Walsh's death. The main point is that where Mannix expected to find favour and support, he found a disconcerting thrust away from the institution he had served and administered over for thirty odd years. This chapter will trace the early years of Mannix's Melbourne episcopate and highlight his rise to the forefront of Australian national politics. De Valera's transformation from teacher to revolutionary politician will also be traced culminating in his meeting with Archbishop Mannix in America in 1920.

On 6 October 1912, Daniel Mannix was consecrated as the new coadjutor archbishop of Melbourne. All the highest-ranking Irish church officials were present, except ironically Archbishop Walsh. All the guests spoke highly of the new coadjutor and the influence he would have in his

---

[1] Joe Broderick, 'De Valera and Archbishop Daniel Mannix' in *History Ireland*, 2 (3) 1994, p. 38.

new parish of Melbourne. The most prophetic statement came from another cleric who also had a close relationship within the ranks of the Irish independence movement, Rev Michael Fogarty, Bishop of Killaloe. Fogarty was a close friend of Michael Collins and pointed out that Mannix "would be a glory to Ireland and a friend of every cause for which Ireland had to struggle in the future".[2]

Fogarty's prophecy offered little consolation to Mannix. His body was even telling him maybe this sudden upheaval for a distant land such as Australia was too much. Mannix's departure was delayed by a severe case of pneumonia, which he had contracted within a month of his consecration as coadjutor.[3] Although delayed substantially, he finally left Ireland in February 1913. Mannix may have been leaving the headlines behind him, but he certainly created new ones, along with a new public image for himself, in Australia. He realised quickly that Australia was his new home and responsibility. However, he never relinquished his desire to one-day return to Ireland. Mannix stated:

> I am an Irishman, and love Ireland and its people. I am bound to Ireland and the Irish people by the strongest ties that could bind a man to his fellow-creatures; and it is especially hard to leave Ireland at a time when the Irish people, after years of walking in the desert, seemed in sight of the promised land[4]

The promised land he spoke of was finally in sight for the generations of Irish nationalists. From Robert Emmet to John Redmond, Irish men and women had fought hard to achieve some degree of autonomy through the method of self-government for Ireland, labelled Home Rule. Mannix left Ireland anticipating, like so many more expectant Irish men and women, Home Rule to pass into law through the British Parliament in 1914. The Irish Parliamentary Party had recovered from the Parnell split, and under John Redmond had done superbly to lobby the British Parliament continuously for Home Rule in Ireland. They had nominally achieved Home Rule for implementation by 1914, as the House of Lords had utilised its last safety net of its veto. The veto ultimately meant a stay of execution on any bill for a maximum of two years. With the eventual passing of the Home Rule Bill, introduced in 1912, the end was in sight for Redmond and his followers. Could Redmond achieve more independence

---

[2] Frank Murphy, *Daniel Mannix* (Melbourne: Advocate Press, 1948), p. 15.
[3] Rev. Walter Ebsworth, *Archbishop Mannix* (Armadale, Vic.: H. H. Stephenson, 1977), p. 98.
[4] J O'Sheehan, *Archbishop Mannix: a sketch of his life and work* (Dublin, n-b.), p. 7.

Figure 3.1: St. Patrick's Cathedral, Melbourne, Australia. Image kindly courtesy of Mrs Winifred Cross.

for Irish men and women than any other public figure before him in the history of the island? An anxious two years would follow not just for Irish people, but Europeans alike.

One of the most disturbing periods in Irish history was the period between 1913 and 1916. The country saw five armed armies occupy the tiny island. The introduction of the Home Rule Bill fuelled old sectarian divides between Catholics and Protestants, particularly in the north, over the fear that Home Rule was "Rome Rule". This "Rome Rule", as it was presented in Ulster, was seen as something, "that could not legitimately be decided by party votes at Westminster".[5] The introduction of the Home Rule Bill would act as a spur to the militant bodies on the island. Britain's delay in implementing Home Rule for Ireland ultimately led to a military insurrection in 1916. Ireland was not a secluded state in which a war would take place within a buffered environment. The events in Ireland in the lead up to the implementation of Home Rule, which in any other circumstances, would have garnered significant universal attention due to its effect on the British Empire, were largely side-lined internationally for one reason, the outbreak of World War One.

Mannix arrived in Melbourne in 1913 on the cusp of great historical change that would not only affect his beloved Ireland, but also his new home, Australia. During his long voyage, he read the book, *Stolen Waters*, which was provided to him by the future Governor-General of the Irish Free State, T. M. Healy.[6] The book details many events including the 1641 rebellion. The scenario that resonated most with the departing archbishop was the pressure put on the Earls of Ulster by the British to flee their country. Mannix may too have felt as if he was being compelled to leave Ireland. The gift of the book also shows the range of connections Mannix held within Irish political circles even before his departure to Australia. His primary objective in Australia was the promotion of the cause of education for the ever-growing Catholic lower classes of Australia, but particularly in his own diocese of Melbourne. This is in fact was one of the main reasons, why his predecessor, Archbishop Carr had sought out his appointment. Mannix's inclusion of Maynooth into the National University of Ireland, as well as the raising of education standards there, had shown his leadership and this was needed in tackling such a contentious issue in Australia. Cardinal Logue argued that "he believed they could not find within the four seas of Ireland, or perhaps in the whole British Empire, an ecclesiastic better prepared or qualified to assist in that

---

[5] R. F. Foster, *Modern Ireland 1600-1972* (London: Allen Lane, 1989 c1988).

[6] T. M Healy, *Letters and leaders of my day* (London: T. Butterworth, 1928), p. 523.

great work" in education.[7] Aged fifty, Mannix's biographer and protégé Santamaria argues that, "if one puts aside his own formidable gifts of intellect and character, the influence of parents and family, then the primary constituent factors of that personal formation were his view of the realities, as distinct from the fictions of Irish history".[8] Mannix's firm grip on the education question in Australia allowed him to catapult himself into the Australian public arena. The "apostle of modern methods in education" was seen as the man to tackle the educational inequality that existed between Catholics and Protestants in the country.[9] By tackling the education question in the manner he did, it found him rapid favour amongst the Catholic community in Melbourne, who for so long had lived in the shadows of the Protestant Ascendancy. The major commentator on Irish-Australian history Patrick O'Farrell believes that:

> ... the Catholic Irish were the key creative element in Australia in the nineteenth century and the first half of the twentieth. He argues that the Irish Catholics operated like a loyal opposition. They acted as a constructive irritant in the general polity, questioning the consensus on values.[10]

For all the great work of his predecessors, Cardinal Moran and Archbishop Carr, they were not natural born leaders like Mannix. He bought Australian Catholics a new sense of belief and had the air of church royalty surrounding him. This prince of the church was to be described by his predecessor Carr as "Ireland's most precious gift to Australia".[11]

Australia had long been an outpost for British penal servitude and the Irish church had long been aware of the plight of its people. It sent out clerical envoys to continue its sphere of influence among the next generation of Irish descendants. This is detailed quite accurately by McGovern and O'Farrell, who argued:

> ...the strength of the Irish element lay in its provision of a distinctive Catholic identity related to a real past and to a living religious tradition, and in the simple fact that the dominant force within the Church – the

---

[7] Ebsworth, op. cit., p. 97.
[8] B. A. Santamaria, *Archbishop Mannix: his contribution to the art of public leadership in Australia* (Melbourne: Melbourne University Publishing, 1978), p. 7.
[9] Murphy, op. cit., pp 6-7.
[10] Patrick O'Farrell quoted in Donald Harman Akenson, *The Irish diaspora: A primer* (Belfast: The Institute of Irish Studies, 1993), pp 113-114.
[11] Ebsworth, op. cit., pp 112-113.

clergy – was Irish. It was on this strength, on Australianism fitted into an
Irish mould for the last time that Daniel Mannix drew.[12]

Figure 3.2: Raheen, Melbourne, Australia - Former Residence of Archbishop
Daniel Mannix of Melbourne. Image kindly courtesy of Mrs Winifred Cross/ Mrs
Patricia Wallis McCombe.

The occasion of his first speech on Easter Sunday 23 March 1913, was the
opportune moment for Mannix to pronounce himself as leader of the
Victorian Catholic body, but especially the Irish body throughout Australia.
He immediately goaded the politicians to acknowledge him as the
representative and head of his new flock. Mannix asked for 'fair play from
any political leader or party who will come out to meet those (Catholics)
and to treat with them on the borderland of reason and just concession'.[13]
This ploy by the coadjutor to draw the politicians from behind their public
lecterns, and into an open debate on the education question. He used
political brinkmanship to test the waters for a ripple of intent from any
party for an alignment with the Catholic vote, growing rapidly. The only

[12] J. J McGovern & Patrick J. O'Farrell, 'Australia' in P. J. Cornish (ed.), *A History
of Irish Catholicism* (Dublin, Gill & Macmillan, 1971), vol. 6, part 6, p. 67.
[13] Cyril Bryan, *Archbishop Mannix: champion of Australian democracy* (Melbourne:
The Advocate Press, 1918), p. 19.

concern from a democratic perspective was that either the inclusion or exclusion of the Catholic education question, by successive Australian governments, would lead to eventual sectarian fuelled riots, similar to the threat already in place in Ireland.

Archbishop Mannix's tackling of state funding for Catholic education in Australia was certainly fuelling sectarianism. It did not however, look like erupting into open warfare between the two religious bodies as it did in Ireland. The issue of religious division was not always at the forefront of constitutional politics in Ireland. Ironically, for a period leading up to the Dublin Lockout of 1913 "it appeared that the critical confrontation in early twentieth-century Ireland would take place not between the British government and Irish nationalists but between Irish capital and Irish labour".[14] De Valera had formally met his future ally Mannix by now. He did not however, even contemplate the scenario that saw their eventual reunion less than a decade later. The political environment in Ireland became a hotbed of militant activity in the lead up to implementation of Home Rule. Ulster Unionists vehemently opposed the idea fearing they would be ostracised by Home Rule. Therefore, the Unionists decided to take to arms through the Ulster Volunteer Force. This was counteracted by the nationalists in the south with the setup of an army of their own, the Irish Volunteer Force. De Valera, although now head of a family, among others of the nationalist persuasion, joined a rapidly expanding Irish Volunteer Force. This force would bring him into contact with some of the influential figures of Irish history including Pádraig Pearse and Thomas Clarke. As Michael McInerney states, he was "soon attending arms drills and successively became a lieutenant, captain, and commandant of the Third Battalion of the Dublin Brigade, and later still adjutant of the Dublin Brigade".[15] De Valera had now become entangled in a series of events that would lead to his participation in the Rising of 1916.

Donal McCartney argues "the outbreak of war in 1914 put the question of Home Rule into cold storage, but the heat that had been generated over the past few years was not so readily turned off".[16] Due to the nature of the war, supplies and fresh recruits were also in desperate demand. John

---

[14] Foster, op. cit., p. 443.

[15] Michael McInerney, 'Eamon de Valera 1882-1975: controversial giant of modern Ireland' in Peter O'Mahony (ed.), *Eamon de Valera: a survey in text and pictures by the Irish Times of the life and influence of a famous leader* (Dublin: The Irish Times, 1976), p. 13.

[16] Dr. Donal McCartney, 'From Parnell to Pearse (1891-1921)' in F. X. Martin & T. W. Moody (eds.), *The course of Irish history* (Cork: The Mercier Press Ltd., 1984), p. 306.

Redmond, leader of the Irish Parliamentary Party, had recognised the substantial growth of the Irish Volunteers. The force would rapidly grow to a membership of 180,000 men. Redmond, hoping to seek British favour decided to call on the Volunteers to participate in the war for Ireland's cause. The I.R.B. members of the Provisional Committee, of the Irish Volunteers Force chose to remain silent and bide their time as Redmond still held a strong position in the English Parliament. However, their hopes of a strong unified nationalist front were destroyed with the split of the Volunteers. Prominent opposition to Redmond's Woodenbridge speech included MacNeill, Connolly and Griffith. They along with others did not believe Britain's promise for Home Rule valid after the war. The Volunteers split into Redmond's National Volunteers and MacNeill's Irish Volunteers who now only numbered 2,000 men.[17] The I.R.B. opposed to participation in a war remained with the Irish Volunteers, along with de Valera, and began to set the wheels of insurrection in motion. Diarmuid Ferriter sees the prelude to 1916 as "an Ireland with a variety of organisations and movements, sometimes with conflicting aims, personalities and visions of the future. This was why deception and secrecy played such an important role in the organisation of the Rising".[18]

One such personality who was central to the events of 1916 was Pádraig Pearse. His vision of the future entailed a free Ireland and unless this was achieved, he argued that "Ireland unfree shall never be a peace".[19] Pearse believed heavily in sacrificial themes similar to that of Cúchulain and other mythological figures, and many examples are found in his works. "Self-sacrifice" had been used for many years before the Rising in poems and plays arousing patriotic fervour, and investing heavily in this, Pearse pushed ahead with the Rising knowing in a sense what lay in store.[20] The Easter Rising was largely destined to failure, and as he refused to take the secret oath of the I.R.B., de Valera had little to do with the actual overall planning of the botched insurrection. The I.R.B. military council including among others MacDonagh, Plunkett, and Pearse decided that the battle should commence on Easter Sunday, a symbolic day of regeneration in the Catholic calendar, and equally so for Pearse and his men. They had hoped that the combined forces of the Irish Volunteers and

---

[17] Jerome Aan de Wiel, *The Catholic Church in Ireland 1914-1918: war and politics* (Dublin: Irish Academic Press, 2003), pp 2-6.
[18] Diarmuid Ferriter, *Irish Independent*, 'Birth of a nation part 1-The Rising', 27th April 2010, p. 6.
[19] Mark Tierney, *Ireland since 1870* (Dublin: CJ Fallon, 1998), p. 175.
[20] George Sweeney, 'Irish hunger strikes and the cult of the self-sacrifice' in *Journal of Contemporary History*, 28 (1993), p. 423.

the Irish Citizen Army would seize Dublin and other key strongholds, subsequently setting up a Provisional Government forcing British Rule out of Ireland for once and for all. However, MacNeill, leader of the Irish Volunteers, issued a countermanding order, which was published in *The Sunday Independent* of 23 April 1916, calling off orders for special action; the Rising looked dead in the water. It was too late though as preparations had gone too far to go back. A substantially smaller group of rebels, largely confined to Dublin instead of other parts as originally planned, took to capturing key points on Easter Monday. The Rising commenced at twelve noon on Easter Monday with the reading of the proclamation on the steps of the G.P.O by Pádraig Pearse, declaring the Republic of Ireland.[21]

The Rising was predominantly an urban conflict and largely focused around close quarter house-to-house combat in the centre of Dublin city. Although initially catching the British off guard the rebels were quickly outnumbered and surrounded. De Valera fought in a difficult area close to Beggars Bush barracks. He was ordered, as commandant of the Third Dublin city Battalion, with their headquarters at Boland's Mills, to defend against enemy reinforcement and supplies from Kingstown, now called Dún Laoghaire. De Valera and his men inflicted severe casualties on the British on various routes into the city, particularly along the Northumberland Road. However, the rebels could not contain the numeric and military advantage of the British for long and "by the next Monday, when fighting was at the end and the inferno of the GPO had been evacuated, 450 had been killed and 2,614 wounded; 116 soldiers and 16 policemen were dead".[22] Knowing that the Rising was over after receiving confirmation from MacDonagh, de Valera was the last to surrender after six days.[23] The fate of de Valera ultimately rested on three great historical arguments, his non-membership of the executive of the IRB and subsequent exclusion from the Proclamation signatories,[24] the well documented case of his American citizenship[25], but most importantly the ultimate delay of his court-martial.[26] This book will not enter into these arguments for the purpose of its aims of outlining the alliance between Mannix and de Valera. It will focus rather on the fact that instead of de Valera's contribution to Irish history ending with the execution of the 1916 leaders,

---

[21] Tierney, op. cit., pp 180-181.
[22] Foster, op. cit., p. 483.
[23] McInerney, op. cit., pp 14-16.
[24] Constantine Fitzgibbon & George Morrison, *The life and times of Eamon De Valera* (Dublin: Gill & Macmillan, 1973), p. 55.
[25] Diarmuid Ferriter, *Judging Dev* (Dublin: Royal Irish Academy, 2007), pp 29-30.
[26] McInerney, op. cit., p. 16.

he would survive to serve a greater role than that of Commandant in the 1916 Rising. De Valera's survival concluded with his confinement to a series of English prisons including stints in Dartmoor, Maidstone and Lewes. These prisons would become hotbeds of revolutionary activity and allowed him to create huge political opportunities for himself in terms of future leadership. This would all begin to manifest itself upon his release when he returned to Ireland in June 1917. In Ireland, the political and social climate had changed substantially in just over a year.

Mannix was also beginning to make headway in his push for alignment with the political leadership of the day in Australia. His public statements were creating many new enemies among the Australian Establishment just as his actions had previously done so with the Irish Ascendancy. Santamaria contends that:

> ... one can generalise that his process of disillusionment with both began with the repudiation of what were conveniently entitled Catholic education claims during the Victorian State election of 1914 and was confirmed by the execution of the leaders of the Easter Rising in 1916. Both were directly impressing the one mind at the same time.[27]

The events of 1916 and its aftermath had begun to reach the news wires of America, Australia and every corner of the globe where the Irish diaspora were focused. As the true sequence of events were still unclear, it was unwise to comment on the developments hastily. The Rising had not gained the popular legitimate support of the Irish public and had left Dublin in ruins and under martial law in a time when the Great War had made life extremely difficult. However, Mannix refused to jump the gun and gave a reasoned reply to the press. It was not just an emotional time in Ireland but also in Australia where the Irish immigrant community were looking for answers. Mannix was castigated by the Australian Ascendancy for his part in the preparation of Archbishop Carr's official statement on the Rising, which was published in Irish papers. It is however, debatable as to just how much influence Mannix actually had on Carr's statement. A more accurate estimation of Mannix's true feelings on the Easter Rising can be taken from his first official speech on the Rising at the opening of a Floral Fete at West Melbourne, 30 April 1916, three days before the executions of the leaders began. Mannix lamented how the Rising was

> ... the natural regrettable sequel and response to the campaign of armed resistance and civil war which the Carsonites had been allowed to preach

---

[27] Santamaria, op. cit., pp 20-21.

and prepare for within the last few years ... I am quite clear in my own mind that the British Government, by its failure to deal with the treason of the Carsonites, and by its shifty policy in regard to Home Rule has, unwittingly I suppose led to the result which we must all deplore. Before condemning the misguided leaders of this movement to be shot, they should remember that the leaders of another movement were taken into British Cabinet'.[28]

Cearbhall O'Briain commented how amongst:

... the welter of damning interviews and resolutions that flooded the columns of the press, the calm review of the events leading up to the Rising, given by His Grace, showed up like an oasis in the desert and caused Australia to sit up suddenly and ask itself if there was not another side to the case.[29]

It was just what the Australian public had come to expect from the archbishop. The Irish Catholic hierarchy either openly condemned the Rising or declined the opportunity to comment, with one notable exception, Bishop O'Dwyer of Limerick. As Tomas Ó Fiaich writes, "several clerical condemnations of the Rising found their way into the newspapers in the weeks after Easter, and of the nine bishops whose comments are reported, seven including Cardinal Logue, condemned it strongly".[30] Oliver Rafferty on this point would argue that "it is often said that the Catholic Church will never support a revolution until it is successful" and this was certainly the case with the Irish hierarchy after seeing the growing influence Sinn Féin were acquiring coming up to the general election of 1918.[31] Why then did Archbishop Mannix, like Bishop O'Dwyer, go against the views of the Irish hierarchy, which he had been so faithful to for so long? Considering that the archbishop must have known by the time of his Floral Fete speech who the ringleaders of the Rising were, it is amazing to consider his response. One might recall how Pádraig Pearse had publicly questioned Mannix's Irish loyalties with regard the Irish question in Maynooth. Was this the reason for his response or had his Australian appointment allowed

---

[28] Ebsworth, op. cit., p. 146. (See Appendix A for full speech)
[29] Cearbhall O'Briain, *Dr. Mannix in Australia the brief story of seven strenuous years under the Southern Cross (Dublin, 191-?)*, p. 7.
[30] Tomás Ó Fiaich, 'The Catholic clergy and the independence movement' in *The Capuchin Annual* (1970), p. 481.
[31] Oliver J. Rafferty, 'The Catholic bishops and revolutionary Ireland: some 19th and 20th century comparisons' in *Studies: An Irish Quarterly Review*, 83 (329) 1994, p. 30.

him to express his deep-seated nationalist views which were confidentially confined during his presidency at Maynooth? One thing is for sure, the Rising had called into question the reason for Britain's entry into the war especially among sections of the Irish diaspora. This is portrayed effectively in the case studies of the Irish and Australian conscription cases.

The establishment in Australia were now beginning to question Irish Australian's loyalty to the Empire and as McGovern and O'Farrell point out "the Empire loyalists associated with the war effort were outraged by what was seen as Ireland's treachery at Easter 1916".[32] If Mannix's comments on the Rising were interpreted as publicly backing the rebels then the establishment would be hard pushed to find support for the forthcoming conscription referendums. In an attempt to re-affirm Australian support for the Empire during the war conscription was sought in the country during 1916. In September of that year, Prime Minister Billy Hughes returned from England after failing to persuade the Labor Party to enact conscription by Act of Parliament. This led to a referendum in Australia on the issue. Mannix was not the organiser of this anti-conscription campaign, but instead became the figurehead for a very powerful campaign launched and supported by a combination of forces, particularly the Labor Party and the trade unions. Mannix stood firmly against conscription although he "claimed seriously that he had not wished to be involved".[33] However, when his views were called upon "he believed it was proper for him to provide a corrective by stating that, in his belief, Australia was doing as much as it should be called upon to do".[34] The Australian people followed his lead and subsequently voted "No" on 28 October 1916 defeating the "Yes" campaign by less than 75,000 votes.[35] This defeat embittered the Australian Establishment, but particularly Prime Minister Hughes who began to make his conscription fight "definitely an anti-Mannix fight, as a matter of tactics" according to New South Wales Labor Premier Holman.[36] The issue of conscription also brought to a head the deepening social conflict of where the true loyalties of Irish Catholics lay. Mannix became the focus of stringent attacks from the establishment as he was seen as the figurehead of the Irish Catholics. However, he always maintained that Catholics were Irish and could maintain loyalty to

---

[32] McGovern & O'Farrell, 'Australia' in P. J. Cornish (ed.), *A History of Irish Catholicism* (Dublin, Gill & Macmillan, 1971), vol. 6, part 6, p. 68.
[33] ibid, p. 68.
[34] Santamaria, op. cit., p. 25.
[35] Byran, op. cit., pp 61-67.
[36] Santamaria, op. cit., p. 25.

both the Commonwealth and their own people. Mannix's strongest critics included *The Argus* newspaper, which claimed that to accept that there were two loyalties at stake, was the equivalent of disloyalty.[37] The war raged on and with it the push for a second referendum on conscription, which was to be held on 20 December 1917. Personal attacks on Mannix continued not just in the Australian press, but also in Ireland. One Irish Unionist wrote:

> it is all the more a pity that a man of his position and ability has not got the foresight to see that, if we – i.e., the Allied Powers – do not beat the Hun, the Hun will beat us. In this titanic struggle it is obviously not fair that some countries have conscription and others not.[38]

However, Mannix also had sizable support in Ireland evident in his clerical colleague Dr Michael Fogarty, Bishop of Killaloe's letter. He outlined how it seems: -

> that he (Mannix) seems to have become a Sinn Féiner. If so this is the greatest boom that Sinn Féin has got since the illustrious Dr. O'Dwyer, Bishop of Limerick, was laid in his grave. Dr. Mannix is the last man in the world to patronise either "madness" or "wickedness." All true Irishmen will rejoice to know, on your authority, that the national instincts of our race are as potent in this great Archbishop in far away Australia as they are in the humblest peasant at home in Ireland.[39]

His detractors in Australia often tried to misrepresent him. One noteworthy misrepresentation, of his 28 January speech caused particular consternation. Here he made his famous, or infamous, "trade war" speech. Mannix argued that "the war was like most wars – just an ordinary trade war ... trade jealousy on both sides had seemed, for many years past, to make a great war inevitable".[40] Although repeating what had been said previous, by people such as Mr Hughes, the establishment set out on a personal attack against Mannix even using the annual index of *The Argus* to manipulate his words as a "Sordid trade war". As the second conscription campaign progressed, his audiences were captivated by his rhetoric and firmness on the issue. James Murtagh contends how "a study of his speeches

---

[37] McGovern & O'Farrell, op. cit., p. 70.

[38] *The Irish Times*, 'Letters to the editor', "An Irish Unionist", 3 December 1917, p. 3.

[39] Michael Fogarty Bishop of Killaloe, *The Irish Times*, 'Letters to the editor – Archbishop Mannix and Mr. Hughes', 1 December 1917, p. 8.

[40] Murphy, op. cit., p. 37. (See Appendix B for full speech)

Figure 3.3: Archbishop Daniel Mannix postcard 1920. Author's private collection.

reveals a logical case, based on the principles of democratic freedom of speech, national self-determination, and the human and economic resources of the country".[41] The second referendum on 20 December 1917 was defeated even more heavily this time. The establishment now realised that due to his influence on the conscription issue, Archbishop Daniel Mannix had officially entered the world of politics. Following the death of his predecessor Archbishop Carr in May 1917, Mannix was essentially left to his own devices.[42] Mannix had become the "hero in history" as Sidney Hook lamented. The Catholic masses had propagated this by instigating a cult around him, publishing pictures, postcards and all sorts of memorabilia. The popularity of the prelate seems to have been moulded around that 'critical moment' in history when he became an articulator of Australian self-consciousness.

This was in direct conflict to the British imperial consciousness. "His famous phrase "Australia first, the Empire second', was as nourishing to the spirits of Australian nationalists as it was shocking to British Australians".[43] This articulation was following on from the legacy of Pádraig Pearse, amongst other Irish nationalists, and would be continued by Eamon de Valera in the coming years. This is in fact one of the reasons why they struck up such a unique and personal relationship.

By now, the true nature of the Rising had become known and the political prisoners who remained would play vital roles in the series of events leading to the War of Independence, especially Eamon de Valera. The Great War in Europe was also close to an end, but not before conscription would become an issue once again, but this time with the Irish people. The British government were to continue their miscalculated judgements that had prevailed since the events at Easter 1916, and introduced the Military Service Act in April 1918. Lloyd George, by pressing conscription, achieved what no single event since the Land War had achieved, solidarity amongst all the major Irish bodies including the bogeyman of the Catholic Church. The eventual withdrawal of the idea by the British government only served to heighten Sinn Féin's popularity and indeed turned up the heat on its other political opponent, the Irish Parliamentary Party. The I.P.P. under John Dillon, who took over the leadership of the party following John Redmond's death, had contemplated

---

[41] James G. Murtagh, *Australia: the Catholic chapter* (New York: Sheed and Ward, 1946), p. 186.
[42] Ebsworth, op. cit., pp 155-180.
[43] Edmund Campion, *Australian Catholics: the contribution of Catholics to the development of Australian society* (Ringwood: Penguin Books Australia, 1988), p. 84.

support of conscription in return for a promise of Home Rule implementation by Lloyd George. The I.P.P., however, were ultimately forced to fall in under the banner of Sinn Féin's abstentionism programme from Westminster. This alignment with Sinn Féin would ultimately cost the I.P.P. dearly particularly if the three previous by-elections of 1917 were a benchmark for the forthcoming general election of 1918, where Sinn Féin won 73 seats out of 105. De Valera would officially make his entrance onto the political stage with his victory in the east Clare by-election of 1917. Along with Count Plunkett and Joseph McGuinness, the Sinn Féin candidates would leave the Irish Parliamentary Party in the shade. The first sign of Mannix's influence on de Valera's career is the promotion of de Valera with the Irish Catholic hierarchy. Mannix's appointment of de Valera to Maynooth in 1912 had put de Valera in a position that allowed him contact with members of the hierarchy. He later used this to his advantage once in power.

The British government's ineptitude towards the Rising culminated in the carte blanche response they allowed the new military regime in Ireland. With Lord French appointed as Viceroy, they fabricated a so-called "German plot" to allow the British army to reinforce British order through the arrest of the leaders of various nationalist organisations such as Sinn Féin, the Gaelic League and the Volunteers. This played directly into the hands of the Sinn Féin leadership and reinforced their ideals for an independent government for Ireland. This was bolstered by the sizable democratic mandate they had received from the people in the general election of 1918. As Tierney wrote "it was a landslide victory for Sinn Féin, which got forty seven percent of the total vote; in twenty five-constituencies Sinn Féin candidates were returned unopposed". However, as Tierney continues, "of the seventy-three Sinn Féin candidates elected, forty-seven were in prison".[44] The electoral nirvana experienced by Sinn Féin ultimately sealed the Irish Parliamentary Party's political fate. De Valera would later declare "that the vote for Sinn Féin was 'not a form of government so much, because we are not republican doctrinaires, but ... for Irish freedom and Irish independence".[45]

Sinn Féin had gathered significant support not just in Ireland. Their popularity amongst the Irish diaspora particularly in America and Australia was increasing, helped by individuals such as John Devoy and Mannix. Archbishop Mannix made such public occasions as the St Patrick's Parade his own, capitalising on the public display's of Irish

---

[44] Tierney, op. cit., pp 210-212.
[45] John A. Murphy, *Ireland in the Twentieth Century* (Dublin: Gill & Macmillan, 1975), p. 7.

fervour that surrounded him. These displays along with his use of evocative language certainly grabbed the headlines and the attention of the "loyalists". During the parade of 1918 as Ted O'Riordan outlines:

> ... two events were a source of "horror" to them. Dr. Mannix appalled them by not standing up or recognising in any way the playing of "God Save the King" by one of the bands, and at the conclusion of his address at the National Concert that night, they considered him guilty of sedition in his advice to his listeners ... 'Let Ireland bide her time and let Ireland watch her opportunity'.[46]

He was certainly a big thorn in the side of the pro-imperialist Australian governments. Mannix became an embodiment of Sinn Féin's policy towards successive British administrations. Frank Murphy reiterates this by outlining that "the archbishop's moral support to the Sinn Féin movement, and Ireland's cause, was invaluable, and in the latter end of 1919 he sponsored a great Australasian Irish-Race Convention which drew delegates from every quarter of Australia and New Zealand".[47] This served to highlight the Irish cause to the vast diaspora, but more importantly fuel Mannix's popularity as one the key figureheads of Irish nationalism abroad.[48] The Irish-Race Convention was to prove a great success and would attract significant publicity overseas. *The Irish Times* in its "Foreign News" section outlined how:

> ... the Irish Race Convention which is meeting in Melbourne is representative of all the Australian States, but it has a large proportion of priests and is obviously dominated by Archbishop Mannix, who appears to intend using it to insist on self-government for Ireland and the Hughes policy for Australia.[49]

The convention was seen as a huge propaganda success for Sinn Féin's cause. Being backed publicly by significant elements of the Roman Catholic Church, not just in Ireland, but also in Australia helped Sinn Féin to push for American solidarity with its cause. The result of the convention was the affirmation of the resolution stating, "the right of the people of Ireland was to choose their own form of Government, and to govern their

---

[46] Ted O'Riordan, 'Great men we have given to history' in *Charleville and District Historical Journal*, 2 (1987), p. 69.
[47] Frank Murphy, *Daniel Mannix: Archbishop of Melbourne* (2nd ed., Melbourne: The Polding Press, 1972) p. 71.
[48] ibid, p. 71.
[49] *The Irish Times*, 'Foreign news', 8 November 1919, p. 1.

country without interference from any other nation". It backed "Ireland's appeal to the nations for international recognition", and it pledged support to "Ireland's chosen leader". [50] Now that the First World War was officially over on 11 November 1918, Sinn Féin had an added incentive to push for self-determination for Ireland considering that the Allies had originally fought for this exact principle, to be granted to small nations such as Belgium. Their national convention of 1918 showed that "the heart of the national revolution was gathered there. It spoke for the nation with unquenchable clarity and with resolute strength". [51] With the public backing of the Irish diaspora across the globe, following events such as the Irish-Race Convention, the final hope for self-determination lay in the Paris Peace Conference and the Treaty of Versailles. These were called in the aftermath of the war to seal the future set-up of Europe. Following Sinn Féin's programme of abstentionism from the British parliament and its vast majority obtained from the general election, they decided it time to set up their own parliament, which they duly did on January 21 1919, naming it Dáil Éireann. The first major step for the illegal government was to secure international recognition under the terms of the Treaty of Versailles. Therefore, as Tierney outlines, "the Dáil appointed three delegates to go to France to plead Ireland's cause. They pinned their hopes on President Wilson, but he proved unwilling to champion the Irish cause, lest he endanger his country's good relations with Britain". [52] This proved to be a major obstacle for the hopes of the new government for recognition by the international community.

Whilst Mannix was continuing to align more followers to Irish hopes for a government of its own, de Valera was sitting out the political action in an English jail cell at Lincoln Gaol. However, this all changed due to the ingenuity and cunning of Michael Collins and Harry Boland, who would help de Valera to make a dramatic escape. [53] This sequence of events allowed his presence at the meeting of the second Dáil, on 1 April 1919. Here he was elected as *Príomh Aire* and proceeded, as Dwyer argues, to appoint a "cabinet truly representative of the various factions within Sinn Féin". [54] The main crux for the illegal government remained the failure to secure international recognition. It was with this in mind that

---

[50] T. P Boland, *James Duhig* (Saint Lucia : University of Queensland Press, 1986), p. 152.

[51] George Morrison, 'Mise Éire' (Produced by Gael Linn, 1959)

[52] Tierney, op. cit., p. 215.

[53] ibid, p. 223.

[54] T. Ryle Dwyer, *Eamon de Valera : The Man & the Myths* (Dublin : Paperview/Irish Independent, 2006) p. 38.

the new president decided to depart and commence a tour of America. Here he hoped to secure American recognition and much-needed funds to allow the government to gain a foothold of authority in Ireland. The trip commenced in May 1919 and as Diarmuid Ferriter contends "the American tour was a long, exhausting, occasionally exhilarating but often frustrating journey, and it is perhaps no surprise that historians have given contrasting assessments of whether or not it was successful".[55] The tour would prove to be a great popularity boost for de Valera on an international scale. He would now begin to command the same degree of public recognition that Mannix had recently achieved in Australia. The year 1920 was to prove to be the significant crux in the development of the alliance between the two men. The archbishop had come a long way since his days in Maynooth and he had not set foot in Ireland since his departure in 1913. The time had come for the members of the Australian Catholic hierarchy to make their *ad limina* visit to the Vatican. This visit was undertaken once every five years. Mannix cleverly utilised this opportunity to make his trip home but not before making a stopover in America.[56] De Valera decided to go to America to seek moral and financial reassurances for the new Irish state not only from the American public, but also from the large Irish diaspora that resided there. He travelled to America with the three-fold title of President of Dáil Éireann, of the Irish Republic and of Sinn Féin.[57] By 1919, Mannix had firmly nailed his colours to the political mast in favour of the Sinn Féin cause. This trip would, however, allow him as Colm Kiernan describes "to be brought up to date on the Irish question" and hence allow him "to be able to decide on the best line of action to adapt".[58] This was essential with an imminent trip planned to Ireland and to the Holy Father in Rome. It also allowed him, as the Irish in Australia saw it, to represent them in solidarity with the Irish-Americans for the cause of Irish freedom.

Mannix made his aims clear before he departed, he was very careful not to dealign himself with the ordinary Australian citizen who had little interest in Irish affairs. With this in mind, he did not forget to promote Australian national identity by announcing that:

---

[55] Diarmuid Ferriter, *Judging Dev* (Dublin: Royal Irish Academy, 2007), p. 34.

[56] Dermot Keogh, 'Mannix, de Valera and Irish nationalism', in John B. O'Brien and Pauric Travers (eds.), *The Irish emigrant experience in Australia* (Dublin: Poolbeg, 1991), p. 200.

[57] Tierney, op. cit., p. 223.

[58] Colm Kiernan, *Daniel Mannix and Ireland* (Morwell, Victoria: Alella Books, 1984), p. 130.

... he hoped to have an opportunity of visiting the graves of the Australian soldiers who fell in the field. It would be his privilege to kneel by the graves of these men who went out from Australia to fight for the little nations, and for Ireland as they thought, and pray over their ashes that the cause for which they fought and bled and died may triumph in their death.[59]

This rhetorical play made some of those Australians who had lost loved ones in the war bitter towards the establishment. Mannix hoped this action would align the general population behind the Irish cause, something similar to what de Valera was aiming to achieve in America. The other Irish bishops in Australia including Duhig and Kelly and in America, Hayes and Foley may have all had different perspectives on events in Ireland and the forthcoming tour of America, but they generally declined to make their personal feelings publicly known. Mannix on the other hand was from a different breed of cleric. Dermot Keogh argues that "Mannix said in public what many bishops, out of prudence, were only prepared to say in private. He took sides while many bishops chose to use their good offices to mediate between the two warring factions".[60] Mannix had become the "darling" of the Australian public and this was evident no more so than on the day of his departure from Melbourne to Sydney, America bound. The archbishop had to spend an extra un-planned night in the city due to his failure to meet the delayed train. The throngs of people who had flocked to wish him well on his departure prevented him from making his scheduled departure. In the true nature of the archbishop he jokingly commented, "People have suggested difficulties about my return to Australia. I think it will be much easier to return than it is to get away"![61] Mannix had been the champion of anti-conscription and he would now become the champion of Irish nationality. On foreign soil, he would meet his political ally and together they would lecture on the need for Ireland to find salvation through the form of self-determination. De Valera would later praise the arrival of the Mannix on American shores outlining how:

---

[59] Ebsworth, op. cit., p. 221.
[60] Keogh, op. cit., p. 200.
[61] Ebsworth, op. cit., p. 221.

We looked for help, and where did we get it? From the other end of the earth, from a great man who remembered his race, who remembered how often the Irish people had been fooled, who once said he never turned his back to a foe or to a friend; and in that he was characteristic of the Irish people.[62]

—Eamon de Valera

---

[62] ibid, p. 232

CHAPTER FOUR

THE BELLIGERENT PRELATE (1919-1920)

As de Valera set sail for America in June 1919, Ireland was in the midst of a battle for its independence. A battle as Anne Dolan suggests that was:

> ... almost like a series of snapshots. Familiar images, incidents and individuals map out the two and a half years of ambush and execution, of reprisal and assassination, of fear, terror, curfew and martial law.[1]

As President of the Executive Council, de Valera was now, in Irish eyes, the essential playmaker in the upcoming struggle with the British. This chapter will focus on Mannix's contribution to the cause of Irish independence and the early political career of Eamon de Valera. The political isolation that surrounded de Valera during the Irish Civil War has its origins in his decision to go to America. Despite Michael Collins pleading with him to stay, de Valera saw the necessity for American approval of an Irish nation as more important. Collins' pleas were well founded. De Valera was still a wanted criminal and faced the possibility of being extradited back to Ireland and returning to an English jail cell. This turned out to be a moot point The rumour mill had begun to flow amongst Irish Americans that the surviving leader of 1916 was about to grace them with his presence in America and went on to have a successful trip. However, Collin's concerns did not go unheeded, as Niall Brennan discusses, "de Valera had no welcome at all until he was safely ashore" and out of the way of British interference.[2]

Both Mannix and de Valera arrived a year apart in the United States on different sides of the country in San Francisco and New York respectively. Their journey to the centre of the country where they eventually met, at Omaha, took different paths. According to James Griffin, Mannix claims

[1] Anne Dolan, *Irish Independent*, 'Birth of a nation part 2 - The War of Independence', 28 April 2010, p. 3.
[2] Niall Brennan, *Dr. Mannix* (Adelaide: Rigby, 1964), p. 187.

"he had not corresponded with de Valera" prior to the trip.[3] There is no evidence to suggest otherwise in the de Valera archives. De Valera essentially made the first steps at forging a relationship with Mannix because he realised that adding such a high profile international figure as Mannix to the bill would increase the success of the tour. It is true that Mannix had hoped to meet de Valera, but it is extremely unlikely he had anticipated such involvement. De Valera had pre-arranged to meet the archbishop as he sent an envoy, Judge Dermot Fawsitt to meet him. Fawsitt outlined a pre-ordained series of high profile public meetings including the eventual rendezvous with de Valera at Omaha, Nebraska.[4]

Events in America, however, had long since left the front pages of the Irish newspapers as de Valera's tour began to take shape. On that iconic day when the first Dáil met in January 1919, effectively the first shots of the War of Independence were fired, with the death of two policemen at Soloheadbeg, Co. Tipperary. What had become clear was that the British government were unwilling to negotiate with Dáil Éireann over these events. By doing so, it helped to heighten the recognition of the Dáil, which is what de Valera was striving to achieve in the United States. As Dolan points out, the War of Independence "slowly escalates through 1919, with the Irish Volunteers drilling, training, arming, with more attacks on policemen, with the year ending in an assassination attempt on the Lord Lieutenant, Lord French, and in Britain's decision to recruit the soon infamous Black and Tans."[5] The hopes for a peaceful settlement to the conflict, as many historians argued, had vanished along with de Valera and Harry Boland to America. Ireland had been left in the hands of the military minded republicans such as Dan Breen and Seán Tracey, as well as the military astute such as Michael Collins and Richard Mulcahy. The war was dominated by guerrilla warfare, ambushes, raids on police barracks and reprisals, executions and civilian disruption as the Black and Tans and British military fought the "flying-columns" of the Volunteers.[6]

Against this backdrop of fear, terror and uncertainty, Ireland's president made the first speech of his tour at Fenway Park, home of the Boston Red Sox. This famous sporting venue had seen many crowds and another sizable gathering filled the stadium when the president spoke on 29 June 1919. As Dave Hannigan outlines "the main thrust of his argument centred

---

[3] James Griffin, 'Archbishop Daniel Mannix' in *The Old Limerick Journal*, 27 (1990), p. 30.
[4] Brennan, op. cit., p. 187.
[5] Dolan, op. cit., p. 3.
[6] Donal McCartney, 'From Parnell to Pearse' in T. W. Moody & F. X. Martin (eds.), *The course of Irish history* (Cork: The Mercier Press Ltd., 1967), p. 311.

on the signing of the Versailles Treaty. Since it promised to protect each member against external aggressors, Article X of that agreement was perceived by de Valera as guaranteeing England's right to rule Ireland".[7] He spoke fluently, and was forthright and uncompromising in his arguments, all the while never forgetting his primary objectives in America:

> ... now I shall not attempt to plead Ireland's cause to you. It was sweet to my own ears, sweeter than I could tell you, to listen to Ireland's cause being pleaded by Americans, and I hope that on all the platforms on which I shall stand it will be the people of America pleading Ireland's cause and I shall be there only to represent Ireland.[8]

Mannix maintained the momentum that de Valera was building in America through his public appearances. He offered the Irish diaspora an outlet through which they could voice their opinions when it came to Irish national affairs. Having accepted Judge Fawsitt's requests, the archbishop followed the programme set out for him crossing America through Nebraska, Illinois and Ohio "never losing a chance to launch scathing attacks on the British occupation of Ireland".[9] Mannix arrived in America almost a year after de Valera and they eventually met in June 1920, at Omaha, Nebraska at the head house of the Irish Mission to China, St Columba's Missionary College. It cemented the relationship of both men and confirmed the alignment of the diaspora not just in America, but also in Australia, behind Ireland's fight for independence. This meeting has largely been sidelined historically due to events in Ireland during this period. Irish history has paid little attention to this meeting up until now, but due to its importance, the book will deal with it in detail. The exact details of the conversations that took place between both men at Omaha were not recorded, as they "wanted to be alone to talk Irish politics".[10]

---

[7] Dave Hannigan, *De Valera in America: The rebel president's 1919 campaign* (Dublin: O'Brien Press Ltd., 2008), p. 53.
[8] *The Boston Herald*, 'De Valera begins his address in Gaelic', 30 June 1919, p.6. [See Appendix C for full speech]
[9] Joe Broderick, 'De Valera and Archbishop Daniel Mannix' in *History Ireland*, 2 (3) 1994, pp 38-39.
[10] Account of Fr E. J McCarthy regional director of Columban Fathers USA, p. 20. [Fr McCarthy's file is housed in the Columban Fathers HQ in Omaha, Nebraska and is reproduced courtesy of the Columban Fathers] Fr McCarthy was one of the first members of the Columbans in 1918. He was born in Cork and became regional director (USA) before he was assigned to the Philippines in the 1930's. He was present during the meeting of Mannix and de Valera at Omaha.

Figure 4.1: Father Flanagan, founding dir. of Boys Town, standing left of visitors: Archbishop Daniel Mannix of Melbourne, Australia, unknown, President of Irish Republic Eamon De Valera and Bishop Foley of Ballarat, Australia during their visit to Boys Town, Nebraska, USA 1920. Image kindly courtesy of Mrs Mary Ellen McCarthy.

Sadly, neither of them kept any memorandum of this event, but one source that survives is the account of their driver for the afternoon, an unnamed Columban Father. He outlined how "he had the privilege of serving the last Mass the Archbishop celebrated at Maynooth before he left for Australia".[11] He also wrote of a conversation he had with de Valera that confirms his son Terry's earlier conceptions regarding his father desire to enter the priesthood. He writes "talking to me in a quiet moment at Bedford Avenue he remarked, "I'd be going with ye, if I were a younger man". He looked quite sincere and I accepted his statement as a genuine expression of his good will".[12]

---

[11] Fr E J. McCarthy account, op. cit., p. 20.
[12] ibid, p. 21.

Figure 4.2: Signed photograph of Eamon de Valera. Image kindly courtesy of Mrs Mary Ellen McCarthy.

De Valera followed Mannix eventually on to New York where a mass meeting was scheduled for 18 July. Mannix would most certainly add brimstone and fire to this occasion by superseding it with a speech at Cliff Haven. At Cliff Haven, he outlined to the crowd:

> No, England never was friend of the United States. When your fathers fought it was against England. Ireland has the same grievances against the same enemy only ten times greater. I hope Ireland will make a fight equally successful. England was your enemy; she is your enemy today; she will be your enemy for all time. England is one of the greatest hypocrites in the world. She pretended to be your friend in the war. Now the war is over she tells you to mind your own business.[13]

The reasoning behind such an outburst is unclear as the archbishop was usually very rational in his public statements. Dermot Keogh suggests one reason behind the outburst in the United States. "Mannix had come into contact with many radical nationalists – lay and clerical – and his rhetoric had become quite extreme".[14] This is most certainly the case, but Mannix was definitely not someone weak enough to be influenced by the rationale of others when in fact it was known that he was quite a stubborn and independent prelate. It is possible that events in Ireland preceding this speech had filtered through to him, such as the Republican prisoner hunger strike and the Milltown Malbay murders, and these possibly infuriated Mannix to the degree where he was to become public enemy number one for a period to the British Empire.[15]

These very public statements made by Mannix had become, much more of a problem for the British now than de Valera, who was seeking support in the harsh American political circuit. Mannix on the other hand was a well-respected figure in both clerical and lay circles and the British authorities could not just as easily arrest the archbishop of Melbourne. It also threatened to fuel further unrest in Ireland and could threaten relations with America, Australia and indeed any other country who had a significant number of Irish immigrants. How then would the British solve this problem of the belligerent prelate?

The public attention was focused on Lloyd George, the British Prime Minister. He had to prove his mettle against Mannix. If not he risked facing

---

[13] Bruce Duncan, *The church's social teaching: From Rerum Novarum to 1931* (Melbourne: CollinsDove, 1991), p. 183.

[14] Dermot Keogh, 'Mannix, de Valera and Irish nationalism' in John B. O'Brien and Pauric Travers (eds.), *The Irish emigrant experience in Australia* (Dublin: Poolbeg, 1991), p. 200.

[15] Dolan, op. cit., p. 24.

the same political climb down as Prime Minister Hughes in Australia, who had previously tried to counteract the archbishop's views on conscription. As well as the scheduled matter of Mannix's arrival in Ireland, the British also had other problems to contend with. As Thomas Hachey outlines "cabinet members were wary of the effect which such a step might have upon public opinion and seemed more concerned with a rumour hinting that the Australian prelate was about to be appointed Archbishop of Dublin."[16] Hachey's assumptions were correct. The British feared Mannix more so than de Valera at this juncture. In an extract from a draft conclusion of a cabinet meeting held on 24 June 1920 the British cabinet agreed that the Secretary of State for Foreign Affairs should:

> ... indicate the undesirability in the present acute state of Irish affairs, of appointing as Archbishop of Dublin a person of pronounced and publicly-proclaimed anti-British sentiments. He should also suggest to the Vatican the desirability, if possible, of finding some employment for Archbishop Mannix outside the United Kingdom'.[17]

This was not an issue that the British could take lightly. If Mannix were appointed to the diocese of Dublin the British would have a very formidable opponent right on their doorstep. In America, Mannix was not only testing Britain's resolve with regards his statements, but also the sincerity of their threats of not allowing him to visit Ireland. This decision had been taken at a British Cabinet meeting of 23 July. At the meeting the cabinet outlined to the Consular General in New York that "Archbishop Mannix who is believed to be about to sail from New York for the United Kingdom cannot be permitted to land in Ireland. Please take steps to acquaint him with this decision before he sails."[18] If appointed to Dublin they could not avoid confrontation with Mannix. The task of dealing with Mannix was left to the British Foreign Office who were stretched to capacity by the 1920 tour of America by de Valera and Dr Mannix. They now had to intercede with the Vatican on behalf of the British government to quell any rumours that Mannix was about to be appointed to succeed Archbishop Walsh as archbishop of Dublin. The government through Count de Salis, Her Majesty's Representative to the Holy See, outlined to the

---

[16] Thomas E. Hachey, 'The quarantine of Archbishop Mannix: a British preventive policy during the Anglo-Irish troubles' in *Irish University Review*, 1 (1) 1990, p. 115.

[17] Cabinet Draft Conclusion 37 (20), 24 June 1920 (National Archives of the UK, CO 537/ 1144).

[18] Hachey, op. cit., p. 116.

Vatican that "if their representations on the subject were disregarded we might have to consider the bearing of such a decision upon the question of our future relations with the Holy See."[19]

Whilst the British delegation was attempting to intercede with the Vatican, the tour and public demonstrations continued in America. De Valera was glad to have Mannix on his side as he was proving a bigger distraction to the British authorities than he was. Mannix's influence amongst the Irish diaspora was widely needed as friction began to appear between the Irish-Americans and de Valera over a number of issues early on. Propaganda was the order of the tour from the beginning with the constant use of underhanded tactics in the press. Both sides used such tactics to win the hearts and minds of the American public. The British were covertly undermining de Valera's attempts at sealing American loyalties to Irish self-determination and would have been delighted to learn of the fractious relationship that had developed between the Irish Americans and the Irish president. The alliances developed into de Valera and McGarrity on one side and Judge Cohalan and Devoy on the other. Although an attempt to push for a united front to fight for Ireland's cause was made and "despite surface appearances of unity, serious differences of opinion had arisen between the president and the leaders of the Clan na Gael and the Friends of Irish Freedom under Devoy and Cohalan."[20] The dispute largely centred on the use of funds gathered during the tour. Judge Cohalan argued that the money be spent in America however, Irish born, McGarritty argued for it to be used in Ireland. As Donal McCartney points out, the use of money engendered an air of mistrust amongst the Irish diaspora. There were "many references in the correspondence of Cohalan, Devoy, McCartan, and McGarrity reveal how the two sides suspected each other of 'flinging money away recklessly', wasting it, misusing it, and even making off with it".[21]

Either way the money was badly needed for the Irish cause. Mannix was close to leaving for Ireland, as the headlines from Ireland did not make for pleasant reading in August 1920. Within the next few months, his subsequent refusal of entry into Ireland would vie for headings with such events as the last stages of Terence MacSwiney's hunger strike, Kevin

---

[19] Cypher telegram to Count de Salis, 24 June 1920 (National Archives of the UK, CO 537/1144).

[20] Seán Nunan, 'President Éamon de Valera's mission to the United States of America 1919-1920' in *The Capuchin Annual* (1970), p. 244.

[21] Donal McCartney, 'De Valera's mission to the United States 1919-1920' in Art Cosgrave and Donal McCartney (eds.) *Studies in Irish history* (Naas: Leinster Leader, 1979), p. 310.

Barry's incarceration, Bloody Sunday and the Kilmichael ambush, closely followed by the burning of Cork city.[22] The tour was coming to a successful conclusion for Mannix but was it as successful for de Valera. The archbishop was to sail from New York on 31 July. Before this, however, on 25 July at a reception in honour of the archbishop at Gonzaga Hall, Washington D.C, de Valera continued to fan the flames that Mannix had earlier lit at Cliff Haven. He outlined the terms needed to achieve Irish independence:

> The truth is that the British Government does not want peace in Ireland or with Ireland except on terms which no real Irishman will accept – on the basis of Ireland's subjugation as a mere province of Britain. Peace will only come when the last British soldier is removed from Ireland, or when Britain is ready to treat Ireland as a separate and independent national state.[23]

Mannix arrived in New York on 17 July, led by archbishop (later Cardinal) Patrick Hayes. Mannix was escorted through the streets of the city by none other than the most famous of U.S regiments, "the Fighting Sixty-Ninth". Among the functions attended by the archbishop was the celebration of mass in St Patrick's cathedral on the Sunday morning, 18 July 1920. Mannix also addressed a monstrous meeting in Madison Square Gardens along with de Valera, which saw 18,000 people pack the arena.[24] After accepting the Freedom of New York city, the most loyal gathering was accorded to him by the Maynooth Union at a banquet in the Hotel Astor on July 20. Here we really get a sense of how de Valera had come to develop a close relationship and reverence for the archbishop. He lauded Mannix's "brilliancy as a professor, the magnificence of his personality, his austerity … his sincerity and his plain-dealing".[25] Archbishop Mannix was the last to speak and he did not disappoint. The high esteem the archbishop held for the president of Ireland can be seen from his many speeches during the tour. His speech at Madison Square Garden's amply demonstrates this trend:

> This was a gathering of priests, and in a certain sense the President did not belong there; but he made for himself a place in the Irish nation which entitled him to sit not merely with the laity and the clergy, but even on the

---

[22] Michael Hopkinson, *The Irish War of Independence*, (Dublin: Gill & Macmillan, 2002), p. 84.
[23] News release, 25 July 1920 (UCD Archives: De Valera Papers, P150/ 2912).
[24] Frank Murphy, *Daniel Mannix* (Melbourne: Advocate Press, 1948), p. 91.
[25] ibid, pp 91-95.

bench of bishops almost … You can see the man has gone to a great more
trouble to put himself right before God than those who are his meanest
critics. I only wish all politicians were like him. I am glad he is not a
politician at all. I am glad the President of the Irish Republic is a statesman
on a different plane.[26]

It seems clear that not alone did the American tour cement these two
men's relationship, but it also provided an opportunity to discuss various
ideas and formulate a clear united republican discourse. De Valera had
constructed the stage and Mannix duly arrived as the main actor in this tour
outshining the president to a large degree, but not taking away from him by
any means. The Americans had found it easy to gather sympathy for the
Irish cause due "to the earlier American struggle for liberation … and in
the incipiently anti-English atmosphere". Archbishop Mannix played to
this sympathy using powerful rhetoric such as "All that Ireland asks of
England is that she takes one of her hands off her throat, and the other out
of my pocket" that enthralled the large crowds and fired up the media
circus to no end.[27] His powerful use of evocative rhetoric would stand him
in good stead as he prepared to set sail for his homeland with the eyes of
the world press focused on him, as well as the nervy British Cabinet. Any
influence Mannix had on Irish affairs was exemplified by the British
decision to arrest him forcing the Irish Catholic hierarchy into a catch 22
situation. Ultimately it forced the hierarchy to give their backing to
Mannix. The main reason for British agitation was the possible positioning
of Mannix as a strong clerical backer to the Irish government and effective
global propagandist for their cause that no other Irish cleric could indeed
attract at this time. The British also feared the arrival of the prelate on Irish
shores would be a big boost to the morale of the Irish men who had fought
a largely successful war against the Crown forces up to this point. As
Brennan suggests "the Irish forces in Ireland were militarily more
successful than their enemies" communiqués cared to admit. By May 1920
the I.R.A. was able to claim that the "King's Government had virtually
ceased to exist west of the Shannon and south of the Boyne".[28] The scene
was set for a clash upon the high seas that would see the mighty royal navy
come up against "the Pirate of Penzance".

Mannix would not be allowed leave New York without incident. Like
so many times before, the archbishop brought public attention everywhere

---

[26] Rev. Walter Ebsworth, *Archbishop Mannix* (Armadale, Vic.: H. H. Stephenson,
1977), pp 231-232.
[27] Brennan, op. cit., p. 189.
[28] ibid, p. 187.

he went and as he boarded the S.S. Baltic the situation was no different. Ted O'Riordan describes the situation on board as being very tense "as there were rumours that some of the crew would strike if Dr Mannix was allowed to stay on board, but the dockers, who were predominantly Irish or of Irish descent, threatened every English ship in the Harbour with strike action if the 'Baltic' did not sail".[29] The stand-off was curtailed and the "Baltic" eventually set sail for Ireland. The Irish people prepared to welcome home their new found hero and "a wave of hope passed over Ireland at the prospect of anyone of Mannix's position and authority coming to Ireland to see for himself the things the British Government was doing its utmost to hide from the rest of the world".[30] Mannix bade his farewells to de Valera expecting possibly to see him in Ireland again in the near future. The seed of their relationship had been sown at Omaha and would grow strong against the ineptitude of British disapproval. De Valera had captured Mannix's loyalties. T. P. Boland argues that from 1920 onwards "Mannix never mentioned Ireland without mentioning de Valera. At this stage Mannix was already a 'Dev Man', not a simple Irishman".[31] This argument had strong credence as many Australians particularly those loyal to the crown argued that Dr Mannix in his capacity as archbishop was no longer speaking on behalf of the ordinary Australian citizen, but had been engulfed by the tide of Irish nationalism. In a letter to the *New York Times*, one Horace Alderson wrote "I wish to emphasise the fact that Archbishop Mannix is not an Australian, nor does he in any capacity, officially or unofficially, represent that country".[32] Mannix's persona was even more charismatic than de Valera's and this was shown in the fact that Judge Cohalan visited the archbishop the day before he left for Ireland giving thanks for his support and offering his well wishes. Mannix effectively telling the diaspora organisations in America what they wanted to hear stated, "I do not know what is before me in my coming travels but I am willing to go to prison, even to be put in chains, for the cause of Ireland's freedom."[33]

As the S.S. Baltic sailed across the Atlantic on a collision course with the British Navy, the War of Independence raged on in Ireland. From

---

[29] Ted O'Riordan, 'Great men we have given to history' in *Charleville and District Historical Journal*, 2 (1987), p. 74.

[30] Moirin Chavasse, *Terence MacSwiney* (Dublin: Clonmore & Reynolds; Burns & Oates, 1961), p. 140.

[31] T. P Boland, *James Duhig* (Saint Lucia: University of Queensland Press, 1986), p. 157.

[32] Horace Alderson, *The New York Times*, 'Australian Sentiment', 23 July 1920.

[33] Hachey, op. cit., p. 119.

Soloheadbeg, events accelerated out of control that neither side effectively could claim control of. Was Mannix's imminent arrest by the British another vindication for retaliation by the I.R.A? It may not have played any part at all, but it did offer them yet more international credence for their actions due to a series of incompetent British Cabinet decisions. Mannix, meanwhile, had learned through the now ever expanding world-press that Lloyd George intended to prevent him from returning home. Obviously irked by any such action, he prepared a statement in which he said:

> One would scarce get a better proof of the jumpy and frenzied condition of British politicians than in Lloyd George's fears to allow me to set foot in my native land. Of that English rule in that country has gone beyond recall. Perhaps, like the dying wasp, he wishes to sting something, no matter how futile and pathetic his efforts should appear.[34]

Mannix now became known to young and old alike in Australia and America as "The Champion of Democracy". All kinds of iconography began to manifest itself around the Mannix name and this was best demonstrated in the various pickets held at events where the archbishop himself was present. On his way to Pier 60 to board the S.S. Baltic, a group of women calling themselves "The American Women Pickets for the Enforcement of America's War Aim" grabbed the crowd's attention with colourful pickets. These were decorated with slogans such as "Mannix the world looks to you to save democracy" and "Freedom – America 1776, Ireland 1916" along with "There can be no peace while British militarism rules the world".[35] The cult of Archbishop Mannix was steadily gathering pace due to his role in the conscription referenda and stance on British involvement in Ireland. Aboard his ship, Mannix could not have predicted the events that would see his popularity rise even further on the international stage. His ship, the Baltic was so close to Ireland on 8 August 1920, that Fr Vaughan, the archbishop's secretary could see the shoreline, along with the possibility that the British would still recant their original threat. Fr Vaughan however, soon realised that two Scotland Yard detectives present on board the Baltic had now spotted a British Naval Destroyer on the horizon making for contact with the Baltic. Night fell as the naval destroyer, the Wyvern, accompanied by a second naval destroyer, ordered the Baltic to a halt. Shortly thereafter, the archbishop and Fr Vaughan, who detailed all the events off the coast in a letter to his family

---

[34] Murphy, op. cit., p. 98.
[35] Joe Doyle, 'The American womens picket' in *The Irish World and American Industrial Liberator and Gaelic American*, 21 April 1984, p. 5.

in Melbourne, were summoned to the captain's quarters. Here Mannix was issued with two summonses on behalf of her Majesty's Government. The summons prevented the archbishop from landing on Irish soil and secondly denied him entry to the cities of known Irish immigrant strongholds such as Liverpool, Manchester and Glasgow.[36] These cities were often the focus of issues such as class and sectarian tensions due to the high volume of Irish emigrants present there.[37] The British argued that Mannix's arrival could possibly stimulate these tensions further. Fr Vaughan wrote of the events on board the Baltic:

> We took our time in getting ready for the transhipment. When quite ready we went to the deck, where the gangway was let down to the waiting pinnace with its crew of British Jack Tars. The Archbishop then quietly and deliberately said: 'I refuse to leave this vessel', thereby throwing the onus for his removal entirely on the British Government. One of the Scotland Yard men then placed his hand on the Archbishop's shoulder, which amounted to a technical arrest.[38]

This was a cunning masterstroke by Mannix and played nicely into the hands of Sinn Féin propagandists, who were closely monitoring the situation. Mannix made folly of his arrest and compared it to other British ineptitude. In his first interview on British soil, he mocked the British Navy claiming that:

> Since the Battle of Jutland, the British Navy has not scored any success comparable with the chasing of the Baltic from the Irish shores and the capture without the loss of a single British sailor of the Archbishop of Melbourne. The British authorities possibly think that the naval victory was worth winning and that the money involved has been well spent. But even their own friends in the Press scarcely venture to share that view.[39]

The British government had now brought the great orator and master propagandist to their own doorstep. As well as having to contend with international censure over their military tactics in Ireland, they now had to fight a constant public battle with Mannix. He revelled in making daily

---

[36] Frank Murphy, *Daniel Mannix* (2nd ed., Melbourne: The Polding Press, 1972), p. 91.
[37] Diarmuid Ferriter, *The transformation of Ireland 1900-2000* (London: Profile Books, 2005), p. 330.
[38] Fr Arthur Vaughan, 'The Vaughan letter' in *Footprints: quarterly journal of the Melbourne Historical Commission*, 1 (8) 1972, p. 15.
[39] *The Times*, 11 August 1920, p. 10.

swipes at Lloyd George and although prevented from entry into the cities of major Irish extraction "his followers proceeded to organise mass demonstrations of support on the outskirts of the principal cities of England and Scotland".[40] Mannix's movements, as well as being followed closely across the Irish Sea, were also attentively outlined to his parishioners back in Melbourne. When he had left them over a year ago, a sizable majority of the Irish Catholics in Melbourne and the vast community throughout Australia feared they would never see their "champion" again. Mannix became a fearless champion to the majority of the Irish and Australian prelates of his time. His influence was felt in a letter from the Australian hierarchy to *The Times* in England, outlining their unequivocal support for the archbishop:

> One of the offences laid to his charge is that he has been the fearless champion of the principle that underlies the just and permanent settlement of the Irish question – namely, the right of the people of Ireland to choose their own form of government. In the advocacy of this principle he has not only the unanimous support of the whole Episcopacy, but also of the Irish people of Australia and New Zealand, as manifested at the Irish Race convention held recently in Melbourne.[41]

An interesting aside with regard to this letter is that where Archbishop Clune of Perth signed the letter, Archbishop Duhig of Brisbane did not. Duhig was the antithesis of Mannix and preferred to seek private co-operation with the British authorities both in Australia and in Ireland. He did not seek the limelight like the Charleville native and instead of signing the letter "he sent a private cable to Mannix to congratulate him on his courage. He also made no public protest and said nothing that might have seemed to endorse the republicanism of Mannix's American speeches."[42] Meanwhile, Mannix continued his imposed "tour" of England "regaling huge crowds with his denunciation of the Black and Tans and his call for total British withdrawal from Ireland. His words taunted the British authorities. 'I venture to think they will come to regret, the day they captured me off the coast of Ireland".[43]

Time proved Mannix's presumptions correct. However, he continued to irk Lloyd George and his cabinet by making himself a nuisance to the

---

[40] Joe Broderick, 'De Valera and Archbishop Daniel Mannix' in *History Ireland*, 2 (3) 1994, p. 39.

[41] *The Times*, 13 August 1920, p. 10. [See Appendix D for full letter]

[42] Boland, op. cit., p. 154.

[43] Broderick, op. cit., p. 39.

authorities. Ireland and its war-weary population were in the midst of a tense struggle. The reprisals on both sides began to intensify and the Roman Catholic Church was the pillar to which society looked towards for support. The Australian hierarchy had shown their hand by supporting Mannix and in October, the Irish bishops would soon follow suit. In a very striking and calculated statement, the bishops outlined where their support lay:

> There has been brutal treatment of clergymen, and, certainly, to ban a distinguished Archbishop of Irish birth, who is the trusted leader of democracy in Australia, is the most unwise step that purblind and tyrannical oppression could take. And still more cruel, and not less destructive of any prospect of peace is the continued imprisonment of the Lord Mayor of Cork, and the other hunger-strikers, who think nothing of their lives if they can do anything for Ireland in the sad plight to which the stranger has reduced her.[44]

Archbishop Mannix became firmly aligned with Sinn Féin. This was not alone due to his appearances during the American Bond Tour of 1920 and his friendship with de Valera, but also in his association with the republican Lord Mayor of Cork, Terence MacSwiney. The religious mentality that had become prevalent in republican ideology bore witness to a new martyr. Following the assassination of his predecessor Tomás MacCurtain by Crown Forces, MacSwiney proclaimed:

> The liberty for which we today strive is a sacred thing, inseparably entwined with that spiritual liberty for which the Saviour of man died, and which is the inspiration and foundation of all just government. Because it is sacred, and death for it is akin to the Sacrifice of Calvary, following far off but constant to that Divine example, in every generation our best and bravest have died...No lesser sacrifice would save us.[45]

MacSwiney was prepared to take any measures to continue the legacy of religious martyrdom instilled in republicanism, even through a hunger strike, following his arrest on 12 August 1920.[46] Many distinguished prelates would visit the Lord Mayor in Brixton prison during his hunger

---

[44] Ebsworth, op. cit., p. 243. [See Appendix E for full statement]

[45] Terence MacSwiney quoted in John Newsinger, 'I bring not peace but a sword': the religious motif in the Irish War of Independence' in *Journal of Contemporary History*, 13 (3) 1978, p. 622.

[46] Mark Tierney, *Ireland since 1870* (Dublin: CJ Fallon, 1998), p. 230.

strike, but the archbishop's three visits would be the most high profile.[47] In an attempt to discredit the staunch Catholic MacSwiney, the issue of his approaching death was brought into question as suicide, which was looked upon as a sin in Catholic theology. In an article by P. J. Gannon in 1920, entitled *The ethical aspect of the hunger strike*, Gannon refused to condemn the Lord Mayor's death:

> ... suicide, so defined, is never lawful according to Catholic teaching ... To abstain from food *in order to put an end to one's life* would doubtless be sinful. The primary intention here is death, and abstinence from food is the means chosen to compass an illicit end. But no hunger-striker aims at death. Quite the contrary; he desires to live. He aims at escaping from unjust detention, and to do this, is willing to run the risk of death – a very different frame of mind.[48]

The archbishop, reminiscent of his days in Maynooth stood to the fore on the matter. During one of his visits, the archbishop administered the Sacrament of the Sick to the Lord Mayor and gave his most famous interview while in England, to the London correspondent of the French paper *Liberte*. He argued that:

> ... in leaving Terence MacSwiney to die I think the English Government is committing a tragical error. His death will be an incalculable disaster for British prestige, and will, on the other hand, be the best propaganda for the Irish Republic. As so many discussions have been raised on the subject, I may tell you that I do not consider the act of the Lord Mayor as that of suicide, and I cannot conceive how any priest could refuse him the Sacraments on that ground.[49]

The Vatican had difficult questions to contend with due to the remonstrances of Archbishop Mannix and Terence MacSwiney's death. The Pontificate was looked to for clarity on MacSwiney's hunger strike. In a statement issued from Rome Pope Benedict XV "had found widely divergent opinions among learned Cardinals and other prominent figures in the church with whom he had discussed the situation and therefore had laid the problem before the Congregation of the Holy Office which settles questions of faith and morals and judges heresy".[50] Mannix on the other

---

[47] Chavasse, op. cit., pp 174-175.

[48] P. J Gannon, 'The ethical aspect of the hunger strike' in *Studies: An Irish Quarterly Review*, 9 (35) 1920, p. 450.

[49] Ebsworth, op. cit., p. 244.

[50] *The New York Times*, 26 October 1920.

hand did not wait for a judgment on the matter and continued to support the Lord Mayor. As a former professor of moral theology, and archbishop, it gave MacSwiney the prominent ecclesiastical support that he needed. Mannix was also to preside over the funeral of the Lord Mayor following his death on 25 October 1920. In a display of fervent nationalism, Archbishop Mannix led the funeral of Alderman MacSwiney through the streets of London in full view of the British Government. Other distinguished prelates such as Archbishop Cotter of Portsmouth accompanied the cortege to Euston Station where Mannix was again forbidden to accompany the body to Ireland.[51] The British Government were pressing the Vatican to act accordingly to silence or discipline its prelate, but their efforts were to no avail. As a Catholic editor outlined in a letter to *The Times*, "the question of ecclesiastical propriety they leave to the Holy See, which necessarily gives great liberty to prelates in questions of politics, upon which it is itself neutral".[52] Mannix took this piece of string and firmly intertwined the Catholic religion with the republican ideology proclaiming "it is for a nation of martyrs to cultivate consistent self-restraint. Our people were a great Christian nation when pagan chaos reigned across the Channel. They will remain please God, a great Christian nation when the new paganism that now prevails there has run its evil course".[53] Lloyd George and his government effectively realised after MacSwiney's funeral they had made a grave error in bringing Mannix to their own doorstep. They had allowed his charismatic personality to fill the pages of the British and world press ridiculing their every decision. Fr Vaughan would later add that "when everything was divulged the public would be surprised to know of the efforts that were made by the Government to induce the archbishop to go to Ireland. When the facts were made known they would see that the authorities almost went on their knees to get His Grace to go to Ireland".[54]

Fr Vaughan, as secretary to the archbishop was in a good position to understand the overall situation. He detailed what was later described by Mannix as, the option to visit Ireland on Lloyd George's terms. However, according to Thomas Hachey "once it became apparent to Dr Mannix that London, despite public demonstrations and private intercessions, would not alter the terms for lifting the ban, Mannix steadfastly continued his verbal attacks upon the British Government".[55] He outlined how he "could have

---

[51] Broderick, op. cit., p. 39.
[52] *The Times*, 17 August 1920, p. 6.
[53] *The Irish Times*, 'The state of Ireland', 20 October 1920, p. 6.
[54] Frank Murphy, *Daniel Mannix* (Melbourne: Advocate Press, 1948), p. 105.
[55] Hachey, op. cit., p. 128.

got over to Ireland with Archbishop Clune, to participate in the negotiations which ended in nothing, if he had only been willing to pay a price which should not be paid by any decent man".[56] Truce negotiations in 1920 had been attempted by various parties including Archbishop Clune and Father O'Flanagan, but amounted to nothing. O'Flanagan had acted on his own accord and may have even pre-empted Archbishop Clune's hopes at a resolution due to the confusion over the true representative of the Sinn Féin diplomatic attempt. The break down of negotiations was a disappointment for many sides. The public along with both sides involved were growing war weary. The British public were anxious for an end to hostility after the human loss of World War One and did not want to get involved in a prolonged guerrilla war in Ireland. Sinn Féin also "found it increasingly difficult to seize the initiative from an enemy that possessed overwhelming military superiority and to continue the fight in a country growing weary of hostilities".[57] Mannix through his stature and rhetorical skills would have been a possible candidate for diplomacy, however, "by taking sides so openly, could never have been a peacemaker. Clune, by his support of conscription in Australia, was a more tolerable fellow from the British point of view, but any churchman would have found it hard to penetrate the mind of Lloyd George", all except as Brennan argues "Dr Mannix".[58]

The original purpose of Mannix's exertions abroad had long been forgotten in the events that had taken place during his tour, however, his *ad limina* visit would still go ahead to the Pope as planned. The archbishop would depart England in March 1921. Frank Murphy and Brennan wrote that Mannix did not get to meet his mother one last time. Ellen Mannix did in fact get to meet her son, although not on Irish shores as she had originally hoped.[59] Mannix's cousin "Bishop Foley, who had accompanied the archbishop on his trip abroad, was not taken from the S.S. Baltic, which eventually landed in Liverpool. The Bishop would bring Ellen Mannix aged 88 to Hammersmith, London to see her son, as it turned out, for the last time."[60] As the archbishop travelled to Rome, via Paris, for his highly anticipated meeting with Pope Benedict XV, de Valera was still entertaining the idea of gaining American support. He hoped to repair the

---

[56] *The West Australian*, 16 May 1921, p. 6.
[57] Thomas E. Hachey, 'The British Foreign Office and new perspectives on the Irish issue in Anglo-American relations 1919-1921' in *Éire-Ireland*, 7 (2) 1972, pp 11-12.
[58] Brennan, op. cit., p. 214.
[59] Murphy, *Daniel Mannix*, (Melbourne: The Polding Press, 1972 2nd Edition), p. 128. Brennan, op. cit., p. 228.
[60] 'Daniel Mannix – a grandson of Croom' in *Crom Abú* (5) 1984, p. 12.

rift between the two factions in America. However, "the conflict between de Valera and Cohalan over control of the separatist movement in America had climaxed at the Republican Convention. From then on the Irish president commanded a greater degree of influence over Irish-American activities at the expense of Justice Cohalan."[61] By the time of de Valera's departure in December 1921, Ireland was on the brink of a historic treaty with the British Government. Historians have often discussed the virtues of the tour. Donal McCartney argues that:

> In the minds of his severest critics de Valera's prolonged absence in America ranks only second in disastrous consequences to his absence from the Anglo-Irish treaty negotiations in London one year later. They see him as the wrong man in the wrong place at the wrong time at two critical moments of Irish history.[62]

Historian Dave Hannigan sums up the tour effectively:

> Even if he ultimately failed to get official recognition from Washington, the scope and ambition of the entire campaign, from the slick pr machine to the hard lessons learned duelling with John Devoy and Justice Cohalan, ensured de Valera was returning as a savvier and more battle-heartened politician.[63]

De Valera needed this hard earned political experience in the future. His true character was about to be tested in the upcoming debate over the treaty. The continued support and public image of his great ecclesiastical ally that he had attained in America was vital if he was going to win the long battle ahead. This was not just with the pro-treaty faction, but also with the hierarchy of the Irish Catholic Church. Mannix was endeavouring like de Valera to garner sympathy for the Irish cause. His meeting with Pope Benedict XV provided an ample opportunity for a masterstroke in propaganda. The archbishop became accustomed to large welcomes and his arrival in Rome was no different. In an address of welcome in Irish to the archbishop from Rev Eric Fair D.D., he outlined how:

---

[61] Dennis M. Sullivan, 'Éamon de Valera and the forces of opposition in America, 1919-1920' in *Éire-Ireland*, 19 (2) 1984, pp 112-113.

[62] McCartney, Donal, 'De Valera's Mission to the United States 1919-20', in Art Cosgrave and D. McCartney (eds.), *Studies in Irish History* (Naas: Leinster Leader, 1979), p. 317.

[63] Dave Hannigan, *De Valera in America: The rebel president's 1919 campaign* (Dublin: O'Brien Press Ltd., 2008), p. 282.

Since that April day three hundred and thirteen years ago when the great Hugh O'Neill was welcomed like the Prince that he was into this city, even though the hand of England lay heavily upon him, no more illustrious guest of Irish birth has ever set foot on Roman soil and we are glad to owe so deep a debt.[64]

The meeting with Pope Benedict XV lasted for an hour in total. Mannix intelligently played upon the fact that it was feared the Vatican was being influenced with regard to Ireland. He intimated that:

... not only was there a general feeling of surprise that the common Father of Christendom who had words of sympathy for Belgium and Poland was silent with regards worse things in Ireland and there was also a widespread fear or impression among Irishmen that the Vatican was allowing itself to be influenced by considerations of policy.

Eager to reinforce the independence of the Vatican diplomatic corps from outside influences, the Pope attempted to rectify the situation. Instead of the Pope Benedict XV disciplining the archbishop, as the British had hoped, and as well as many in the Australian establishment, their cordial meeting ended with Mannix drafting a letter of support to the prisoners of 1916 families for the Pope also including a sizable amount of money totalling 20,000 lire.[65] This event shows the esteem which Mannix held in Vatican circles and how he was able to turn a tricky situation to his advantage. This was a severe blow to the British Foreign Office who could not be rid of the Irish prelate. Mannix left Rome after spending the last two years of his life playing a role in the push for Irish independence. He returned to Australia in April 1921, hoping for an end to the bloodshed in his native land that had devastated a population and its country. The "champion of democracy" had become a "champion of propaganda", and continued to put pressure on England for a final resolution to the Irish question, which his friend de Valera was working tirelessly to achieve.

---

[64]Typescript [draft] and copies with handwritten amendations for a speech [given by Dr. Eric Fair, Irish
College Rome] from the 'Gasra of the Fáinne', welcoming [Archbishop Mannix of Melbourne], 27 March 1921 (Irish College in Rome: Msgr. Hagan letters, HAG 1921/171).
[65] Ebsworth, op. cit., p. 255.

I pray that the ideals of President de Valera might be realised and that we may visit an Ireland, both free and prosperous and that Ireland might be one of the great if one of the small nations of the world.[66]
—Archbishop Daniel Mannix

---

[66]Handwritten account by […] of a meeting at the Irish college 'on Sunday last' to welcome Archbishop Mannix, 27 March 1921 (Irish College in Rome: Msgr. Hagan letters, HAG 1921/174).

CHAPTER FIVE

UNCHANGED AND UNCHANGEABLE: FOREVER ANTI-TREATY (1920-1925)

A defiant leader resisted pressure and his evocative language showed how far he was willing to go against signing the Anglo Irish Treaty. De Valera stood firm telling Ireland's pro-treaty camp: "Go to the devil. I will not sign".[1] This sums up his opposition to the treaty. The devil himself could well have scripted the aftermath and disastrous implications the signing of the Anglo Irish Treaty in December 1921 had on Ireland's future. On the 7 January 1922, "the Dáil accepted the treaty by a majority of 64 votes to 57. De Valera led his followers out of the Dáil and proceeded to set up his own underground government drawn from anti-Treaty members of the Dáil".[2] The manner of the result still allowed the republicans enough credence, as they saw it, to continue in the manner that manifested itself with the Four Court occupation and subsequent actions. This chapter will focus on the Civil War in Ireland and Mannix's final return to his home country. De Valera's entrance into Dáil Éireann and the influence Mannix had on this decision will also be analysed. The chapter will highlight the political distance by 1925 between Mannix and the religious, as well as political leaders in Ireland at this time.

Eamon de Valera became either the great protagonist or devil's advocate due to his role in the Civil War. He symbolised for many the political opposition towards the Anglo-Irish Treaty. Mannix returned to his primary role as the episcopal head of Melbourne with his return to Australian shores in July 1921. Like the vast diaspora, Mannix kept a close eye on the key events happening in Ireland in the run up to the treaty debate. He placed his hopes for a resolution firmly behind de Valera and showed the esteem in which he held him: "I never met an Irishman for whom I had more admiration and in his hands the interests of Ireland are

---

[1] Diarmuid Ferriter, *Judging Dev* (Dublin: Royal Irish Academy, 2007), p. 68.
[2] Tim Pat Coogan, *Irish Independent*, 'The birth of a nation – Civil War', 29 April 2010, p. 8.

perfectly secure".[3] The treaty discussions would set the tone for future Irish politics as well as clerical relations with the newly formed state. De Valera and Mannix acted as two renegades in response to the discourse set by the Anglo-Irish Treaty. Both combined to offer the concrete base for opposition to the treaty.

The archbishop of Melbourne finally arrived back in his diocese, but not with such ease as one might have expected of a prominent cleric. He was now attempting to gain entry into a country which was part of that Empire and of which he was not a citizen. The Prime Minister, Mr Hughes had threatened a prohibition on the archbishop entering Australia following his departure on his *ad limina* visit to the Pope. Despite Mr Hughes rhetoric of refusing entry to archbishop Mannix to enter Australia, he did not have the legal power to do so.[4] With this knowledge behind him, the prelate made a triumphant return to his adopted country. He had become a master of public rhetoric and always kept his audience in mind wherever he was. The night after his arrival in Melbourne a crowd of over 30,000 people gathered to hear an attempt by Mannix to enthuse nationalist spirit in the large audience present. In a vain attempt to instil a nationalist mindset in the Australian people, Archbishop Mannix outlined how:

> ... as an Australian, he had made it his constant text to remind Australians that their country had come of age. He had reminded them that Australia was a nation and held a proud place among the nations, and that, therefore, in the minds of Australians, Australia's interests ought to be dominant, and the Australian flag ought to be at the top of the pole.[5]

Mannix was not alone re-affirming his commitment to the Catholic laity of Melbourne and Australia, but he was also protecting himself from the slanders of Hughes and his associates to claims of disloyalty to Australia and the Empire. They had long attempted "to smear his name and accuse him of putting Ireland before Australia, and politics before his religious calling".[6] However, Mannix, although still deeply involved in affairs

---

[3] Dermot Keogh, 'Mannix, de Valera and Irish nationalism' in John B. O'Brien and Pauric Travers (eds.), *The Irish emigrant experience in Australia* (Dublin: Poolbeg, 1991), p. 208.

[4] Rev. Walter Ebsworth, *Archbishop Mannix* (Armadale, Vic.: H. H. Stephenson, 1977), p. 258.

[5] Frank Murphy, Daniel Mannix (Melbourne: Advocate Press, 1948), p. 119. [See Appendix F for full speech]

[6] Ted O'Riordan, 'Great men we have given to history' in *Charleville and District Historical Journal*, 2 (1987), p. 76.

relating to Ireland, now began a period of sustained pastoral duties pertaining to his original appointment to Melbourne almost a decade ago. De Valera's primary duty as president of the first Dáil Éireann was to gain recognition of Dáil Éireann as the de facto government of Ireland, and hence secure finalisation of its claims to national self-determination. In correspondence between Lloyd George and de Valera, prior to the start of treaty negotiations, it is easy to see how astute a politician Lloyd George was. He tried using previous historical references from fervent nationalists such as Thomas Davis to justify England's claims to Ireland quoting a letter from 1845 whereby, Davis declared to the Duke of Wellington, "I do not seek a raw repeal of the Act of Union. I want you to retain the Imperial Parliament with its Imperial Power". De Valera responded to Lloyd George's brinkmanship with a firm rebuttal claiming "the history that you interpret as dictating union we read as dictating separation".[7] The Anglo-Irish Treaty did not guarantee Ireland, as an island, the right to full self-determination.   T. P. Boland outlines the travails of the treaty as follows:

> In one way, the treaty brought an end to seven hundred years of the suzerainty of the English crown. In another, it divided Ireland into north and south and preserved a nominal suzerainty through a governor-general and an oath of allegiance. It allowed the presence of British forces in strategic bases for external defence.[8]

Although the oath would prove to be an arduous point in itself, even for the pro-treaty faction, the division of Ireland into north and south would also prove a prevailing factor in Irish men and women taking up arms against each other. False pretentions for the treaty opponents had been thrown up by the treaty signing, as pages in *An Cosantóir*, the magazine of the Irish Armed Forces revealed "it looked at last as if the long struggle was over, that peace with honour had come to Ireland for few thought that partition could last for more than a year or so".[9] However, it only proved a false dawn as the Civil War would quickly follow suit. Graham Walker sees the Civil War "as a distasteful last act in the revolutionary drama

---

[7] Tim Coates, *The Irish uprising, 1914-1921: papers from the British Parliamentary Archive* (London: Tim Coates, 2000), pp 179-185.

[8] T. P Boland, *James Duhig* (Saint Lucia: University of Queensland Press, 1986), p. 158.

[9] Major General Hugh MacNeill, 'Na Fianna Éireann: senior corps of the old army' in Terence O'Reilly (ed.) *Our struggle for independence: Lessons from the pages of 'An Cosantóir* (Cork: The Mercier Press Ltd., 2009), p. 185.

begun by the Easter Rising in 1916. It claimed some 4,000 lives in its ten months duration and it provoked acts of inhumanity on a greater scale than the Anglo-Irish War of 1919-21". [10] Mannix still maintained his unwavering support for his friend, de Valera. In January 1922, at Queen's Cliff, he predicted that:

> Deep down in the hearts of the Irish people, the most popular man in Ireland today was De Valera. Even if I am wrong, I will make a prediction and say that in the near future the man whom Ireland will honour as one who never turned his country down, as one who never yielded the smallest fraction of an inch, as the man who has stood out as Ireland's idealist, and who deserved the greatest possible honour is President De Valera. History will say that, and history will be doing De Valera only the barest justice. [11]

In fact, after the Dáil walkout, de Valera held very little influence over his republican colleagues particularly the more militant ones like Rory O'Connor, who eventually occupied the Four Courts in April 1922. Diarmuid Ferriter believes that the republicans would have "fought regardless of whether de Valera rejected the Treaty or not, but it has remained a common belief" as Ferriter puts it "that while de Valera did not start the civil war, neither did he do enough to stop it". [12] The nationalist movement was split and both Collins and de Valera became the figureheads of a violent traumatic period of Irish history. The diaspora was also split along the same lines and although "Mannix posed as a neutral, he made it clear in whose favour he was neutral. He was for de Valera, against the treaty". [13] While de Valera had been in America, Michael Collins built up a fearsome reputation and strong support. This put him into direct conflict with de Valera in many ways, and after he undermined his former president in June 1922, they were on a direct collision course, which saw fruition in what ultimately became the Civil War. Collins had undermined de Valera by publishing the new Free State Constitution before the polls were opened on 16 June 1922, for a new coalition government. He urged the populace to negate the earlier pact he had made with the former president to set up a coalition government containing both factions, destroying all hopes of a peaceful resolution. [14]

---

[10] Graham Walker, 'Propaganda and conservative nationalism during the Irish Civil War, 1922-1923' in *Éire-Ireland*, 22 (4) 1987, p. 92.
[11] J.J O'Sheehan, *Archbishop Mannix: a sketch of his life and work* (Dublin, n-d.), p. 32.
[12] Ferriter, op. cit., pp 70-71.
[13] Boland, op. cit., p. 158.
[14] Walker, op. cit., pp 94-95.

Diehard republicans refused to give up arms and continued to take the fight to the newly formed Irish Free State, which was heavily backed by British military equipment and expertise. The British were keen to see the treaty accepted, namely as they could not contemplate de Valera in charge of Irish affairs among other reasons. The Irish Civil War began on 28 June 1922, with the Four Court bombardment by the Provisional Government. Occupation of the Four Courts was more of an attempt by the I.R.A. men to make a bold statement as opposed to a strategic occupation. The men of the anti-treaty faction army stood little chance of success against the well-equipped Free State Army who numbered 38,000 men particularly, when guerrilla warfare was only successful against a foreign army, not their own countrymen and former comrades in arms.[15] Michael Collins was winning both battles against de Valera. Firstly, he had the upper hand on the I.R.A. forcing them to slowly retreat to the Munster Republic eventually seizing the initiative, by attacking from the coast. Collins also began to win over Irish public opinion, which by the time of his death in August 1922, had largely rowed in behind the Free State, apart from the hardliners. The population were sick of bloodshed and destruction therefore, the I.R.A. knew that as time progressed they were fighting a losing battle. If de Valera was to have any hope of winning the Civil War against the Free State, he needed the backing of the main foundation pillar of Irish society in twentieth century Ireland, the Roman Catholic Church. This aspiration for clerical solidarity was dashed when the entire episcopate of Ireland in October 1922 condemned the war as unjustified and "morally only a system of murder and assassination ... killing in an unjust war is as much murder before God as if there were no war".[16]

De Valera was highly critical of the Irish hierarchy and he turned to his last episcopal ally for a shoulder to lean on, Mannix. He outlined in a very personal letter how, "never was charity of judgement so necessary, and apparently so disastrously absent. Ireland and the church will, I fear, suffer the consequences".[17] This letter highlights the bond that had been forged between the two men over the course of the previous two years. It shows a fragile, deeply conceited man in desperate need of reassurance from a fatherly figure. Mannix not only dispensed advice, but also acted as caretaker of de Valera's soul. De Valera continued:

---

[15] Coogan, op. cit., pp 14-17.

[16] Bruce Duncan, *The church's social teaching: From Rerum Novarum to 1931* (Melbourne: CollinsDove, 1991), p. 184.

[17] Eamon de Valera letter to Archbishop Mannix, 6 November 1922 (UCD Archives: De Valera Papers, P150/2909). [See Appendix G for Full Text]

> I crave your Grace's blessing, and I assure you of the affection and esteem
> of all who are striving now that the way may not be closed for those who
> may be destined to complete the work towards which the hopes of the
> nation have been set definitely since Easter 1916.[18]

The archbishop largely refused to comment publicly on affairs in Ireland
during this period, breaking his silence only following the death of
Collins, Brugha and Griffith in August 1922. This public statement may
have worried de Valera as it perhaps showed a leaning towards the Free
State with his statement: "In this tragic day, mourning over the graves of
Brugha, Griffith and Collins, Ireland will surely expect her sons to turn to
the arbitrament of reason. Arbitration may succeed, force will certainly
fail". [19] De Valera need not have feared though, as his ecclesiastical
guardian and political sentinel "was the only bishop or archbishop
anywhere to reject the treaty". This stance had secured Mannix many
enemies, but his support never wavered as detailed in a letter to Monsignor
Hagan in Rome from Fr Liam Connick:

> ... yourself and Dr. Mannix are today as far as I can see two Irish
> churchmen, who are respected by all sections of the Irish people and who
> hold a grip on the hearts of the people. This is not my own opinion alone
> but that of the laity around me.[20]

Mannix persevered with his stance against the treaty. He reiterated his
position with his most passionate plea of the Civil War on 2 December
1922. In his speech, he called for the unconditional release of the anti-
treaty political prisoners. He pleaded the following:

> We are here irrespective of our divergent political views, to ask, with
> absolute unanimity, or if you wish, to demand, the release of the Irish
> political prisoners, and that not so much for the sake of the prisoners
> themselves – though that object appeals to our hearts – as because we
> know that their release is the only way to peace in Ireland.[21]

---

[18] ibid.

[19] Ebsworth, op. cit., p. 265.

[20] Fragment holograph letter from [Liam Connick], Seaview House, Rosslare to
Msgr. Hagan, 13 November 1922 (Irish College in Rome: Msgr. Hagan papers,
HAG1-1922-493-0002).

[21] *The Advocate*, 'Irish political prisoners: unconditional release demanded', p. 18,
2 December 1922 (National Archives of Ireland/NAI, D/Taoiseach, S1369-13).

Mannix's support as Kiernan suggests allowed "the Republican cause to propose that there was no clear religious answer, that it was a matter of opinion, that they had Mannix with them". [22] The rebuttal by the archbishop of his former ecclesiastical superiors and brethren in Ireland did not sit well with them as well as those who had backed the treaty. Although all of the Irish hierarchy firmly supported the treaty, the clerical population also included renegades who, against the wishes of their superiors, continued to support the underground I.R.A. movement including Fr William Hackett and Fr O'Flanagan. Archbishop Mannix's support of de Valera gave these renegades the episcopal umbrella they needed to continue their support of the I.R.A., and hence de Valera. The archbishop would come into conflict with both the Irish hierarchy but also the Australian Catholic hierarchy. They now threatened to ruin his iconic image among the Irish in Australia due to their support for the treaty. By daring to question the Irish and Australian Catholic hierarchies during the Civil War, both Mannix and de Valera risked public unpopularity. Unfortunately, while de Valera realised this risk and attempted to repair the bond, Mannix continued to isolate himself further, not just from the Irish Catholic hierarchy, but also the majority of the Irish public. It seems that both men appealed more to the lower echelons of the Catholic Church during the period 1920 to 1925. They garnered significant support to maintain their status as authoritative voices in Irish public opinion, sometimes in direct opposition to the Irish and Australian Catholic hierarchies. De Valera, who came so close at one stage in his life to becoming a priest, certainly never underestimated the power of the Catholic Church. His son Terry argues this:

> It is true that the Catholic Church (then so deeply conservative) held a much greater influence, but again it was only reflecting the perceived views and attitudes of the greater part of the Irish population. This must have been so considering the radical changes in their attitudes in modern times. [23]

The main supporters of the treaty in Australia included Archbishop Duhig and Kelly. They outlined their support of the Free State government when Archbishop Kelly telegraphed Logue outlining that, "nineteen Archbishops and Bishops of Australia strongly deprecate National dissension. They look for practical union of action according to majority

---

[22] Colm Kiernan, 'Appréciation: Archbishop Daniel Mannix of Melbourne, 1864-1963' in *Éire-Ireland*, 19 (3) 1984, p. 126.

[23] Terry De Valera, *A memoir* (Dublin: Currach Press, 2004), p. 166.

vote".[24] Mannix was beginning to make enemies where he had once been able to rely on popular support. His foundations were beginning to crack and split in stark contrast to three years earlier, when the Australian hierarchy were fully behind him following his arrest. The split in his support from the Australian hierarchy was evident in March 1923. Against the wishes of Duhig and Kelly, Archbishop Mannix entertained Fr O'Flanagan and J.J O'Kelly in their self-appointed capacity as Republican envoys from Ireland. Mannix's association with O'Flanagan was particularly troublesome. O'Flanagan had hampered peace negotiations two years earlier in his capacity as Vice-President of Sinn Féin where again he appointed himself as an envoy without any formal declaration from Sinn Féin.[25] De Valera's political and ecclesiastical aide was, however, to step up to the mark as expected and by backing Fr O'Flanagan and O'Kelly he firmly stood against the Irish Free State government. Joe Broderick sees his verbal tirades as putting "himself at odds with the entire hierarchy of the Catholic Church in Ireland, as well as provoking profound division amongst Irish Catholics in Australia".[26]

Although Mannix was deeply saddened by what was happening in Ireland, he wished for a speedy resolution to the conflict. His steadfast support of de Valera and the republican cause did not waiver. The archbishop was not the only influential clergyman backing de Valera during the Civil War. Other notable clerics in high office such as Monsignor John Hagan, rector of the Irish College in Rome and the Reverend Peter Magennis, Prior General of the Carmelite Fathers maintained constant contact with the republican cause however; Mannix was the only bishop siding with the anti-treaty faction against the wishes of the Irish hierarchy and Rome.[27] The people of Melbourne, along with the press, had long become accustomed to the use of the St Patrick's Day parade by their archbishop as an outlet for his public persona. Mannix's speech on that day left his untainted iconic status in tatters with the pro-treaty supporters. Mannix pulled no punches and outlined in a one-sided pro-de Valera statement the current implications for Ireland of a country led by the Free State:

---

[24] Patrick Murray, *The political involvement of the Roman Catholic clergy in Ireland 1922-37* (PhD. Thesis: Trinity College Dublin, 1998), p. 68.

[25] ibid, p. 68.

[26] Joe Broderick, 'De Valera and Archbishop Daniel Mannix' in *History Ireland*, 2 (3) 1994, p. 40.

[27] ibid.

There are two sides to almost every question, and certainly, there must be two sides at least to the present Irish question. On one of these sides, we have been hearing a great deal. At the disposal of the party on that side is the daily Press right through the whole of the British Dominions. The patent fact is – whatever the reason or the significance of the fact may be – that throughout the wide world every enemy of Ireland, without exception, as well as many who profess to be Ireland's friends, is a supporter of the Free State Government.[28]

Following on from this, Mannix urged Melbourne to remember that there was a duty on both sides:

If you complain of the loss of life, do not forget to enquire about Childers and Mellows and their sixty or more companions whose lives have been taken in the gaols of the Free State.[29]

The speech coincided with the visit of Fr O'Flanagan and Mr J.J. O'Kelly to Melbourne. In his speech, the archbishop as well as re-iterating his position on the treaty re-affirmed his commitment to his lay protégé, de Valera. He boasted to the crowd gathered that "the delegates have come out here with credentials from a man who deserves our respect and homage, no matter how we may differ from him in some things, if indeed any of us do differ from him. I refer to Eamon de Valera".[30]

One could argue that Mannix made such speeches as he was ill informed due to his distance from the situation at hand. This case was put forward through a letter from W.T. Cosgrave to the archbishop on 17 December 1923. Here the president outlines how:

I have observed with sincere regret that on a few recent occasions Your Grace has been induced by misleading and inaccurate information to give publicity to statements which are calculated to produce an impression entirely to fact.[31]

The president quotes a speech from *the Catholic Press* from the 23 October 1923, whereby, the archbishop claims the 44 men on the losing side of the election of August 1923 were associated with the anti-treaty

---

[28] *The Monitor New Jersey*, Saturday 28 July 1923 (Maynooth College Archives, 20-7-16).
[29] ibid.
[30] ibid.
[31] W.T Cosgrave letter to Archbishop Mannix, 17 December 1923, p 6. (National Archives of Ireland/NAI, D/Taoiseach, S1369-13). [See Appendix H for full letter]

faction. Cosgrave highlights this speech due to its presentation of false facts. The president continues:

> Your Grace will perhaps permit me to say that the implication contained in this statement is … an absolute perversion of fact and which will be strongly very strongly resented by the gentlemen in question … May I venture to express the hope that our task will not be rendered more difficult by injudicious and inaccurate pronouncements, however well intentioned, circulated amongst those of our far-flung race whose distance from their native land makes it impossible for them to receive correct impressions of the day to day happenings here.[32]

Concurrently, however, de Valera argued previously that Mannix had kept well up to date on such matters. He achieved this by talking to visiting priests from home or those who had been in close correspondence with events taking place back in Ireland. One Jesuit priest in particular, Fr William Hackett, would prove to be at the heartbeat of the Civil War for Mannix not solely to his correspondence, but indeed through his first hand involvement in the Irish Republican movement. Michael Collins indeed eulogised that Father Hackett was worth more than five hundred men in arms for his help in the fight against the British.[33] Fr Hackett's first visit in March 1923 to "Raheen", Mannix's home in Melbourne would have been an intimidating experience for any newly arrived priest. He need not have worried, however, as himself and the archbishop instantly struck up as close a chord as any of Mannix's other aides, including Fr Vaughan. Hackett's biographer Brenda Niall suggests that Mannix always having an attentive ear "is likely to have benefited from a point of view much closer to the people than he could ever be. The archbishop had nothing like Hackett's direct experience of violence, and probably fewer close friends to mourn".[34] As events progressed in Ireland, the one true friend that the archbishop would have been truly fearful for was de Valera. Considering the Civil War had already robbed Ireland of some of its favourite sons, Mannix was eager that the same fate did not meet de Valera.

On 24 May 1923, de Valera issued a proclamation to the anti-Treatyites, often referred to as his Legion of the Rearguard speech, ordering them to lay down their arms.[35] Many of the republicans felt that

---

[32] ibid, p 10.
[33] ABC Australia, 'The riddle of Father Hackett', *Late Night Live*, 10 September 2009.
[34] Brenda Niall, *The riddle of Father Hackett – A life in Ireland and Australia* (Canberra: National Library of Australia, 2009), pp 134-135.
[35] Mark Tierney, *Ireland since 1870* (Dublin: CJ Fallon, 1998), p. 267.

the fight should have continued, but de Valera realised that militant republicanism was not the way forward. Although he managed to avoid jail in the intermittent period, he re-emerged to contest the general election of August 1923. He was arrested at the election meeting in Ennis, Co. Clare, but was surprised at how well Sinn Féin performed winning 44 seats.[36] With this success of Sinn Féin, Mannix continued to believe in his lay protégé. In an article from the *Gaelic American* brought to the attention of the government by Seán Lester, Director of Publicity dated 15 December 1923, he outlines how:

> Dr. Mannix is for de Valera right or wrong and is as inconsistent and illogical in regard to the situation in Ireland as de Valera himself ... but now he demands the unconditional release of the author of all this orgy of destruction and assassination – which is at least tacit approval of it all. He is greatly moved by the fakes about 'Freak State Atrocities' but is heedless of authentic reports of real savagery and moral turpitude.[37]

It is evident from this letter by Lester that Mannix had now become a firm enemy of the Free State. He stood firm in his resistance and even petitioned for the republicans release from prison. As outlined in a cable to the Irish delegate in Paris the archbishop, following a meeting of Irish societies of Victoria, informed him:

> ... having learned with indignation and shame that, despite the cessation of hostilities and the lesson of the recent election and in defiance of all democratic principles, thirty-five of the elected representatives of the Irish people and at least fourteen thousand other Irish men and women are held in gaol by the Free State Government as political prisoners, and under conditions which led to a general hunger-strike, this meeting unanimously protests against this outrage upon freedom and calls for the release of these prisoners as the first essential step towards peace in Ireland.[38]

It would take a mammoth shift of political direction from Mannix for his opinions to change, even considering Cosgrave's previous intervention. This showed little sign of taking place. In January 1924, the archbishop visited New Zealand where the effects of "Mannixism" had already been seen through the trial of Bishop James Liston. The bishop was facing trial

---

[36] Ferriter, op. cit., p. 101.
[37] Letter from Seán Lester Director of Publicity, 28 December 1923 (National Archives of Ireland/NAI, D/Taoiseach, S1369-13).
[38] Cable to Irish delegate in Paris, 1 November 1923 (UCD Archives: De Valera Papers, P150-2909).

on charges of sedition against the Empire. It was obvious whom the blame lay with for influencing Liston. Bishop Brodie told how, "Bishop Liston was made to suffer for the hero-worship won by other members of the Hierarchy of Australasia who had ventured into the political or semi-political sphere, and thereby gained for themselves fame and unbounded popularity".[39] Direct swipes at Mannix mattered little to him. He was surprised that the host of his visit to New Zealand Bishop Redwood "begged him to keep off the Irish issue in his public utterances".[40] The archbishop was an independent prelate, but his public statements were slowly making him more enemies. At the end of 1924, "he sponsored new delegates in Australia. One was a sister of Kevin Barry, herself a battler for de Valera in the Civil War". Duhig cautiously sponsored £20 but also kept a close eye on Mannix.[41] Archbishop Duhig had firmly sided with the Free State government. In a private letter to president Cosgrave, he assured him how:

> ... every one of our priests who has been home, has come back a convert to the Free State, and Australia is being slowly but surely permeated with a favourable impression regarding all of you who have stood out against the extremists. Father O'Flanagan and Mr O'Kelly created a good deal of trouble here. Brisbane proved to be their Waterloo. They were soon afterwards deported'.[42]

Eamon de Valera was released from prison in 1924. The former president saw that the Free State government were keen to sideline him. His political influence was declining requiring his immediate attention or possible exile into the political wilderness.[43] He had reason for hope as "during the grimmest phase of the Civil War, he told Dr Mannix that there had been 'nothing more cheering through these months than the unerring instinct which enabled Your Grace to appreciate the situation truly".[44] De Valera was correct. Mannix's constant support of the republican cause in the newspapers and backing of the prisoners, including those on hunger strike, as Seosamh Ó Broin contends, "was having a powerful effect on the

---

[39] Rory Sweetman, *Bishop in the dock: the sedition trial of James Liston* (Auckland: Auckland University Press, 1997), p. 266.
[40] ibid, p. 268.
[41] Boland, op. cit., p. 166.
[42] Letter from Archbishop Duhig of Sydney to Cosgrave, 22 July 1924 (National Archives of Ireland/NAI, D/Taoiseach, S1369-21).
[43] Tierney, op. cit., p. 287.
[44] Patrick Murray, *Voices of de Valera* (M. Litt Thesis: Trinity College Dublin, 1995), p. 153.

people and that their propaganda was skilfully playing upon popular emotions".[45] This had been effectively portrayed through the case of Mary MacSwiney, the sister of Terence, whom Mannix had a close affiliation with. Ms. MacSwiney went on hunger strike and received the full support of the archbishop, just as her brother had received two years previous. Mannix encouraged "all Catholics to support MacSwiney in her courageous struggle for an Irish Republic and to denounce the inhumanity of the Free State Government".[46] The pressure and republican propaganda worked, they released her from prison.

Mannix had been through a harrowing and demanding five years. This saw him balance his role as episcopal leader of the Irish diaspora abroad particularly in Melbourne, and being the clerical rock on which republican fortunes including de Valera has relied. This position had already seen him miss a triumphant return to Ireland and saw his popularity evaporate slowly with many of the Irish population both at home and abroad. No one could deny that Mannix still harboured hopes of a return to his native Charleville and the opportunity duly presented itself from an unlikely source. Archbishop Duhig, often Mannix's antithesis in previous years, was the secretary to the conferences of the Australian hierarchy. Duhig in his capacity as secretary "intimated to Dr Mannix that it was the unanimous wish of the Archbishops and Bishops of Australia that he should head the first Australian Pilgrimage to Rome".[47] This was a significant decision considering the events of the previous few years, and the animosity that Archbishop Duhig had shown in private towards Archbishop Mannix. Regardless of this, it showed the respect and esteem that Mannix could still muster from his clerical brethren in Australia. The year 1925 was a defining year in the relationship between de Valera and Dr Mannix. De Valera still keen to use the archbishop's Vatican influences asked Mannix to intercede to the new Holy Father once again, but this time on behalf of the republicans. He wrote to the archbishop:

> Your Grace will have an opportunity of seeing the Holy Father. I fear that the Republican position has never been properly presented to His Holiness. Want of a proper understanding has wrought much havoc here, which only

---

[45] Walker, op. cit., p. 101.
[46] Charlotte Fallon, 'Civil War hungerstrikes: women and men' in *Éire-Ireland*, 22 (3) 1987, p. 78.
[47] Frank Murphy, *Daniel Mannix* (Melbourne: Advocate Press, 1948), p. 136.

the Holy Father himself can undo. Things have gone from bad to worse, but Your Grace will understand without my writing this.[48]

This meeting would also set out the future path for de Valera towards constitutional nationalism, as he stood on the brink of political isolation. The archbishop left for Rome on 14 April 1925, harbouring proud ambitions of representing Australia at the Holy Year. The trip gave him the opportunity to update himself firsthand on matters relating to Ireland, firstly in Rome through Monsignor Hagan and Fr Magennis, and in the near future through de Valera. The archbishop had maintained close contact with the rector of the Irish college in the previous few years. Before Mannix departed for Rome, he made a telling remark to Monsignor Hagan. His only wish was that he could tell the new Pope, Pope Pius XI what he had told his predecessor about his countrymen being solid and united.[49]

Mannix was correct on this in many ways. The Civil War had not only left a divided people due to their stance on the treaty, but also due to the Irish hierarchy's endorsement of it and subsequent rejection of the irregulars' actions. The people not for the first time in Irish history were divided on the Catholic Church's opinions. As Cardinal Logue was to emphasise in 1924, the divisions of the Civil War were not just in the political field, "we will have to meet a divided people...who have lost much of their reverence for religion and the Church".[50] The Catholic Church was also divided on the imminent arrival of Mannix as can be seen by the hierarchy's representation at the funeral of Mannix's mother Ellen. She died on 4 January 1925. In a letter to Monsignor Hagan from Seán T. O'Ceallaigh, he outlines how:

> The arrival of Dr. Mannix in Ireland, as well as in Rome, will be embarrassing for a number of people. I don't see the Irish daily papers so only learned accidentally that Dr. Cotter was the only Bishop to be present at the funeral of Mrs. Mannix. This shows the hostility of the Bishops generally towards Mannix. I suppose you may take it that he won't get many invitations from his hierarchical colleagues.[51]

---

[48] Eamon de Valera letter to Archbishop Mannix, 9 May 1925 (UCD Archives: De Valera Papers, P150-2909).

[49] Archbishop Mannix letter to Msgr. Hagan, 17 November 1924 (Irish College in Rome: Msgr. Hagan papers, HAG1-1924-542).

[50] J. H Whyte, *Church & state in modern Ireland 1923-1970* (Dublin: Gill & Macmillan, 1971), p. 24.

[51] O'Ceallaigh letter to Msgr. Hagan, 17 February 1925 (Irish College in Rome: Hagan papers, HAG1-1925-90-0001).

Mannix had not yet realised the extent of the division amongst the Irish hierarchy and would only learn so through his conversations with Monsignor Hagan upon his arrival in Rome. Hagan in a letter to de Valera outlined the intentions of the archbishop upon his visit to Ireland. He wrote to de Valera:

> I have placed him in possession of any information I have or any conclusions and impressions I have been able to form relative to the trend of events in Ireland, particularly in recent months, and I think he understands the situation in most of its bearings. On his part he has been good enough to outline the attitude he proposes to take up and maintain in Ireland. Any utterances he may feel called upon to make will be to the effect that everyone knows his views, that he has nothing to unsay.[52]

De Valera obviously worried by this interpretation of Mannix's intentions by Hagan, hastened to Rome to meet his episcopal ally before his arrival in Ireland. Here he tried to persuade Mannix "to refrain from public statements; he was anxious to avoid an open breach between the Irish bishops and his sole episcopal supporter". Mannix, however, as independent and stubborn a prelate as ever refused to take de Valera's advice.[53] De Valera may have been unsuccessful in his attempt to manipulate his ally's future public pronouncements in Ireland, but he still sought his advice on political manifestations. Any steps he was about to make in political circles were discussed and confided in with his strongest episcopal ally. De Valera had been duly informed before he made his secretive trip to Rome that:

> The Bishops were doing their utmost to prevent the Archbishop coming to Ireland and are sending Bishop Foley to meet him for that purpose, since then I have learned that a movement is on foot to ask him to meet both sides and try and find a means of having the Republicans be induced to enter the Free State Parliament and I believe some of the so call national party and their influential Free Staters are going to ask him to use his influence to get the oath removed.[54]

---

[52] Msgr. Hagan letter to de Valera, 31 May 1925 (Irish College in Rome: Msgr. Hagan papers, HAG1-1925-293).
[53] Joe Broderick, 'De Valera and Archbishop Daniel Mannix' in *History Ireland*, 2 (3)1994, p. 41.
[54] Letter from unknown to de Valera, 9 May 1925 (UCD Archives: De Valera Papers, P150-2909).

It was highly imperative that de Valera met the archbishop before his ally met the "Free Staters" in case they undermined his attempt to regain his political stature. Before his arrival in Rome on 30 May, disguised as a priest de Valera had been duly informed by Monsignor Hagan of the viewpoints held by all three clergymen, Mannix, Hagan and Magennis, on the possibility of taking the oath of allegiance. It is interesting to note Dr Mannix's stance according to Hagan:

> We [Hagan and Mannix] discussed the subject of the oath. While our guest [Mannix] did not commit himself to any expression of opinion, I am inclined to gather that he would not be disposed to balk at the idea if it could be entertained without danger of a split. On this head I remarked that there was a possibility of a split arising sooner or later even if the present policy was maintained, and that in the face of two dangers the practical line would be to try and ascertain was the lesser. At any rate he has an open mind and is prepared to discuss all possibilities and any help he may be able to give will be gladly rendered in the way that seems best calculated to serve the interests of the country, present and remote ....[55]

There is no doubt that de Valera returned to Ireland from Rome in June 1925 with the words of his clerical advisors ringing in his ears, particularly the words of Archbishop Mannix. This is re-affirmed by his secretary on the trip, Seán Mac Bride who ascertained that "such advice was what de Valera wanted to hear from this eminent Churchman".[56] De Valera and Sinn Féin, elected members of the Dáil, objected to taking the oath of allegiance and the terms in the treaty thereby, continuing a policy of abstentionism from the parliament. Niall Brennan contends that this led to an "unsatisfactory state of affairs that was not achieving much for anyone, and it savoured of that occasional touch of unreality with which Irish extremists approached the solution of their problems". [57] Mannix's imminent trip home was more troublesome to de Valera than he realised. Public perceptions had changed immensely regarding the public persona of Mannix of 1921 and the returning Mannix of 1925, due in large part to his views during the Civil War. Dermot Keogh states that "de Valera certainly faced a serious problem with Mannix in 1925. If the archbishop

---

[55] Msgr. Hagan letter to de Valera, 31 May 1925 (Irish College in Rome: Msgr. Hagan papers, HAG1-1925-293).
[56] Anthony J. Jordan, *Seán MacBride: a biography* (Dublin: Blackwater Press, 1993), p. 41.
[57] Niall Brennan, *Dr. Mannix* (Adelaide: Rigby, 1964), p. 228.

was to help the anti-treatyite site, he had to be tutored in the 'realities' of Irish politics".[58]

The political landscape had changed since Mannix had last been in Ireland. The old pillars of society were now used to stabilise newer ones until they could support themselves. After 1923, the Free State turned to the Catholic Church, for support and willingly sought its inclusion in all prominent matters of the newly founded state. As Patrick Corish discusses:

> ... the government was as anxious as the clergy to preserve what were regarded as traditional values. Its favoured method was to consult interested parties when these issues arose. The Catholic hierarchy, naturally, was usually among them. The government awaited a consensus and legislated accordingly.[59]

The arrival of Archbishop Mannix to Irish shores threatened this newfound relationship. The Catholic Church was more eager than the state to copper-fasten this relationship by denying the archbishop the chance to publicly upset their *de jure* control of state affairs. Mannix arrived in Dublin on 29 June 1925 "in a semi-public capacity against the advice of Hagan and de Valera".[60] His arrival, as de Valera feared, would be "passed over almost in silence by the Dublin pro-treaty Press, and though, according to one report, he was 'totally ignored both by the Free State Government and the official representatives of the Roman Catholic Church". The same report added that "enormous crowds' greeted Dr Mannix at the pier".[61] He travelled the length and breadth of the country, addressing many civic receptions. However, the Free State government strongly backed by the Catholic hierarchy ostracised the archbishop of Melbourne. As Joe Broderick comments: "although he professed to speak for peace and for unity amongst Irish people of all opinions, in fact he was undisguisedly taking sides and reopening wounds still fresh from the recent Civil War".[62] As well as being anti-treaty, the irregulars were split over their loyalty to the Catholic Church, due to their stance of support for the Free State government. Mannix's arrival offered a glimmer of hope to devout republican Catholics. They had viewed the Irish hierarchy's interference in

---

[58] Dermot Keogh, 'Mannix, De Valera and Irish Nationalism', in John B. O'Brien and Pauric Travers (eds.) *The Irish Emigrant Experience in Australia* (Dublin: Poolbeg, 1991), p. 215.

[59] Patrick Corish, *The Irish Catholic experience: a historical survey* (Dublin: Gill & Macmillan, 1985), p. 244.

[60] Keogh, op. cit., p. 219.

[61] Murphy, op. cit., p. 140.

[62] Broderick, op. cit., p. 41.

Civil War politics with disdain. As John A. Murphy contends "that while they saw the priest's spiritual authority must be respected, politics was none of his business".[63] The archbishop's visit in June "demonstrated to those many Irish Catholics who must still have felt that opponents of the treaty were beyond the ecclesiastical pale that an Archbishop could be an eloquent voice on their behalf".[64] The archbishop would display this representation at the numerous civic receptions afforded to him including the conferral of the freedom of Limerick City, on 5 August 1925. Mannix would confirm de Valera's worst fears. He lamented after his conferral how:

> ... he never made any secret of the fact that if he had been in Ireland at the time he would have refused to put his name to the document which was now unfortunately inflicted on the country. He might have been wrong, he was not infallible. He never surrendered his own opinion, no matter who differed from him. When the Treaty was signed he would have endeavoured to get an admission from those who signed it that it was done under duress, and he would have been endeavoured if he had been in this country then, to help the Collins-De Valera pact which gave a ray of hope for a united Ireland. He would also have endeavoured to keep the oath out of the constitution'.[65]

This frank and open address proved de Valera's mission to Rome was unsuccessful in advising Mannix against such public addresses. If de Valera maintained any hopes of reconciling Civil War divides, Mannix was not helping his cause. Particularly if he hoped to gain support for his new political party from the Free State supporters. Mannix still had strong admirers and this was clear on the archbishop's visit to Killarney town on 1 July. At the civic reception afforded to him by the Urban District Council, the address pronounced how:

> we in Ireland who know what alien and class oppression have been to ourselves watched with high gratification and approval your unyielding and successful attitude in vindication of the rights of labour and of the citizen against hostile and powerful interests.[66]

---

[63] Cited by J. H Whyte, *Church & state*, op. cit., pp 11-12.
[64] Murray, op. cit., p. 157.
[65] *The Times,* 'Archbishop Mannix', 6 August 1925.
[66] Killarney Urban District Council, *To His Grace the most rev. Dr. Daniel Mannix D. D. Archbishop of Melbourne on the occasion of his visit to Killarney 1 July 1925* (1925). [See Appendix I for full speech].

The occasion also showed how iconic language had now become firmly associated with the imagery of Mannix in the minds of many Irish men and women. The Killarney Rural Council presented an address to Mannix outlining this fervent language:

> As Irishmen we honour you as a fellow-countryman whose weapon is the sword of truth and sincerity, whose bold advocacy had saved the young new manhood of Australia from old war's worst lust, democracy's worst sin, compulsory military carnage; whose strength of mind and tongue have been consecrated to defend our children's right to religious liberty and education, and, last of all, whose steadfast fidelity to the principles on which alone the great war can be justified, viz., the independence of small nationalities.[67]

The Irish Catholic Church's hierarchy were loath to acknowledge the public receptions afforded to Dr Mannix. One occasion was the appointment of Archbishop Byrne to the diocese of Dublin. Mannix had previously been touted by sections of the press for the vacant see in Dublin following the death of Archbishop Walsh but these endorsements proved unsuccessful.[68] O'Brien suggests that British intervention with the Vatican played a large part in this affair. The British sent their Secretary of State for Foreign Affairs to the Vatican to indicate to the church authorities that they were fearful "in the present state of Irish Affairs of appointing as Archbishop of Dublin a person of pronounced and publicly proclaimed anti-British sentiment".[69] An invitation was however, forthcoming from Archbishop Byrne to Mannix.[70] Mannix would return to Ireland's capital city as archbishop of Melbourne where he had received the Freedom of the City. Another rebuttal from the hierarchy was evident when Bishop Browne of Cloyne, visited the archbishop at his hotel-room during his stay in Cork. Here he offered a slanderous rebuke to Mannix claiming he had "come at last, like Nicodemus, in the night".[71] If Bishop Cloyne had hoped for a recantation from Mannix, he was mistaken. The prelate remained as stubborn as ever and the treatment of the Irish hierarchy possibly only solidified old wounds that to him were still fresh from his days at Maynooth. History varies on the overall reception received by Mannix as detailed earlier through the coverage of the Dublin Press. Another example

---

[67] *The Kerry News*, 'Archbishop Mannix arrives', 3 July 1925.
[68] Ebsworth, op. cit., p. 280.
[69] O'Brien, John B., 'The British Government and Archbishop Daniel Mannix' in *Journal of the Cork Historical & Archaeological Society*, 93 (1988), p. 57.
[70] Keogh, op. cit., p. 219.
[71] Ebsworth, op. cit., pp 278-279.

Figure 5.1: Archbishop Mannix date/location unknown. Image kindly courtesy of Mrs Winifred Cross/Mrs Patricia Wallis McCombe.

of this appears during Mannix's visit to his hometown of Charleville. Many sources claim that the archbishop was locked out of the parish church altogether. This is not entirely accurate as local historian Ted O'Riordan outlines, "the sad event of the death of his nephew, Rev. William Mannix, who was a curate in Youghal, was possibly the only time he publicly officiated at a ceremony in Holy Cross Church during his visit".[72] It is true that the archbishop officiated over his daily masses in the Sisters of Mercy chapel during his stay in Charleville. This shows the extent of clerical animosity towards him. As O'Riordan continues "he should have got a one hundred per cent genuine welcome, but unfortunately his political affiliations out-weighed his clerical renown, at least in the minds of those who saw it in that context, and the welcome he received was by no means as warm and magnanimous as he deserved".[73] These displays of public clerical degradation would not sit well with Mannix and he would not forget them. Not all the clergy were against the archbishop and he was still idolised by many of his Irish clerical brethren. The night

---

[72] O'Riordan, op. cit., p. 81
[73] ibid, p. 77.

of 25 October in the Pillar Room of the Rotunda, Dublin, offered the "opportunity for the many priests who sympathised with de Valera and Archbishop Mannix to demonstrate their support in a public forum".[74] This was the crowning glory of Mannix's visit and became known as the "Night of the Priests". This was the perfect platform to allow Mannix to criticise the Irish clerical hierarchy for their treatment of him and his fellow republican priests. He firmly outlined that:

> ... when a man becomes a priest he does not cease to be a citizen, and, being a citizen, he has the right to his own opinions like other citizens. (Applause). These priests who are gathered round me tonight, these are not men who claim that they must be right, and that they are always right. They make no claim to infallible sanction in political matters; for they know right well there is no infallible sanction in political matters.[75]

Mannix would return to Melbourne later that year having given these assurances to the republican laymen and priests during his 1925 visit. The endorsement of republicanism is hardly surprising as: Patrick Murray contends "Mannix was not given public recognition by either Church or State, that he was ignored by the hierarchy and not invited to visit Maynooth".[76] Mannix also, as the Free State government feared, alienated further the northern Unionists through his attempts to visit Belfast during his tour. In an open letter to the press, the Minister of Home Affairs for Northern Ireland, Sir Dawson Bates, reiterated the Unionist stance on republican activities:

> I feel that everyone is anxious that the peace which we have secured here should not be endangered, and I venture to hope that Dr. Mannix will not persist in his intention. His utterances elsewhere would make his visit here highly undesirable, and are calculated to revive dissension and ill-feeling. As I said I hope he will reconsider his intention, but if he persists in coming here he will only put the Government to the disagreeable necessity of exercising the same powers as have been used in the case of other persons whose presence in Northern Ireland was considered prejudicial to the maintenance of order.[77]

---

[74] Murray, op. cit., p. 157.

[75] Dr. Daniel Mannix, *Speeches of His Grace most rev. Dr. Mannix, Archbishop of Melbourne in the Rotunda Dublin, October 22nd and 29th 1925*. (Dublin: Mellifont Press, 1925]), p. 16.

[76] Patrick Murray, *The political involvement of the Roman Catholic clergy in Ireland 1922-37* (PhD. Thesis: Trinity College Dublin, 1998), p. 166.

[77] *The Times*, 'Ulster and Dr. Mannix, 5 October 1925.

The archbishop did not proceed to the North in the end. De Valera still wanted to maintain a strong relationship with his episcopal ally. With this in mind de Valera largely played to the crowd about the significance of their relationship, as he knew Mannix retained considerable support around the country. In de Valera's address to the Pillar Room, he lamented how:

> It is a pity he cannot stay in Ireland, where he is so badly wanted, and not have to go back to the farthest end of the earth, but in Australia he will do good work for Ireland too. As he told you, the heart of Ireland is sound, and he is going away in that belief, and the Irish people will come back and do what they proved they were able to do.[78]

This window dressing from de Valera glorified Mannix and secured their relationship and his support in the intermittent period. Joe Broderick contends that, de Valera felt "the archbishop's approach was too blunt; Irish politics would be requiring men capable of more sinuous and subtle manoeuvrings".[79] The archbishop left Ireland in October 1925. He may not have made his feelings public, as he was a very lonesome figure, particularly with regards personal matters. Mannix must have been disappointed and heartbroken of the affairs the previous month. The realisation of the remonstrations he had received from members of the Irish hierarchy would forever be etched in Mannix's mind. Although he had many great occasions, Mannix left knowing he had been away from Ireland for far too long.

---

[78] Mannix, op. cit., p. 23.
[79] Broderick, op. cit., p. 41.

CHAPTER SIX

A CONTINUING PRESENCE
(1925-1960)

The Civil War had left a deeply divided nation. Core divisions had manifested themselves in the religious arena due to the Irish hierarchy's support of the Free State government. However, as de Valera would state "Ireland remains a Catholic nation, and as such, sets the eternal destiny of man above the issues and idols of the day."[1] The pro-treaty camp under de Valera's political foe, William T. Cosgrave, had the unenviable task of reconstructing a country separated by division through partition and politics. Dermot Keogh contends that while Mr Cosgrave "did not give inspiring leadership, he had a safe pair of hands and was intent upon providing popular legitimacy for the Free State".[2] The final chapter of this book will focus on the relationship between Mannix and de Valera as the latter rises to power. It will show how Archbishop Mannix still maintained his support for de Valera and maintained a personal relationship with him.

Cosgrave looked to safeguard the legitimacy of the state all the while leaving de Valera facing political obscurity. As the validity of the Free State continued under Cumann na nGaedhael, in the mindset of the Irish public, the further de Valera and his irregular colleagues were from achieving their aim of a united Ireland independent from Britain. Archbishop Mannix and Dr Hagan had reiterated these points to de Valera during his secret trip to Rome, as well as the further consultations between the archbishop and de Valera during Mannix's visit home in 1925. The clerical intervention given by both men, but particularly by Mannix, gave de Valera the confidence he needed to confront the Sinn Féin Ard Fhéis in March 1926, with a radical proposal. Here he put forward the following motion: "That once the admission oath of the 26-county and six-county assemblies is removed, it becomes a question not of principle but of policy

---

[1] John Cooney, *The crozier & the Dáil: church & state 1922-1986* (Dublin: The Mercier Press Ltd., 1986), p. 19.
[2] Dermot Keogh, *Twentieth century Ireland: nation and state* (New York: St. Martin's Press, 1995), p. 18.

whether or not Republican representatives should attend these assemblies".[3] The treaty had divided the Irish people and with the end of the Civil War; the population was still divided. Worse was to come, with the issue of the oath of allegiance set to split the anti-treaty side even further, tearing dreams of a united Ireland even further apart. Although, de Valera had large support, including that of his clerical rearguard in Rome, it was another cleric, Father O'Flanagan whose intervention at the Ard Fhéis of 1926, derailed attempts at Sinn Féin unity on abstentionism. He proposed to his Sinn Féin colleagues "an amendment to prohibit representatives of the party from entering into any usurping legislature set up by English law in Ireland".[4] The motion was put to a vote and once again, de Valera came out on the losing side by a narrow margin. De Valera felt very disillusioned with politics at this stage of his career and this disenchantment has been documented by Ryle Dwyer, who quotes him as saying to Seán Lemass after the motion defeat, "I have done my best, but I have been beaten. Now that is the end for me. I am leaving public life".[5]

The political heavyweight could not resist the temptation to depart the Irish political arena on such a low point. De Valera needed to set up his own party; a party, which would cradle and manifest his political ideals and ambitions. The inaugural meeting of Fianna Fáil took place on 16 May 1926, with de Valera becoming its first president. With "the Chief" at its helm, the party prepared both financially and strategically for the next general election. It would do this by securing funds from America and transferring grassroots support from the dominant Sinn Féin political supporter's base and I.R.A. support there.[6] These preparations would stand the party in good stead for the general election of 1927 almost a year after the foundation of the party. The successful introduction of his party into the Irish political arena allowed for what some would argue greater democratic transparency and representation in the political system. Before the election, his great clerical ally Archbishop Mannix once again publicly spoke in favour of the Fianna Fáil president. He said in a cable:

> ... desperate ills need desperate remedies. Proposed legislation left you choice between entry of the Dáil and possible renewal of violence, which

---

[3] Keogh, op. cit., p. 42.
[4] T. Ryle Dwyer, *Eamon de Valera : The Man & the Myths* (Dublin : Paperview/Irish Independent, 2006), p. 150.
[5] ibid, p. 151.
[6] Mark Tierney, *Ireland since 1870* (Dublin: CJ Fallon, 1998), p. 289.

could mean disaster. Your opponents overreached themselves, and Ireland at the forthcoming election, will, I hope, say you have chosen well.[7]

Not alone, did the archbishop rhetorically generate support for de Valera but his financial worth to Fianna Fáil was also very valuable. Mannix was able to generate substantial funds for any aims he advocated. Along with his cable to de Valera in 1926, he also launched "a fund to assist de Valera in early elections" shortly following this with a thousand pound subscription "towards the September General Election Campaign".[8] The archbishop's support was not in vain, as the election was a success for the new party and 'in the end, the voting went very much in Fianna Fáil's favour: de Valera's party returned 44 deputies, only three less than Cumann na nGaedhael. De Valera now had an opportunity to topple the government if his Fianna Fáil members were to enter Leinster House'.[9]

Archbishop Mannix's support proved vital to de Valera's initial success with Fianna Fáil. A large part of this was due once again to Mannix's return to America in June 1926 to visit the International Eucharistic Congress in Chicago, as head of the Australian hierarchy's delegation. This significant event in the clerical calendar was an opportune moment for Mannix to offer public support for de Valera and to the large international clerical community as well as the worldwide Irish diaspora. During his previous visit to the U.S in 1920, the archbishop had received many distinguished honours and this trip was no different. He used his high civic standing to revisit the cities of Boston, New York and Philadelphia and similar to events five years previously, he attracted huge attention through his public appearances. At Philadelphia, we can gather just how much influence de Valera now commanded over the pair's relationship. Mannix through his speeches continued to castigate the Free State government and offer his full endorsement to de Valera, support vital for the forthcoming Irish general election. He regaled the crowd in Philadelphia with the story of his first meeting with the Fianna Fáil president back in Omaha in 1920. He had what he deemed the greatest honour of his life:

---

[7] Archbishop Mannix telegram to de Valera published in *The Advocate*, 18 August 1927, p. 27. (UCD Archives: De Valera Papers, P150-2909)
[8] Patrick Murray, *The political involvement of the Roman Catholic clergy in Ireland 1922-37* (PhD. Trinity College Dublin, 1998), p. 220.
[9] Keogh, op. cit., p. 45.

Figure 6.1: Archbishop Mannix aboard the Oceanic Liner June 15 1926. Author's private collection.

I had the opportunity for the first time of standing upon the same platform, of preaching the same doctrine, and upholding the same principles, as the greatest man that Ireland has produced in my time, and possibly in any time – Eamon de Valera'[10]

It is clear from this bombastic assessment of de Valera that the Fianna Fáil president had indeed clearly influenced the opinions of Mannix since their first official meeting in 1920. Since then their subsequent encounters had only strengthened this influence. The reverence de Valera commanded from Mannix was significant, considering the independent nature and relative preferred social isolation of the archbishop. Most historical commentators would argue that Mannix's visit to Ireland in 1925 showed how out of touch the archbishop was with the Irish situation. Mannix's continued support of de Valera through the early stages of Fianna Fáil shows that he had a distinct foresight that was often portrayed as chance by his critics. He would comment again in 1926 of his visit the previous year that:

... when he went to Ireland, he said, he found that instead of a republic for Ireland, almost more than ever the whole of Ireland was evidence of British ascendancy. He had been up and down Ireland and he had put his finger on the pulse of the people of Ireland and he could say from his own experience there that the people were as sound at heart as ever they were. The Free State Government had very few friends'.[11]

His detractors are correct when they argue that he was out of touch with Ireland in 1925 and did not indeed have his finger on the pulse as he claimed. However, the archbishop's ability to assess a situation would prove true in 1932 with the election of Fianna Fáil to power. Mannix indeed had his finger on the pulse of the Irish nation; it was a faint pulse in 1925.

Although Fianna Fáil had performed exceptionally well in the election of 1927, they still had to contend with the oath of allegiance if de Valera's policy to re-enter the Dáil was to come to fruition. His clerical backers firmly outlined the stance the Fianna Fáil president should take towards the oath as he entered Leinster House. Monsignor Hagan advised de Valera that:

---

[10] Colm Kiernan, *Daniel Mannix and Ireland* (Morwell, Victoria: Alella Books, 1984), p. 207.
[11] Frank Murphy, *Daniel Mannix* (2nd ed.: The Polding Press. Melbourne, 1972), pp 127-128.

This oath, like every other oath, must be judged according to its antecedent and concomitant implications, and in particular must be interpreted in the light of the theoretical and practical value attached to it by theology and history.[12]

The clerical ally that de Valera took most credence from was Mannix. Not alone did his opinion hold considerable weight politically, but Mannix also had been a distinguished professor of moral theology at Maynooth for many years. His opinions on issues relating to moral dilemmas such as the oath would have been widely acknowledged and well received. As J. J. Lee outlines, Mannix "pronounced that the Fianna Fáil T.D's who took the oath 'no more told a falsehood that I would if I sent down word to an unfortunate visitor that I was not at home".[13] Inspired by this theological interpretation and with the threat of relinquishment of their seats within two months, due to the Electoral Amendment Bill Fianna Fáil entered Dáil Éireann. The assassination of Kevin O'Higgins also played a part in this decision. In August 1927 Fianna Fáil "seeing no oath, hearing no oath, signing no oath shuffled into Dáil Éireann".[14] Broderick describes how Fianna Fáil must have been "basking in the aura of Mannix's apostolic benediction."[15] The T.D.'s signed the attendance book and sat in the chamber without actually verbally reciting the words of the oath. De Valera had "convinced them that it was 'an empty political formula' and the registration of their names was simply an 'empty formality".[16] The advice of his clerical backers, particularly the archbishop, along with de Valera's desire to be at the forefront of Irish politics now meant a more balanced political system was in place to continue the democratic process. Under Cosgrave, Cumann na nGaedhael also deserve immense respect for safeguarding the institutions of the new state and guiding the country through its most formative and turbulent years. However, this respect has come with historical hindsight. The Cosgrave administration, now facing a rejuvenated de Valera and Fianna Fáil, could not persuade the Irish public of the period that their government's policies were the correct ones to

---

[12]Dermot Keogh, 'Mannix, De Valera and Irish Nationalism', in John B. O'Brien and Pauric Travers (eds.) *The Irish Emigrant Experience in Australia* (Dublin: Poolbeg, 1991), p. 218.

[13] J. J. Lee, *Ireland 1912-1985: politics and society* (Cambridge: Cambridge University Press, 1989), p. 155.

[14] ibid, p. 155.

[15] Joe Broderick, 'De Valera and Archbishop Daniel Mannix' in *History Ireland*, 2 (3)1994, p. 40.

[16] Mark Tierney, *Ireland Since 1870* (Dublin: CJ Fallon, 1988), p. 291.

guide Ireland through such events as the 1929 Wall Street Crash, and growth of fascism and communism in Europe.

1927 had already proved critical to de Valera's political aspirations and he had passed the first test successfully. By the year's end, his party's true potential was once again tested. Although well prepared for the June election, the party could not have been prepared for the rapidity of successive elections that were necessary due to an unsuccessful vote in the Dáil of no confidence in Cosgrave's government. The result again favoured Cosgrave in the September election, but it also reinforced the notion that the results of the June election were a distinct statement on the part of the Irish voting public; that Fianna Fáil had a long future ahead in Irish politics. In the election "the two major parties increased their parliamentary strength considerably" leaving Fianna Fáil as the dominant and skilful leader of the opposition voice gaining experience invaluable to its future extended period in power.[17] Although firmly backed by the Irish Catholic Church, the Free State under Cosgrave was in no sense of the word a Catholic state. The 1922 constitution as defined by Cumann na nGaedhael was indeed a uniquely, religiously secular document. As John Cooney states:

> ... the Catholic Church was not even mentioned, let alone its status defined. There was no official alliance between the State and the Church: bishops and priests were not invited to participate in either government or parliament. No politician proclaimed his new State to be Catholic.[18]

Independent of Irish Catholic hierarchical approval, Mannix was sharp to recognise an opportunity that he believed would benefit Ireland and Catholicism. Mannix saw the devoutly Catholic and lay priest de Valera, as being a vehicle for religious change in the future. John A. Murphy contends that 'the appearance of Fianna Fáil led by Eamon de Valera held out the hope that there was a second chance to establish a happy, prosperous and united Irish-Ireland'.[19] Although cementing democratic principles in the new state, the international economic depression and subsequent increase in the emigration of Irish people, left Cosgrave and his party badly exposed by the time of the 1932 general election. The time

---

[17] Tierney, op. cit., p. 291.
[18] Cooney, op. cit., p. 11.
[19] John A. Murphy, 'The achievement of de Valera' in *De Valera and his times* by J. P O'Carroll & John A. Murphy (eds.) (Cork: Cork University Press, 1983), p. 13.

had come for Fianna Fáil to seize their "destiny" as Archbishop Mannix had been preaching since 1926:

> The Irish people should not be disunited. They should unite in the common cause. If they fail to stand by the man who has stood by them – who is head and shoulders over every other Irishman – de Valera – if they fail to stand by him, I should not like to be held responsible for Ireland's cause in the near future; but even then I would not despair of it as long as there are ten Irishmen that have genuine Irish hearts in them.[20]

It is hard to believe that Mannix saw de Valera and his Fianna Fáil party as the ones to secure Ireland's political future, but also embed the Catholic doctrine firmly through the infant institutions of the state. The reason for this disbelief is that only five years previous the republicans had been excommunicated from the Catholic Church for their part in the Civil War. Aside from this, the republicans still maintained their reverence for their religion as opposed to the clerical fraternity. The Roman Catholic Church was the powerbroker in Irish political life, as the discussion looked at earlier, therefore; de Valera needed to gain favour once again with the Irish hierarchy.[21] Although Mannix's support proved vital to Fianna Fáil, de Valera feared that if the archbishop's denunciations of the Free State and partition continued it could lead to a public confrontation between his greatest clerical ally and the hierarchy he wished to gain favour from once again. The politician began the clerical juggling act and was greatly helped, as John A. Murphy contends by "his personal piety and his friendship with some clerics which helped overcome the intense hostility of many priests to him and his new party". Murphy feels that de Valera also "lost no opportunity of affirming and demonstrating that Fianna Fáil was as Catholic as, if not more so than, their opponents, and whatever anti-clerical elements existed within the party were kept well under control".[22]

With his political avenue, finally unlocked de Valera set out along the path of dismantling the Anglo-Irish treaty and shaping Ireland through the medium of his own political ideology. He appointed himself to the position of Minister of External Affairs, which he saw as the position along with President of the Executive Council, as most suited to shaping Ireland's domestic politics, but also stamping her political independence

---

[20] Archbishop Mannix in Chicago June 26th 1926, 'Archbishop Mannix on the campaign against the oath', (Limerick City Museum, 2001.0006), p. 2.
[21] J. H. Whyte, *Church & state in modern Ireland: 1923-70* (Dublin: Gill & Macmillan, 1971), p. 41.
[22] Murphy, 'The achievement of de Valera' op. cit., p. 7.

on the international stage. The programme for Fianna Fáil in 1932 started with the oath of allegiance. De Valera secured its abolition along with the

> ... ending of the payment of land annuities, which led to the Economic War with Britain. His quest for international sovereignty also resulted in the abolition of the governor generalship, the creation of the Irish Nationality and Citizenship Act of 1935 which replaced British Citizenship with Irish, and the introduction of a new Constitution in 1937.[23]

As expected, the news of de Valera's ascension to the top of the political polls raced down the wires to the international community, and was met with delight by various segments of the vast Irish diaspora. With de Valera's appointment as President of the Executive Council, it was hoped that the gun could now finally be decommissioned from Irish politics. Australia's large Irish community had mixed views on affairs relating to Ireland, but Melbourne's Irish had largely been behind their ecclesiastical supervisor and his stance on Irish political affairs. Archbishop Mannix's political patronage of de Valera had never ceased and with help from the diaspora in terms of financial support, the republican cause was kept alive. An example of the archbishop and diaspora's patronage can be seen in the position taken towards the Irish Republican Prisoners. Mannix's endorsement of the Prisoners Dependent Fund along with the American diaspora was symbolised by a letter written by secretary of the group Kathleen Barry thanking them, but particularly Mannix for their support. Barry wrote:

> I am directed by my Committee to thank Your Grace for your help sent to us from Australia. It came at a moment when we were absolutely without funds and were it not for the Australian money should have been compelled to close down the fund at least for a few weeks. The American people have been magnificently generous to us and we have endeavoured to raise money at home but our resources were completely used up when the first Australian £1200 came.[24]

On May 5, the Irish Societies of Melbourne held a celebratory night to mark Fianna Fáil's triumph with the archbishop understandably providing the main attraction. Here he made one of his most defining speeches as both a spokesperson for the Irish diaspora and the republican cause in

---

[23] Diarmuid Ferriter, *Judging Dev* (Dublin: Royal Irish Academy, 2007), p. 123.
[24] Letter from Kathleen Barry General Secretary of Irish Republican Prisoners Dependant Fund to Archbishop Mannix, 27 November 1923 (National Archives of Ireland/NAI, D/Taoiseach, S1369-21).

Ireland. For the first time he outlined how there was no threat of war hanging over Ireland. This threat had helped Cosgrave to maintain power as opposed to de Valera's popular endorsement of his political party:

> ... a threat that had won every election since the so-called Treaty of 1921. The Treaty of 1921 was broken in the very act of making it. While forcing Griffith and Collins by threat of war to accept partition, although assuring the Northerners partition would be permanent.[25]

De Valera's immediate focus upon his appointment as President of the Executive Council was to dismantle the aspects of the treaty that had the Civil War. By concentrating on alterations to the treaty and strengthening state foundations, Fianna Fáil was effectively turning its back on partition that had been finalised in November 1925 by the Boundary Commission.[26] The ratification of the existing border by the three political entities of the Free State, Northern Ireland and Britain following the leakage of the report left de Valera's hopes of future reunification lying in the balance. The Fianna Fáil president would later: -

> ... defend his concentration on state-building by claiming that, from 1932, he had been merely following the plan, unveiled at the party's inaugural meeting, to secure the full independence of "this part of Ireland" before moving on to tackle the problem of partition.[27]

The problem was that the party was seeking to develop its own political ideology and plans instead of following his manifesto, as he claimed they were still doing. His main triumph during his first few years in office was the solidification of the Free State as an independent nation, liberated from British subjugation and free to voice her own opinion on international affairs. He achieved this during his reign as President of the League of Nations. De Valera now leading the dominant party in Irish politics by early 1932 turned his focus to re-aligning his government with the Catholic hierarchy. An opportune event presented itself in June 1932, allowing Fianna Fáil to re-align itself firmly behind the Catholic Church. The Eucharistic Congress would allow de Valera show the Catholic hierarchy; both in Ireland and Rome, that Fianna Fáil was firmly committed to a new Irish state firmly entrenched in Catholic morals and

---

[25] Rev. Walter Ebsworth, *Archbishop Mannix* (Armadale, Vic.: H. H. Stephenson, 1977), p. 314.
[26] Tierney, op. cit., p. 281.
[27] Tom Gallagher, 'Fianna Fáil and partition 1926-1984' in *Éire-Ireland*, 20 (1) 1985, p. 35.

values. As Dermot Keogh argues, "this was an occasion to display the strength of the 'special relationship' between Ireland and the Holy See".[28] J. J. Lee reaffirms this view by outlining how the Congress gave de Valera "a timely opportunity to baptise his synthesis of republicanism and catholicism, reminding the papal legate that he was a loyal son of Rome".[29] De Valera rose to the occasion and in his formal welcome to the Papal Nuncio outlined how:

> ... at this time, when we welcome to Ireland this latest legation from the Eternal City, we are commemorating the apostolic mission to Ireland, given fifteen centuries ago to St. Patrick, apostle of our nation. Who can fail on this day to recall to mind the utterance of our apostle, recorded of old in the Book of Armagh: *Even as you are children of Christ, be you also children of Rome.*[30]

Archbishop Mannix was expected to be heralded to Irish shores by an event of such magnitude as the Eucharistic Congress however, this was not to be. Rev Ebsworth explains that "in spite of repeated urgings from priests around him he decided not to go, as he knew too well his very presence would disturb the purely spiritual character of the occasion".[31] His attendance may have re-ignited old Civil War divides, but considering that, the National Australian Eucharistic Congress was to be held in the archbishop's own diocese in 1934, his decision not to attend the International Congress appears strange. Is this the point where cracks began to appear in their relationship? Was it because of de Valera's quick restoration of faith with the Irish hierarchy, whom Mannix still harboured ill feeling against due to his treatment in 1925, that the archbishop declined the invitation. Kiernan suggests that:

> Mannix's radical Irish nationalism was fanned by his alienation from the hierarchy in Ireland. The rise of de Valera to be Taoiseach in Ireland and his reconciliation with an Irish Church, which had changed greatly since Mannix, was President at Maynooth, would result in a sharp diminution in the source of Mannix's alienation and would work towards another synthesis.[32]

---

[28] Dermot Keogh, *Ireland and the Vatican: the politics and diplomacy of church-state relations, 1922-1960* (Cork: Cork University Press, 1995), p. 97.
[29] J. J. Lee, *op. cit.,* p. 177.
[30] Eamon de Valera quoted in Keogh, *Ireland and the Vatican*, op. cit., p. 97.
[31] Ebsworth, op. cit., p. 315.
[32] Kiernan, op. cit., p. 209.

Mannix's suggestion that the Eucharistic Congress' religious ceremony would be affected due to his presence was an overstatement. The state had now firmly secured its democratic principles with Fianna Fáil's transition to power. Subsequently, the party's isolation of partition from its imminent political agenda meant that the archbishop's presence could do little to alter this. The Irish people would not tolerate a return to violence and that included anyone who possibly advocated this to secure reunification of the six counties. Another archbishop over the next few decades offered de Valera the clerical contact network and association that he needed to cement his favourable position with the Irish Catholic Church. John Charles McQuaid facilitated de Valera as president of Blackrock College "by making the ground Blackrock College available for a state garden party. This allowed de Valera 'to avoid the embarrassment of the state function being associated with the Vice-Regal Lodge or with the Representative of King George V".[33] McQuaid had begun to network within Irish political circles and through his position as president of Blackrock; he became very friendly with de Valera. Mannix's public profile in Ireland had begun to diminish significantly after his visit in 1925 and by not attending the Eucharistic Congress what looked like his last high profile engagement in the country had passed.

The 1932 Congress allowed de Valera another opportunity to skilfully dismantle another troublesome aspect of the treaty. This high profile state function would normally demand a formal invitation to any significant public dignitary from the government. The absence of an official invitation to Governor General, James MacNeill, from de Valera "made life impossible for him, especially as the affair was covered widely in the newspapers".[34] The attempt to derail particular treaty clauses by using such events as the Eucharistic Congress, abdication of King Edward (1936) and the Anglo-Irish Trade War (1932-38) shows how well de Valera was able to use these events to Ireland's advantage. He had now turned into a more capable politician well able to utilise current events to his advantage. Archbishop Mannix would belatedly acknowledge how big an event he had missed in 1932 writing in a letter to Dr Maguire that "gradually I am beginning to value the unity and triumph of the Congress".[35] This success did not go unnoticed by the foreign press as the *Illustrazione Vaticana* commented how:

---

[33] Patrick Murray, *Voices of de Valera* (M. Litt. Trinity College Dublin, 1995), p. 175.
[34] Tierney, op. cit., p. 300.
[35] Archbishop Mannix to Dr. Maguire, 2 September 1932 (UCD Archives: De Valera Papers, P150-2909)

... the church is the whole island – the altar is the metropolis, Dublin. Here the very air one breathes is the divine breath of God, Jesus Christ Our Saviour – the vivifying oxygen of all truth. Never before perhaps have foreign pilgrims breathed such an atmosphere of faith.[36]

Of all the changes the new president would make, the passing of the 1937 Constitution would rank amongst his greatest achievements. Not alone would it ensure the country now had a legitimate constitution drafted independently of British pressure, as Archbishop Mannix had claimed previously. It would also cement the "special position" of the Catholic church within the boundaries of Ireland. Essentially, as Patrick Corish suggests:

> ... de Valera's vision of Ireland was embodied in his 1937 constitution. It seems certain that it was essentially his own creation, though he did consult a number of people, and among the clergy consulted was John Charles McQuaid, soon to be Archbishop of Dublin.[37]

The consultation over the constitution involved, as Corish suggested, both lay and clerical intervention with input from both Archbishop Mannix and Archbishop McQuaid. McQuaid made sure that de Valera could not ignore his opinions by consistently bombarding the president with letters. As Ferriter writes "there was certainly extensive consultation between the two men, and McQuaid undoubtedly influenced de Valera with regard to many aspects of it."[38] The new constitution was the independent imprint for the fledgling state and solidified in many ways its position on both domestic and international affairs. Mannix gave de Valera his opinion on the constitution after de Valera sent him a draft copy. Although their relationship had thawed it still showed that de Valera valued Mannix's opinion.[39] Cooney deliberates on how:

> ... the constitution, which states that all authority is from the Most Holy Trinity, reflected Catholic teaching on the family, marriage and education as well as on social matters such as the rights of poverty. But the 1922 provisions on religious liberty remained in the 1937 constitution.[40]

---

[36] Keogh, *Ireland and the Vatican*, op. cit., p. 98.
[37] Patrick Corish, *The Irish Catholic experience: a historical survey* (Dublin: Gill & Macmillan, 1985), p. 246.
[38] Ferriter, op. cit., p. 198.
[39] Patrick O'Farrell, 'De Valera in Australia: 1948' in *The Old Limerick Journal*, 23 (1988), p. 180.
[40] Cooney, op. cit., p. 20.

Although Cardinal MacRory and McQuaid pushed for the provision of Catholicism as the state religion cementing the church-state relationship, de Valera firmly resisted the clerical onslaught, instead offering it "a special position" over other churches. Had Mannix not been relocated to Melbourne he might have had a much more considerable bearing on events in Ireland, as can be judged by his popularity prior to the Civil War. Due to his close relationship with de Valera, he would most definitely have been the theological reference point for the constitution just as he had been in 1925 with respect to the oath. Should Mannix have succeeded Archbishop Walsh to the see of Dublin rather than the actual appointment of Archbishop Byrne in August 1921, Irish politics as well as church-state relations might have been substantially different. This was not the case and McQuaid's influence grew while Mannix's waned, not alone in Irish episcopal circles, but also in the Irish political circuit. De Valera did not have to work on his relationship with Mannix now that he had been in power for a substantial length of time. He had now reached parity with the hierarchy of the Catholic Church in Ireland following the Pope's acceptance of Bunreacht na hÉireann.[41] The archbishop's last direct involvement in Irish affairs was confirmed with the passing of the constitution by referendum on 1 July 1937. De Valera secured a significant victory and Mannix finally seeing his lay priest secure Ireland's religious future.[42] The passing of the constitution "entrenched partition", but as many historians agree "it is less often realised that the Anglo-Irish agreement of 1938 had a similar, though less marked effect".[43] Although for the first time since 1921, Ireland had gained territory for the British in the form of the ports this helped with securing its neutrality before the upcoming war. Although the constitution did envisage reunification, as the years passed by the boundary became more permanent. Mannix like de Valera still retained hope that partition could not continue and hoped through some diplomatic miracle partition might cease to function. The archbishop believed British financial concerns would turn the case around as he outlined in 1938 in a cable to the Taoiseach:

> ... the present British Government one must suppose feels humiliated by the tyranny and injustice which partition imposed by their predecessors in

---

[41] Gallagher, op. cit., p. 37.
[42] Tierney, op. cit., p. 313.
[43] Gallagher, op. cit., p. 39.

office has brought upon a portion of Ulster. It is no less certain that Britain is weary of carrying the financial burden that partition entails.[44]

The diplomatic miracle that both men were hoping for presented itself in the form of British survival rather than Imperial security. The substantial threat of a German invasion of Britain during World War Two, led Churchill to offer the taoiseach the prospect of Irish reunification, in return for Éire's entry into the war on the allies' side. De Valera remained unconvinced for a number of reasons as J. J. Lee contends, "the offer' of Irish unity; however, vague threatened the unity of Fianna Fáil".[45] Although risking the break-up of his political legacy, de Valera also knew that concurrently the prospect of rejecting Churchill's offer and maintaining neutrality would allow him an unprecedented chance to secure Ireland's nationhood. This option he took and accomplished quite successfully during "The Emergency". The virtuoso politician, given the opportunity by Churchill's victory speech after the war, managed to deflect attention away from the confirmation of partition. Instead, he swung the Prime Minister's speech into a verification of his own ideals for a nation independent, competent in the national political arena and free from British pressure. The ramifications for Irish unity of the taoiseach's decision to maintain neutrality were not lost on all the Irish people. Dorothy MacArdle, "hagiographer royal to the Republic, sadly conceded in 1944: 'I want to live to see the day when Emmet's epitaph may be written, and I fear that it is further off now than it was a little while ago".[46] Ever at the defence of the taoiseach, Mannix jumped to support his home country and its under-fire leader. The archbishop had already lived through one world war and was well able to recall tales of numerous foreign battles during his lifetime. He certainly did not harbour any justification for a more brutal Second World War. Indeed, in April 1939, "Mannix blamed the newspapers for stirring up 'war fever'; if there were a threat of war, he advised suppressing the daily papers for a time. He urged a boycott of the secular papers and supported efforts to make friends with Japan."[47] As the death toll began to surpass even that of World War One, Mannix realised that neutrality was Ireland's best policy and yet again, he offered himself as an outlet of support for de Valera. In March 1944, the

---

[44] Archbishop Mannix telegram to de Valera, June 28 1938 (UCD Archives: De Valera Papers, P150-2909)

[45] J. J. Lee, op. cit., p. 249.

[46] Dorothy MacArdle quoted in J. J. Lee, *Ireland 1912-1985*, op. cit., p. 270.

[47] Bruce Duncan, *Crusade or conspiracy? Catholics and the anti-communist struggle in Australia* (Sydney: University of New South Wales Press, 2001), p. 26.

war had swung considerably in favour of the Allies and Ireland's role was beginning to come under question. Mannix always keen to support his homeland just like the vast diaspora elsewhere implied that:

> England is fighting against the enslavement and partition of Poland; but British money and British force is maintaining the slavery and partition of the six counties of Northern Ireland. My advice to anti-Irish people is to cease from stirring up the dark and murky waters of Anglo-Irish politics and history.[48]

The archbishop still bore hopes that de Valera would lead Irishmen from both north and south through the difficult post war period, and secure the reunification of Ireland in the future.

The archbishop now in his eighty-first year must have been harbouring hopes of a final return to Ireland before the final chapter of his life concluded. The relationship he had developed with de Valera also meant that he would not return estranged from the high social rank he had maintained as president of Maynooth. A significant measure of the respect de Valera had for Mannix arrived in 1938. To complete the building of St Patrick's cathedral in Melbourne the taoiseach presented a bronze cross to the archbishop. This would make the spire of the cathedral "the highest in the Southern Hemisphere, and second only in height to Salisbury in the British Empire standing at 350 feet".[49] Although their relationship may have shown signs of cooling this powerful gesture by the taoiseach showed that Mannix and he still maintained a friendly relationship. This gesture also showed Archbishop Mannix that de Valera and his supporters would still welcome him back to Ireland. No better an opportunity would present itself then at the end of the war with the passing of Ireland's Cardinal MacRory in October 1945. Mannix would have been anxious to return home in triumphant fashion following his last visit in 1925. This visit had tainted his public profile with some of the Irish population. Both Archbishop's McQuaid and Mannix had built significant, but differing relationships with de Valera at this stage. However, the decision for the red hat was firmly outside his hands and lay instead on the banks of the Tiber. John Cooney discusses the possibility of "the unlikely event of Rome offering Ireland two Red Hats – for McQuaid and Archbishop Mannix of Melbourne – they should be taken!"[50] The result was that the

---

[48] Ebsworth, op. cit., p. 355.
[49] Details of the Cross (UCD Archives: Eamon de Valera Papers, P150-2906).
[50] John Cooney, *John Charles McQuaid: ruler of Catholic Ireland* (Dublin: O'Brien Press Ltd., 1999), p. 207.

Pope overlooked Ireland, but sadly, for Mannix it was possibly his last real chance of returning to Ireland. As for McQuaid, his position as archbishop of Dublin and his ranking in the Irish hierarchy would allow him as Dermot Keogh contends "to bestride relations between church and state for twenty years".[51]

Albeit overlooked by the Vatican for a "red hat" a newly appointed apostolic delegate to Australia John Panico was causing quite a stir amongst the Irish bishops in Australia. Panico showed particular disregard for the service Archbishop Mannix had done for the Catholic Church there. Arthur Calwell, a Catholic minister in the government outlined in a letter to Rome he saw Panico as having a particular "vendetta against Archbishop Mannix".[52] Although both de Valera and Mannix's relationship may have shown fractures particularly on Mannix's side, he still showed immense loyalty to his most senior clerical advisor when he needed it most. Keogh gives us an idea of how strong both men's' relationship was in 1947. De Valera considered an attack on Mannix strong enough reason to warrant a withdrawal of an audience with the apostolic delegate when he arrived in Ireland in May of that year: "In view of the manner in which Panico has treated Dr Mannix, I doubt very much whether the Taoiseach will be anxious to receive him".[53]

The support was justified as de Valera saw Mannix yet having a role to play. A significant event took place in 1946, which showed how important the Irish government and de Valera viewed the role of its diaspora in Australia. The Irish government appointed Dr T. J. Kiernan in November, as the country's first ambassador to Australia and what welcome could be more fitting than that given by Archbishop Mannix. De Valera had given Dr Kiernan a letter to take with him to the archbishop declaring a last hand of reconciliation for the events of 1925, and the missed opportunity of 1932. Dr Mannix was to be welcomed home as an official guest of the government and president. De Valera outlined in the letter:

> The President, the late Cardinal (MacRory) and I were hoping that Your Grace might find it possible to come home on another visit now that the war is over and see things for yourself. I need not say how welcome you will be if you find it possible. The President is anxious to have you as his

---

[51] Dermot Keogh, 'Éamon de Valera, Fianna Fáil and the Holy See, 1932-41' in *Ireland and the Vatican: the politics and diplomacy of church – state relations, 1922-1960* (Cork: Cork University Press, 1995), p. 150.

[52] ibid, p. 210.

[53] ibid.

guest in the old 'regal' and as a whole we would be overjoyed to see you again one who has been their friend in times of 'loneliness and sorrows'.[54]

Patrick Murray wrote that de Valera had previously travelled personally to Paris in 1932 to meet Mannix and tried convincing him to return with him.[55] However, Mannix declined the request and never set foot on Irish soil again. In his address of welcome to Dr Kiernan, who would become a close friend of the archbishops, Mannix still gave a hint of his hope for reunification in Ireland by outlining that "when we welcome Dr Kiernan our welcome goes to him not simply as representing the 26 counties of Ireland, but the whole of Ireland".[56] Yet again using the opportunity of a high profile gathering, the archbishop re-affirmed the esteem that he held for the Taoiseach:

> Irish patriots died, pointing still to the dawn. So time went on until God in his Providence sent Ireland's man of destiny, Eamon de Valera. He could neither be cowed by threats nor cajoled by diplomacy. He could not be turned from his purpose, because he knew his own mind.[57]

The "man of destiny" looked untouchable in the eyes of Mannix, but this view was undermined a good deal in the spring of 1948. His hopes for the reunification of Ireland, along with de Valera's, were dashed in February, when the general election of that year saw the unification of all opposition parties to form the first ever Inter-Party government. As Mark Tierney wrote, "the de Valera government was criticised for not achieving Irish unity and for allowing unemployment to reach such a high level".[58] This left de Valera and his Fianna Fáil party once again out on the political sidelines and away from the most pivotal decision yet in Ireland's assertion of independence and hopes for reunification of Northern Ireland. Even though promising that if the repeal of the External Relations Act were put to a vote in the Dáil, de Valera would not stand against it. The rapidity with which the new coalition government announced the decision to implement the Republic of Ireland Act in November 1948 must have taken him by surprise.[59] After all the former Taoiseach was himself on an

---

[54] Letter from Taoiseach Eamon de Valera to Archbishop Mannix concerning Dr. Kiernan appointment to Australia, 1 August 1946 (UCD Archives: Eamon de Valera papers, P 150-2906).
[55] Murray, *Voices of de Valera, op. cit.*, p. 159.
[56] Frank Murphy, *Daniel Mannix* (Melbourne: Advocate Press, 1948), p. 209.
[57] ibid.
[58] Tierney, op. cit., p. 339.
[59] ibid, pp 333-344.

anti-partition tour of the world, which would bring him to the final meeting he had with Archbishop Mannix. In a sense, this anti-partition tour forced the government's hand as Michael McInerney contends "the government was trying to be more Republican than de Valera".[60] The trip in many ways became more about boosting de Valera and Fianna Fáil's popularity, instead of really focusing on the main issues at hand at home in Ireland. His support in Australia, largely sustained through the archbishop, was evident in the welcomes he received in both Sydney and in Melbourne – the latter to celebrate the Diocese's centenary year. At Sydney, the Irish National Association President, Sean Kennedy praised the former taoiseach claiming "the status attained by Ireland as an independent Republic is largely attributable to him. In him the Irish people throughout the world recognise the leader of their race".[61] Archbishop Mannix spoke with great emotion and fervour as he proclaimed de Valera "as the greatest of Irish patriots, Ireland's man of destiny and the one man who had given a lifetime trying to make peace and friendship between England and Ireland".[62] Although historians and many others alike would argue with this sentiment, it cannot take away from the position de Valera had attained in Mannix's eyes. De Valera had always recognised Mannix's support as hugely important and at a subsequent dinner by the Irish National Foresters acknowledged that, "Dr Mannix was the one outside Ireland who could always be relied on to interpret correctly the actions of his Republican Party."[63] The reception offered to de Valera and Aiken without prior consultation of his episcopal colleagues in Australia 'annoyed' his clerical brethren. The archbishop cared little for their opinions and independently made sure the former Taoiseach received the welcome of a true friend.[64] De Valera's acceptance of the archbishop's invitation also came as a "surprise to the organisers".[65] He had originally indicated in a draft letter ready to be sent to the archbishop acknowledging where his original decision lay:

---

[60] Michael McInerney, 'Eamon de Valera: 1882 – 1975' in *Eamon de Valera 1882-1975: the controversial giant of modern Ireland* (Dublin: The Irish Times, 1976), p. 72.

[61] Sean Kennedy, 'Public reception and welcome to Mr. Eamon de Valera and Frank Aiken: Sydney Stadium, Rushcutter's Bay, Tuesday, 1st June, 1948, 8 p.m.' (UL Special Collections: Leonard/B/3651).

[62] Ebsworth, op. cit., p. 374.

[63] ibid.

[64] T. P Boland, *James Duhig* (Saint Lucia : University of Queensland Press, 1986), p. 347.

[65] O'Farrell, op. cit., p. 180.

I have delayed until now writing a final reply to your kind invitation to visit Melbourne for the big centenary celebrations. It is for me a heartbreak to say that I will be unable to go. I have taken into consultation the ex-ministers and members of our Party as a whole, and all agree that the conditions here are such that I ought not to leave the country.[66]

Thus was de Valera's eventual attendance a sign of the bond of their friendship, or as O'Farrell details did meeting Archbishop Mannix guarantee de Valera "the certainty of a larger audience for the Melbourne occasion", something he didn't receive in Brisbane and Adelaide?[67] The tour was largely a failure and de Valera's return to the corridors of power is attributed more to the collapse of the patchwork quilt that was the Inter-Party government, than the support garnered by the anti-partition tour. The aim of tackling the issue of partition was a failure, as in 1954, "no internal party backlash arose when de Valera instructed his party to oppose a Dáil motion that all elected representatives of the people of Northern Ireland should be given right of audience in the Dáil".[68] Reunification looked unobtainable and a twenty-six county republic was the best Ireland had achieved by the time de Valera retired from active politics in 1959.

The archbishop never relinquished his public role even as he retreated closer to his centenary year. Many people still came to see him and claim his advice. He retained remarkable longevity of character and mental astuteness up to his final days. In an account given by the Charge d'Affaires to de Valera in October 1962, he regaled on an event that proved that more than half a century later how he was not opposed to the Irish language as originally thought. Mannix in fact rather hoped for its revival long after his decision to oppose compulsory Irish in Maynooth was purely a practical decision:

He spoke about the problem of reviving the Irish language and recalled the Gaelic League had not been pleased with him for opposing a proposal for a compulsory Irish examination for matriculation early in the century.[69]

Although to some extent, Mannix was to retreat from public life and appearances, de Valera never forgot the courtesy shown to him by Mannix

---

[66] Draft letter not sent re Melbourne centenary 1948, 13 April 1948 (UCD Archives: Eamon de Valera Papers, P 150-2906).
[67] O'Farrell, op. cit., p. 180.
[68] Gallagher, op. cit., p. 49.
[69] Charge d'Affaires account to de Valera on meeting with Archbishop Mannix, 9 October 1962 (UCD Archives: Eamon de Valera Papers, P150-2909).

since they first met. After their last meeting in 1948, there always was the cordial yearly telegram greeting a birthday, episcopal anniversary, or Christmas celebration between both men, as displayed in the de Valera papers. One would consider this possibly benign and more out of courtesy than friendship. Two events, one in private and one in public, undertaken by de Valera showed the respect and reverence he still maintained for Mannix. As the Irish government and people separately sent out gifts to Melbourne to mark the magnificent achievement of the archbishop's Golden Jubilee on October 6 1962, de Valera delivered spectacularly on his own accord. Considering that their first official meeting was in Maynooth, the president sent "an illuminated scroll from the National University as well as a gold replica of the 15th century de Burgho chalice".[70] The archbishop was no doubt delighted by the generosity shown to him by the president. It was fitting that for his final mass, which took place on the opening day of the Second Vatican Council, 11 October 1962, the archbishop "wore the vestments presented to him as a jubilee gift by the members of the Maynooth Union and he used the chalice presented to him by de Valera".[71] The second event that showed that their relationship was indeed special was the attempt by the president to petition the Holy See to appoint Archbishop Mannix as Cardinal. In a formal meeting with the Papal Nuncio to Ireland on 31 July 1961, the president paid respects to the Nuncio on the recent death of Cardinal Tardini whilst, also using the opportunity to promote the argument for Mannix's appointment to the Sacred College of Cardinals.[72] This was an unprecedented move particularly by de Valera. It does however; show how far he was willing to privately return a favour to his longest and most loyal clerical backer. The move seemed to be ignored in Ireland therefore in a letter, a year before the death of Dr Mannix, to Cardinal Browne, de Valera petitioned the idea to be presented personally to the Holy Father.

Nothing would give such joy to Irish people throughout the world, and especially throughout Ireland, as his being made a member of the Sacred College. I wonder could the matter be brought to the attention of the Holy

---

[70] Ebsworth, op. cit., p. 421.

[71] Frank Murphy, 'A great Irish archbishop' in *The Capuchin Annual* (1965), p. 101.

[72] Untitled note in de Valera papers dated 31, July 1961 (UCD Archives: Eamon de Valera Papers, P150-2909).

Father? I am daring to make a more formal request through His Excellency the Nuncio here.[73]

This was a monumental gesture on behalf of the president. It would prove to have an unfruitful ending as Archbishop Mannix's chance had come and gone in 1945 and his episcopal reign in Melbourne was meandering to a peaceful close. The president continued to show a more public face of their relationship when he attended the commemoration ceremony for the archbishop's Jubilee in his hometown of Charleville. Here he publicly showed in his capacity as president his willingness to acknowledge the close relationship and respect he held for Mannix. He would not give up in seeing Mannix return to Ireland. In Mannix's final year, he offered a rhetorical invitation to the archbishop knowing that he could not accept it due to his old age:

> I wish it were possible for Your Grace to come on a visit to us. How welcome you would be to me and my wife in this house. With every good wish from my wife and myself and indeed from the whole Irish people.[74]

The archbishop passed away on 6 November 1963 on the "Feasts of All Saints of Ireland" with Dr Simonds, his coadjutor, lamenting, "a cedar of Lebanon has fallen".[75] His legacy has largely been forgotten by the people of Ireland. In Australia, he will never be forgotten as his mark has been most visibly left by the massive buildings and infrastructure he left in his diocese of Melbourne. This great church leader was from a generation of ecclesiastical leaders that have largely disappeared since the implementation of the Second Vatican Council. Mannix always kept the interests of his homeland close to his heart, but also instilled in Australians, particularly those of the Irish Catholic diaspora, a new sense of belonging and collectiveness to achieve their goals of social equality in a time of rampant inequality. In his one and only television interview in 1962 with Australian interviewer Gerald Lyons, the archbishop was pushed into deciding where his loyalties lay with regard his position as either a man of the cloth or a crusader for political rights. Witty, as the archbishop often was, even at the old age of 97, he never relinquished his right, first and foremost as a citizen of Ireland. Secondly, as an adopted

---

[73] De Valera letter to His Eminence Cardinal Michael Browne, 14 September, 1962 (UCD Archives: Eamon de Valera Papers, P150-2909).
[74] De Valera letter to Archbishop Mannix, 19 October 1962 (UCD Archives: Eamon de Valera Papers, P150-2909).
[75] Ebsworth, op. cit., pp 425-426.

citizen of Australia, of whom both countries should be immensely proud of:

> When a man becomes a bishop he doesn't cease to be a citizen, and as a citizen and a responsible man he has the right to make up his own mind and his own conscience and to follow it.[76]

His relationship with de Valera can only be described as unique to both its time and era. Mannix's episcopal motto may have been "all things to all men", but to de Valera he most certainly gave "all things to one man" and the president realised this more than anyone else did, as his episcopal rock was no more. Mannix's character appraisals and supportive relationship with the president had kept de Valera focused on his political path. Almost like the fatherly figure he never had, his constant counsel gave him the motivation he needed to believe in himself and lead Ireland down the road to freedom. Archbishop Mannix was often at times the only one who believed in de Valera when no one else would:

> I know an honest man when I meet him. I think I know a wise man, when I hold confidence with him, and I have never met a man who gave me a better presence of honesty and wisdom that Eamon de Valera.[77]
> —Archbishop Daniel Mannix

---

[76] Archbishop Daniel Mannix in an interview with Gerald Lyons (29 Dec. 1961, ABC Archives)
[77] Archbishop Mannix speaking at Boston USA in July 1926 (UCD Archives: De Valera Papers, P150/2909)

CONCLUSION

There is a remarkable physical resemblance: both being of the same height and build. The facial markings are such as to almost lead one to class them as brothers.[1]
—Father Vaughan

Father Vaughan may have seen the characteristics of a brotherly nature between Mannix and Eamon de Valera in 1920. This book has argued that the relationship between both men was more akin to a paternal one rather than a brotherly one. Mannix was almost like the male paternal figure that de Valera never knew. For Mannix, de Valera became like the son that he never had and saw in him many characteristics of himself. The death of his father, Juan Vivion, left de Valera without any paternal figure. This was not replaced by his uncles so he looked to the natural male dominated influence in Irish society at the time – the Catholic Church. Therefore, de Valera was always favourable to clerical influence and as discussed previous contemplated joining the priesthood in his earlier years. For the archbishop he must have seen in de Valera, after their Omaha meeting, a younger more energetic man than himself made from the same mould. It is as if Mannix, almost decided from that point onwards to take the fledgling politician under his wing and offer him the patronage he needed to succeed in his destiny, which to Mannix was, the chosen leader of Ireland.[2]

The relationship follows a clear path from the Omaha meeting in 1920 right up to their last reunion in 1948. Their relationship, assessed in a historical context, can be seen in the discussion as metamorphosing through five stages. These are formal, friendly, supportive, aloof and finally cordial. A characteristic pattern of the first two stages develops chronologically following from de Valera's appointment to Maynooth to their meeting in Omaha in 1920. However, their bond becomes closer as the political landscape in Ireland changed rapidly over the course of the 1920s into a more empathetic bond. It has been shown that once de Valera gained power in 1932, that the relationship with Mannix became strained.

---

[1] *The West Australian*, 'A striking resemblance', 21 August 1920, p. 7.
[2] Colm Kiernan, *Daniel Mannix and Ireland* (Morwell, Victoria: Alella Books, 1984), p. 132.

Particularly with respect to the refusal of Mannix to attend the Eucharistic Congress in Ireland. He did not contemplate that following Fianna Fáil's ascension to power in 1932 that de Valera or his party would turn so quickly to re-align themselves with their former heretics the Irish hierarchy, which Mannix had grown to loathe since 1913. This may have played a substantial part in the archbishop's decision not to return for the Eucharistic Congress. De Valera from the 1930s onwards proved an adept politician thus, relying on the clerical pillar he needed for support previously. From the archbishop's perspective however, he saw his continued support and that of his diasporic flock as vital to de Valera especially during the turbulent decade of the 1920s and during the anti-partition tour of 1948. Mannix would begin to focus more on Australian politics after the war and was helped by a newfound lay protégé in the form of B. A. Santamaria, who now saw Mannix as the fatherly figure:

> I found it difficult to accept the earthly disappearance of one who, in the face of so many adversities, had seemed so indestructible. It was by the purest chance that my life had become so intertwined with that of a man who was already 50 when I was born; whom I did not even meet until he was 71; who had become not merely the point of reference for every major design or project but also, in a sense, my conscience.[3]

With Mannix's chances of returning to Ireland as a cardinal diminished as time passed by, McQuaid held the position in Irish history that Mannix was once touted for as far back as 1921. Historian J. H. Whyte discusses the links between McQuaid and de Valera as being very interesting. "Politically", he argues, "his appointment was interesting because there were links between Fianna Fáil and Blackrock. Mr. De Valera had once been a pupil there, and he sent his sons there". He continues, but remains sceptical to the point that, some historians see "Dr. McQuaid's appointment to the See of Dublin as being some way influenced by Mr. De Valera".[4] Whyte holds reservations about this as he argues "such interference would be inconsistent with the Irish tradition".[5] If so, then de Valera's attempt to have Mannix in 1961, promoted to the College of Cardinals was most definitely against tradition. This signified the depth of their friendship.

---

[3] B. A Santamaria, *Santamaria: a memoir* (Melbourne: Oxford University Press, 1997), p. 240.
[4] J. H. Whyte, *Church & state in modern Ireland, 1923-70* (Dublin: Gill & Macmillan, 1971), p. 76.
[5] ibid, p. 76.

This also suggests that this was not de Valera's first attempt to influence clerical appointments.

The relationship established by both men was also paradoxically akin to that association developed between the Catholic Church and state in Irish society. In many respects, this was a symbiotic alliance between the two parties. After he gained power in 1932, de Valera set about establishing closer links between Fianna Fáil and the Catholic Church and making amends for his wrong-doing in their eyes. When de Valera needed the Catholic Church's support most in 1932, he set about fraternising with it in return for what he saw as limited demands in what was already a Catholic dominated society. Similar to his relationship with Mannix he used the archbishop's support particularly in 1920 to propel himself into a position of power. When he attained political office in 1932, he felt he did not have to work on his relationship with Archbishop Mannix now that he had gained power. Having now reached parity with the hierarchy of the Catholic Church in Ireland as leader of the Irish Free State, de Valera felt Mannix's relationship could not benefit him further politically. The success of the Eucharistic Congress and the "special position" attained by the Roman Catholic Church through the constitution of 1937, confirmed de Valera's assumption that the Catholic Church and state were once again realigned. He became complacent just like he did with Mannix's support. In 1948 when he lost power, he returned to the pillar that had set his political machine in motion as early as 1920. Similarly, the state returned to church support that had been vital to its fight for independence. Once the Irish Free State came into existence, church-state relations, particularly with the formation of Fianna Fáil, shift dramatically. As historian, Dermot Keogh argues:

> Irish Catholicism in the 1920s sought, as one of its major objectives, to reinforce the legitimacy of the new state. The post-civil war political climate of Saorstát Éireann suited and reassured members of the Catholic hierarchy.[6]

The unique bond between the two men that was categorised by Mannix's constant belief in de Valera during the 1920s, but particularly during the Civil War period. This bond forced both the Catholic Church and Free State to re-evaluate their partnership. This re-evaluation developed into a direct alignment between the church and state over the coming decades particularly with regard domestic political affairs. Therefore, the uniqueness

---

[6] Dermot Keogh, 'The catholic church and the Irish Free State 1923-1932' in *History Ireland*, 2 (1) 1994, p. 47.

of Mannix and de Valera's relationship acted as one of the catalysts in cementing Irish church-state relations. This leaves Dermot Keogh to contend correctly that "Irish Catholicism owes much to Mannix".[7]

Irish history has focused in recent years on the impact the diaspora had on events in Ireland during the country's fight for independence. This focus has largely been directed towards the socially wealthy and powerful Irish diaspora in America. Patrick O'Farrell discusses the Irish-Australian diaspora's impact on events during the War of Independence and Civil War has largely been overlooked. The success of the diaspora in America has superseded its Australian counter-parts in the historical textbooks. McCaffrey describes, through his portrayal of components of Irish nationalism, how the nationalists "used Irish-American success stories as evidence that the Irish in a free environment were ambitious and enterprising."[8] Mannix's ties with de Valera from one of the Empire's furthest outposts, Melbourne, act as a mirror. The influence the archbishop could command over the Irish in Australia was a carbon copy of the influence the Irish-Australian diaspora could command for the support of affairs taking place during Ireland's fight for independence. By using the archbishop as a figurehead for the diaspora in Australia and de Valera as the symbol of Irish liberty, the discussion has shown how their relationship was analogous to those striving for Irish freedom and its vast diaspora. Events such as the annual St Patrick's Day Parades, public demonstrations and subscriptions to causes in aid of Ireland, the diaspora in Australia, but particularly in Melbourne, played as significant a role in maintain Ireland's fight for independence. This support manifested itself through both its physical and financial support as those anywhere in the world. The archbishop played a large part in these remonstrances. He actually turned the Irish question into a Catholic question "linking it with and symbolising for many Catholics their own grievances and their belief that other Australians sought to exclude or demean them".[9] This was similar to a lesser extent with Cardinal Hayes in New York. De Valera realised this support and continued to use it from 1920, right through to his anti-partition tour of 1948, in an attempt to regain power.

---

[7] Dermot Keogh, 'Mannix, De Valera and Irish Nationalism', in John B. O'Brien and Pauric Travers (eds.) *The Irish Emigrant Experience in Australia* (Dublin: Poolbeg, 1991), p. 221.

[8] Lawrence J. McCaffrey, 'Components of Irish nationalism' in Thomas E. Hachey & Lawrence J. McCaffrey (eds.) *Perspectives on Irish nationalism* (Kentucky: University Press of Kentucky, 1989), p. 9.

[9] J. J. McGovern & P. J. O'Farrell, 'Australia' in P. J. Cornish (ed.), *A History of Irish Catholicism* (Dublin, Gill & Macmillan, 1971), vol. 6, part 6, pp 69-70.

Biographers of Mannix argue that the archbishop only developed his stringent form of nationalism after he developed a close relationship with de Valera. However, the discussion has looked at the influence of the Land League on Mannix's formative years. Essentially, we can see that Mannix had a strain of nationalism in his blood long before de Valera could claim any influence on the archbishop. This strain was one of an agrarian nature and came as no surprise considering his background. Mannix did manifest certain hints of where his nationalism lay through his paper given to the Maynooth Union as a student and his previous family involvement with the Land League. The Catholic Church superseded any manifestations he had once he joined Maynooth. Once he escaped the insular politics of Maynooth the archbishop set about trying to create his own niche of nationalism in a time when what it meant to be Irish was still in its formative era. His breed of nationalism as Colm Kiernan suggests "was dedicated and practical and dominated his conscience".[10] The events of 1916 and successive anti-conscription campaigns catapulted the eloquent, charismatic, Charleville native into the public spotlight that he could never have imagined had he stayed in Ireland. He had gone through a significant metamorphosis during his episcopal reign. His clerical style changed and he became very used to being a figure of public attention in Australia for Irish Catholics. Australia and its surrounding environment were completely new to the former Maynooth president and as McGovern and O'Farrell argue it was easy to see why as "in Ireland clerics habitually made the most scathing public pronouncements in an environment where nearly everybody agreed with them, or respected their authority".[11] Mannix's pronouncements were a very attractive prospect for de Valera and his aims at an independent Ireland, which is why he was first to establish an opening to a long and fruitful relationship with Mannix.

Connections between Mannix and de Valera, although proving very beneficial to Sinn Féin and Ireland's push for independence in the end left Mannix ostracised from the annals of Irish history. It has left his historical legacy largely commemorated as contributory to modern day Australia whilst neglecting the role he played in Irish history predominantly during the War of Independence and Civil War. Mannix's firebrand personality seemed to cause uneasiness in their friendship particularly after the divisions of the Civil War, which were still fresh during Mannix's visit of 1925. However, their relationship remained strong throughout the remaining years of Mannix's life. Where de Valera grew into his role as an

---

[10] Colm Kiernan, 'Appréciation Archbishop Mannix', *Éire-Ireland*, p. 121.
[11] McGovern & P. J. O'Farrell, op. cit., p. 68.

international statesman by capably using the "fire and manoeuvre" technique, Mannix seemed to show a preference for direct confrontation particularly where national issues were at stake. This showed one key difference in their personalities and allowed one act as a counterweight to the other.

Mannix's Irish historical legacy is in stark contrast to that of Archbishop John Charles McQuaid who would become in the historical textbooks the iconic religious leader of the Irish Roman Catholic Church during the twentieth century. Mannix strayed too close to the hardened revolutionary militant nationalism of de Valera. He has become less topical in the narrative of modern Irish history. Australia ultimately allowed Mannix to emerge as a "charismatic figure who ran the system". Rev Ebsworth explains that it allowed him "to emerge as an aggressive public figure as well as a progressive churchman" possibly something that he could never have achieved in Ireland.[12] Therefore, the tale of Archbishop Mannix is doubled edged. Had he not been moved to Melbourne he would never had gained the prominent stature that he now holds in Australian history. However, had he stayed in Ireland he may not have had the influence he had on Irish affairs during the War of Independence and Civil War. De Valera wrote in his message of condolence to the people of Melbourne upon the archbishop's death that Mannix's "memory will be revered among us and his name will live forever on in our history".[13] This has not been the case and Archbishop Mannix has remained in a Vatican liked sealed memory box gathering dust that makes it hard to see his true contribution. His removal to Melbourne in 1913 created a rift with the Irish hierarchy that never looked like healing, especially after the reception he received following his return home in 1925. As Kiernan correctly suggests "although Mannix had accepted his posting to Melbourne, it raised doubts in his mind about the probity of the Catholic Church's hierarchy in Ireland and of its seeming support for British rule there".[14] The Catholic Church in Ireland had already disintegrated Mannix's original hopes for an independent Ireland free of the Landlord by "overthrowing Parnell which was only a temporary disruption of the church-constitutional nationalist alliance, and it was precisely the nationalist credentials that the bishops had gained during the Land War that enabled

---

[12] Rev. Walter Ebsworth, *Archbishop Mannix* (Armadale, Vic.: H. H. Stephenson, 1977), p. 124.

[13] 'World leaders pay tribute to his memory', *The Advocate*, 14 November 1963, p. 15.

[14] Kiernan, 'Appréciation Archbishop Mannix' op. cit., p. 124.

them to play a part in his downfall".[15] Mannix did not let the same scenario happen in Australia and remained aloof from the Australian hierarchy with regard to nationalist issues bringing him into conflict with them quite frequently, most notably Archbishop Duhig. He never held any sentimentality towards the Irish clerical hierarchy and after he moved to Melbourne, it would spell the end of his association with them, as the olive branch was never extended from either side particularly after 1925

It is hard for the present-day reader of Irish history to imagine just how high profile a figure the archbishop was, not just in Australia but also for a period at least he was an international figure lauded for his stand during the conscription referendums of World War One. As Lanier laments "the past is rather the relentless drift of the stream of time itself in which we cannot but participate as we strive to move towards an understanding of it".[16] In conclusion, the book has aimed not just to show how unique the relationship was between Mannix and de Valera, but it has also attempted to understand the bond both men had during the key period 1920-1925. As we reassess the relationship, we can now appreciate in full the part Mannix played in the fight for Irish independence, especially how pivotal his steadfast support of de Valera, along with Hagan, was in allowing Ireland to continue on the road to democratic stability. The archbishop realising after the 1920 tour the power he could command on both a national and international level set about cultivating, as James Griffin, would argue "the Cult of Personality".[17] Melbourne and the strong Irish Catholic community allowed him this opportunity, something that he could not have realised in Ireland. The Irish in Australia needed a champion to mobilise them as an effective and cohesive unit and Mannix provided this mobilisation. Fanned by a strong jingoistic sense of his own breed of nationalism and with a newspaper, *The Advocate*, the archbishop was ultimately able to secure his Australian legacy. Mannix's self-proclaimed cult status focused on his adulation as a great man of the Catholic Church. This rhetoric often used in lamentations of Mannix was supported by powerful statistics that showed that the archbishop was not just a man of words but also of action. As O'Brien points out

---

[15] John Newsinger, "I bring not peace but a sword": 'The religious motif in the Irish War of Independence' in *Journal of Contemporary History*, 13 (3) 1978, p. 611.

[16] S. C Lanier, 'It is new-strung and shan't be heard': nationalism and memory in the Irish harp tradition' in *British Journal of Ethnomusicology*, 8 (1) 1999, p. 1.

[17] See James Griffin, 'Daniel Mannix and the cult of personality' in O. MacDonagh and W. Mandle (eds.) *Ireland and Irish-Australia: studies in cultural and political history* (London: Croom Helm, 1986), pp 95-118.

... in 1913 there were 160 churches in his archdiocese; in 1963 there were
300. In 1913 there were 24,000 attending Catholic Primary Schools; in
1963 this had risen to more than 73,000. In secondary education there was
an even higher percentage increase with the number of secondary school
pupils rising from a low of 4,000 in 1913 to more than 28,000 fifty years
later.[18]

These figures suggest that Mannix had shown his capacity as a great
administrator overseeing the expansion of his flock. Ultimately, however,
he failed in his aim of state aid for Catholic education. Up until his death
in 1963, he bitterly continued the fight into the last decade of his life, on
one occasion questioning how the archbishop of Canterbury and other
Anglican bishops asked for state aid for their schools and got it.
Sarcastically as always, he proclaimed "I don't pretend to understand the
difference between Anglican leaders in Britain and Anglican leaders in
Australia".[19] Posthumously, however, his aims were achieved. In 1964,
state aid for private schools was secured "when Menzies honoured his
election promise".[20] The Catholics of Melbourne and Australia indeed
realised effectively the capacity of this influential churchman and clerical
politician to achieve such a goal and were quick to rally to his cause.
Mannix achieved unparalleled cult status that has continued in Australia
with the expansion of the Catholic Church and although not achieving his
main goal during his lifetime, Vincent Buckley contends that:

> ... among barons and princelings in this situation, Archbishop Mannix of
> Melbourne was a king – a republican king on some old Irish model,
> operating according to his own vision of the Brehon law.[21]

In a re-evaluation of Mannix's personal characteristics, Sidney Hook
contends, that "there is a natural tendency to associate the leader with the
results achieved under his leadership even when these achievements, good
or bad, have resulted despite his leadership rather than because of it".[22]
This in effect was the opposite for de Valera. The leadership qualities he
portrayed in his long distinguished public life have constantly been re-

---

[18] John B. O'Brien, *Daniel Mannix: builder of the Australia church* (Dublin:
Veritas, 1988), p. 18.

[19] Ebsworth, op. cit., p. 401.

[20] Colm Kiernan, *Daniel Mannix and Ireland*, op. cit., p. 123.

[21] Vincent Buckley, *Cutting the green hay – friendships, movements and cultural
conflict in Australia's great decades* (Victoria: Penguin Books, 1983), p. 134.

[22] Sidney Hook, *The hero in history: A Study in Limitation and Possibility* (New
York: Transaction Publishers, 1943), p. 4.

assessed. These included his part in such debates as reunification and Ireland's economic stagnation after the war. Most of these re-evaluations have neglected to take these failures in context with his achievements.[23] Although de Valera had created a large following during his life in Irish political affairs, in essence as he withdrew from public life he became obsessed with the legacy that he would leave for future generations. De Valera could never have hoped to re-create the magnitude of popularity or "cult of personality" that Archbishop Mannix had achieved. In essence, Mannix had faced his fiercest critics during his lifetime whilst de Valera's enemies were yet unforeseen, the ones who would evaluate his historical legacy. Mannix had overseen his creation of "Mannixolatry" he did not want as he would claim "posterity to analyse my soul"[24] and ordered "that all personal correspondence be destroyed before his death".[25]

A historian's greatest tool is the primary source and in the case of this book, the evaluation of personal correspondence between both men was critical to forming an evaluation of their relationship. Although the archbishop realised the dominance of his participation in Irish, but particularly Australian, affairs, would warrant an investigation of his papers. Mannix decided that he would ultimately control the course of written history; he achieved this through the actions both verbally and physically. This is opposed to a re-evaluation of his memoirs by historians or researchers. Indeed this perspective on the archbishop's life is unique as:

> ... in his long life he actually wrote very little; apart from personal letters, mostly short introductions to various Catholic publications. His medium was the spoken word, but his spoken word in countless speeches emerged in print as lucid, persuasive and finely tempered prose. He never beforehand wrote any sermon or address not even his noble panegyric on Archbishop Carr.[26]

---

[23] Coogan, *De Valera: long fellow* and Gallagher 'Fianna Fáil and partition' in *Éire-Ireland.*

[24] Griffin, James, 'Archbishop Daniel Mannix' in *The Old Limerick Journal*, 27 (1990), p. 27.

[25] Ebsworth, op. cit., p. 429.

[26] Father James Murtagh, 'The last of a line' in *The Advocate*, 14 November, 1963, p. 11.

Figure 7.1: Archbishop Mannix Raheen 1963. Image kindly courtesy of Mrs Mary Ellen McCarthy.

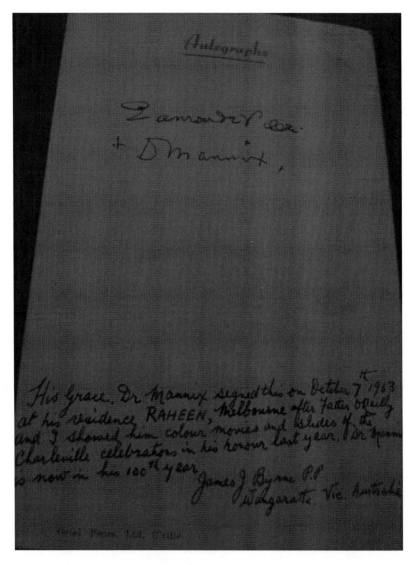

Figure 7.2: Autograph signature of Eamon de Valera and Archbishop Daniel Mannix on Archbishop Mannix's Episcopal Golden Jubilee Commemoration Luncheon leaflet. Image kindly courtesy of Provincial Heritage Centre Sisters of Mercy Convent Charleville, Co. Cork.

De Valera's historical legacy is essentially the antithesis of Mannix, as his actions have for a long time been psychoanalysed by various disciplines. This has largely been achieved due to de Valera's meticulous preservation of all correspondence and publications that he deemed were necessary to the conservation of Ireland's historical narrative. As Patrick Murray debates, "many of de Valera's letters to highly-placed supporters are clearly influenced by his interest in the verdict of history on him and on his political collaborators". [27] Although many decisions have been questioned due to the research of his papers, he has nothing to hide unlike Mannix who remains an enigma for the historical researcher. Thankfully, de Valera believed correspondence from Mannix as being pivotal to Ireland's historical narrative and this has allowed the book to draw its main conclusions. The letters have allowed us to develop a fresh profound perspective on how Mannix related to one of his few closest friends. Father Morley Coyne, a former student of Mannix's, provided a further insight when interviewed by Brenda Niall:

> Fr M.C: He wasn't a man you could know. No one knew him, not even Jerry Murphy [Jeremiah Murphy SJ].
> B.N: Or Father Hackett?
> Fr M.C: No but they knew him as well as anyone. There was always a wall.[28]

This discussion has posed a new historical question. Did de Valera finally manage to break down the institutionalised wall of solitude, isolation and concealment that Archbishop Mannix had built? Fr Hackett's relationship may be described as the closest thing Mannix had to a friend. However, the context of the relationship and correspondence he had with de Valera as seen through the personal letters and declarations of support throughout the years suggests that de Valera became the elite counter-part that Mannix found himself wanting to be more attached to after the American tour of 1920. De Valera held such a position in Mannix's esteem, that a photo of his writing desk published in *The Advocate* shows a framed picture of himself and the taoiseach posing together during one of their numerous encounters. This memory holds pride of place at the top centre of his writing desk along with a picture of his pre-deceased sister.[29]

---

[27] Patrick Murray, 'Voices of de Valera,' (M. Litt. Thesis, Trinity College Dublin, 1995).

[28] Brenda Niall, *The riddle of Father Hackett – A life in Ireland and Australia* (Canberra: National Library of Australia, 2009), p. 136.

[29] *The Advocate,* 'This was the place he called home', 14 November 1963, p. 16.

One of Mannix's lasting legacies to society is the power of his oratory. Through the medium of speech, Mannix was able to summon not just Irish men and women of Australia to the cause of Irish independence, but his voice echoed to the Irish diaspora worldwide. His mesmerising public displays of slick, witty and concise rhetoric, would have proven a marvellous template for the young de Valera as he hoped to achieve the same aims as the archbishop in America. Mannix's strength lay in:

> His power of speech, his simplicity and lucidity of utterance, his telling turn of phrase, his unanswerable logic, his faculty of "getting a firm grip of the subject" and his playful but extraordinary use of banter and irony roused into reckless reaction those who, in the words of Dr. Mannix himself, had been accustomed to praise'.[30]

Lloyd George and Prime Minister Hughes, among many others, could testify to Mannix's ridicule over the decades. De Valera would learn a valuable lesson from the archbishop from 1920 onwards. Violence was not the way to achieve Ireland's gains, but rather through democratic methods, Fianna Fáil would gain power and make de Valera's dreams a reality. Mannix had encountered many great speakers through his days as a student in Maynooth, but he would only come into his own following his appointment as archbishop of Melbourne. The panegyric that he delivered at his predecessor's funeral stands among the most eloquent of speeches given by a prelate. One of de Valera's crowning moments definitely lies in his much-anticipated public rebuttal of Churchill's claims to Irish weakness and selfishness during his victory speech after World War Two. Archbishop Mannix aligned the diaspora particularly the Irish-Australians willingly behind de Valera's cause. As Canetti outlines "a crowd exists so long as it has an unattained goal".[31] Mannix through the education question for Catholics in Australia maintained throughout his episcopal career a strong power base from which he was able to draw constant support. De Valera successfully followed suit with Ireland's independence from Britain standing as his intermittent goal. However, after World War Two, even his Fianna Fáil colleagues could see he would not attain his reconstituted goal of reunification, thus the slow ebb of his political influence began. Although it is recognised that Mannix nurtured de Valera on the road to political involvement, it is wrong, as Hook argues, "to assume that the individual who affects history – that is, who helps redetermine the direction of historical events – must get himself believed

---

[30] *The Advocate*, 'Powerful and lucid orator', 14 November 1963, p. 5.
[31] Elias Canetti, *Crowds and power* (Hamburg: Classen, 1960), p. 32.

in or acclaimed, as a condition of his historical effectiveness".[32] This is a very valid point by Hook, as Mannix, by the time he had reached Melbourne, did not focus on being a crowd pleaser. His encounter in Maynooth with the Irish language enthusiasts had taught him a valuable lesson he would never forget. Do not attempt to play to the crowd, let the crowd follow you through the justification of your actions.

Mannix made numerous predictions particularly those that concerned de Valera and Irish independence. He became so entrapped in the "cult of personality" that had spawned around him that he almost began to see himself as a modern day prophet, a fact to which he admitted in 1924, during the zenith of his popularity:

> Now I venture a prediction. I am getting bolder as a prophet. Nothing I can see can stay the march of events in Ireland. The Republican cause is winning, and will, I believe, win right out.[33]

Similar to the portrayal of the prophet in Luke's Gospel's in the Bible whereby, Jesus laments that "no prophet is accepted in his own country", Mannix would experience this scenario first-hand during his return to Ireland in 1925. Although, the public lamentation of his doctrine may have been proven right in the long term, the archbishop had to endure the humiliation of the Irish hierarchy's public treatment of his office during his return home. Not even his relationship with de Valera could heal the wounds, which the Irish Catholic Church had left with Mannix after 1925. De Valera's strongest clerical ally had now been firmly side lined by those who retained the key to unlocking the social powerbase of support that Fianna Fáil needed facing into the 1927 elections. The discussion has looked at how, before the final return of Mannix to Ireland, de Valera began to manipulate the archbishop towards his own ends. Although, failing to dissuade Mannix from making public utterances, a precedent had been set for de Valera's over Mannix's "cult of personality". Roles had been reversed and the prophet had now become the firm follower and believer of de Valera. Historically, it can be shown that probably the one and only person during Archbishop Mannix's career to dominate him was indeed, Eamon de Valera. Cardinal Gilroy once again gives us a sense of just how much respect and affection de Valera commanded over Mannix when he wrote to the president after the death of Mannix:

---

[32] Hook, op. cit., pp 10-11.
[33] Ebsworth, op. cit., pp 273-274.

No one ever loved the land of his birth more than Archbishop Mannix loved Ireland. No one ever loved and served the land of his adoption more than Archbishop Mannix loved and served Australia. For yourself personally, Mr. President, His Grace had an affection and admiration that knew no bounds – and rightly so.[34]

Mannix's inner feelings and moral foundations have for generations puzzled historians and religious brethren alike as he did not allow his memoirs to be preserved for analysis. The relationship Mannix developed with de Valera offers the reader a window into the crystal ball that was Mannix's inner sanctum. The bond he secured with de Valera and the depths to which he was willing to go to support this perennial tie will forever stand as a lasting reminder to the caricature of one of the Ireland's, and the Catholic Church's most iconic statesmen. Dr Simonds, the archbishop's coadjutor, offers us his perspective into one of Mannix's few offerings of his inner thoughts. He laments how:

Often they discussed Cardinal Newman, who fascinated him...He felt deeply for Newman, who was constantly misunderstood, both in and out of the Church. Newman's writings are full of the unhappiness he felt at this lack of trust. No such complaint can be found in any sentence written or spoken by Dr. Mannix. In the misunderstanding of Newman, he saw his own, and his greatness never became so inhuman that he ceased to feel.[35]

Simonds contends that Archbishop Mannix had a deep respect for Cardinal Newman and would eventually open a Catholic college named after the Cardinal in Melbourne. The archbishop's life in many respects mirrored Cardinal Newman's. Mannix, like Newman, was often misunderstood both in terms of his support for de Valera during the Civil war and even during his role as president of Maynooth. In an interview with the archbishop's grandniece, Mrs Patricia Wallis McCombe, in March 2010, she informed me that Mannix wrote her a very poignant letter. He quoted the famous lines from the poem *Casabianca*, by Felicia Dorothea Hemans, in which he said: "I feel like the boy on the burning dock when everyone else has fled". Mrs Wallace contends that Mannix, who would have been in his early nineties when he wrote the letter, that did not survive, came across as feeling almost alone and exiled maintaining the final stand at his post in Melbourne, which he had taken up in 1913.[36]

---

[34] Cardinal Gilroy letter to de Valera, 6 November 1963 (UCD Archives: Eamon de Valera Papers, P150-2909).
[35] Ebsworth, op. cit., p. 429.
[36] Interview with Mrs Patricia Wallis-McCombe (8 March, 2010).

Mannix maintained his contempt for his treatment by the Irish hierarchy at the end of his presidency, but particularly in 1925 along with a strong disregard for the Cosgrave led government, which opposed and attempted to dissolve his belief in de Valera. Pope Benedict XVI officially beatified Cardinal Newman, on 19 September 2010. The Pope said of the cardinal that he displayed "that tradition of gentle scholarship, deep human wisdom and profound love for the Lord has borne fruit".[37] Archbishop Mannix could also claim to have such attributes and may someday follow Cardinal Newman to the altar of sainthood. His argument for inclusion has not been forgotten and in recent times, his adopted native Melbourne has seen a foundation set up for this very purpose.[38] However, until Mannix's "cult of personality" succeeds in his elevation to the sainthood, the archbishop will remain like Newman before him, an exiled and misunderstood peripheral figure in Irish and Vatican circles. Australia, where he for so long was a beacon of hope and inspiration to the Irish diaspora will keep his flame memory alive.

Since the day they met in Omaha, Nebraska in June 1920 the story of the relationship between Mannix and de Valera is a chapter of modern Irish history that has been waiting to be written. The evidence and facts presented in this book have concluded this chapter of history, by showing just how special the relationship was. The length of time since the character's deaths has removed the sentimentality that may have lingered for two such iconic figures in Irish and Australian history. Now, however, the time has come for a new generation of readers to examine and understand fully the role both men's friendship played in Irish history during the embryonic stages of Ireland's fight for freedom. They offered each other both public and private support when each went through periods of crises. Archbishop Mannix during his early public platform appearances outshone de Valera. It is easy to see why as Rev Ebsworth establishes "in the early decades of this century, few there were with sufficient ability and courage to challenge his unanswerable logic and his laugh-provoking ridicule".[39] De Valera learned many attributes from the archbishop and used them to mold himself into the politician he became.

---

[37] Patsy McGarry, 'Newman, first rector of UCD, beatified' in *The Irish Times*, 20 September 2010.

[38] Archbishop Mannix Foundation has been established by Mr. Tony Grieve the convenor and has the ecclesiastical approval of the then Archbishop of Melbourne, Archbishop Pell who met with Mr Grieve on the 6th November 1997, the 34th anniversary of Archbishop Mannix's death. The address for the foundation is P.O. Box 341, Lilydale Victoria 3140. Australia.

[39] Ebsworth, op. cit., p. 124.

Figure 7.3: Archbishop Daniel Mannix statue Melbourne, Australia sculpted by Nigel Boonham. Image kindly courtesy of Mrs Winifred Cross.

Figure 7.4: Archbishop Daniel Mannix statue Melbourne, Australia inscription on plaque. Image kindly courtesy of Mrs Winifred Cross.

He eventually stood alongside Archbishop Mannix on the public pedestal that he had created for himself. The public arena was not large enough for, as Frank Murphy, described "the two greatest Irishmen of their time".[40] This left Mannix falling gradually out of the Irish public's mindset and clambering for public recognition in Australia. It is widely recognised in Australia that Mannix was one of the greatest orators of his day, as was de Valera in Ireland. It cannot be denied that both men were leaders. Their careers have left them being judged as talented leaders in their respective fields. The iconic legacy of these two men has only been questioned in recent times. Australian historian, James Griffin in the case of Mannix, and by Irish historian Tim Pat Coogan, on de Valera's side. According to Griffin, "publication, republication and admiring commentaries were all directed towards the Mannix personality cult and the political interest it served".[41] This "cult" of Mannix, has most recently been symbolised in the

---

[40] Frank Murphy, *Daniel Mannix* (Melbourne: Advocate Press, 1948), p. 91.
[41] James Griffin, 'Revisionism or reality? Daniel Mannix in ADB 10', in *Irish-Australian studies: papers delivered at the eighth Irish-Australian conference Hobart* (Sydney: Crossing Press, 1995), p. 142.

call for his beatification, and cannot be ignored along with the most recent historical appraisals on de Valera.[42]

Relationships are key to unlocking clues behind many historical events and this bond has proved no different. Sociologist Allan would argue that

> ... friendship is a social relationship, and not just a personal one. Class, ethnicity, kinship, age and whatever other social divisions are most pertinent to that society at that period will impact on the "freedoms" there are to develop forms of informal relationships and shape the consequent solidarities that emerge.[43]

Before both men had met, they shared many similar characteristics. They both grew up in rural areas within a mile of each other as part of the large lower-middle farming class. They received the same education, and their attachment to the social powerbroker in Irish society, as both a cleric and layperson, played a significant role for two extremely pious men. It allowed them to make a distinct connection, but after 1920, the real link appeared in their political outlook. It has been easy therefore to see why they became so close when they eventually became acquainted.

Sociologists Adams and Allan, in studying the topic of friendships have come to many conclusions. The main finding they discovered when it comes to the definition of friendship is that "it is interaction which matters the most, and not just action".[44] For Mannix and de Valera although both sides proved willingly through their actions that they were indeed close friends and allies it is the interaction of both men through their correspondence and meetings which have determined the existence of their friendship. In the Collins Dictionary, a relationship is described as "the mutual dealings, connections, or feelings that exist between two parties, countries or people".[45] This definition certainly pertains to Archbishop Daniel Mannix and Eamon de Valera, but their relationship was by no means just an ordinary relationship. It was a special one between two friends that has left a lasting legacy on Irish history.

---

[42] *The Corkman*, 'First moves to beatify Archbishop Daniel Mannix', 25 November 2004, p. 8.

[43] Graham Allan, 'Friendship and the private sphere' in Adams & Allan (eds.) *Placing friendship in context* (Cambridge: Cambridge University Press, 1998), p. 71.

[44] Rebecca G. Adams and Graham Allan, 'Contextualising friendship' in Adams & Allan (eds.) *Placing friendship in context* (Cambridge: Cambridge University Press, 1998), p. 2.

[45] *Collins English dictionary 3ʳᵈ edition*, (Glasgow: HarperCollins Ltd., 1991), p. 1308.

A special friend can share one's deepest thoughts, hopes and fears and provide another self to share the vicissitudes of life.[46]

—Ray Pahl

---

[46] Ray Pahl, *On friendship* (Cambridge: Polity Books, 2000), p. 1.

APPENDIX A

ARCHBISHOP MANNIX SPEECH AT THE OPENING OF A FLORAL FETE AT WEST MELBOURNE SUNDAY 30TH APRIL 1916

"It is needless for me to say how deeply pained I am by what has just happened in Ireland, and how grieved I am for the lives that are lost. The outbreak is truly deplorable. But we must not lose sight of the facts of the situation. People must expect to reap what they sow. And knowing, as I do, what has been going on in Ireland before and since the outbreak of the war, I am not altogether surprised at the lamentable things that have occurred. They are the natural regrettable sequel and response to the campaign of armed resistance and civil war which the Carsonites have been allowed to preach and prepare for within the last few years. The Carsonites, of course, had no opportunity of coming into collision with the forces of the Crown. They got a free hand, though some of them boasted that they were intriguing with the German enemy. They were assured, on the authority of Mr. Asquith, that the British army would never point a gun at them. Their leader, instead of being sent to prison, was taken into the British Cabinet.

To truckle with treason is never safe for any Government. I am quite clear in my own mind that the British Government, by its failure to deal with the treason of the Carsonites, and by its shifty policy in regard to Home Rule has, unwittingly I suppose, led to the result which we must all deplore. I hope the immediate trouble is already over, or that it will soon be over; and I hope too that those who are already calling out for executions will first pause and try to fix the responsibility for this outbreak. Before condemning the misguided leaders of this movement to be shot, they should remember that the leaders of another movement were taken into the British Cabinet".[1]

---

[1] Rev. Walter Ebsworth, *Archbishop Mannix* (Armadale, Vic.: H. H. Stephenson, 1977), p. 146.

APPENDIX B

ARCHBISHOP MANNIX SPEECH AT THE OPENING OF A NEW CHRISTIAN BROTHERS' SCHOOL AT BRUNSWICK 28TH JANUARY 1917[1]

"They have heard much about the causes of the war, and about the fight for the small nations. It was fortunate for them that they were fighting on the side of small nations. But when all was said and all concessions made, the war was like most wars – just an ordinary trade war. As long as they could remember, Germany was capturing more of the world's trade than other nations thought to be her due. The other nations, or some of them, had equal opportunities; but they could not, or they did not, achieve the same success. Trade jealously on both sides had seemed, for many years past, to make a great war inevitable. How it would come about was a matter of accident. The invasion of Belgium was the spark that lighted the fire in Great Britain. But it was useless to shut one's eyes to all that went before. Trade jealousy was long leading to a trade war, and the war came. Even now people were arranging how the vanquished nations – when they were vanquished – were to be crippled in their future trade. They told us that the victory would be a barren victory, and all the bloodshed vain, if the enemy were to retain after the war a chance of again beating in trade the rivals whom they failed to beat in war. Whatever else may be involved, it was just a truism that the war was a trade war".

---

[1] Frank Murphy, *Daniel Mannix* (Melbourne: Advocate Press, 1948), p. 37.

Appendix C

De Valera Speech at Fenway Park, Boston 29 June 1919[1]

Gaels and Friends of the Gaels

I spoke to you in the tongue of the Gael because that tongue carried in itself the greeting I bring you from 'the white hills of Ireland'. I regret that my voice does not carry to the limits of this meeting because I would like everyone here to hear that greeting which I know will touch a responsive chord in every one of your hearts. They told us during the war that we had lost the sympathy of America (Cries of Liars) Like yourselves, I never mince words and told them as you do now that they lied. I know that the people of your land showed the way to the peoples of the world to true liberty. I know that the land in which I had the honour to be born was not going to misunderstand the struggles of a people fighting against a tyrant far greater than had been charged against Germany;

When an opportunity came, I came to you, as I came to the people of Clare after my liberation from prison. England had branded us as criminals. England said that even our own people despised us as traitors to Ireland. I answered them that I for one was willing to be judged by the Irish people and that if they called us traitors I would accept their judgement and hang my head in shame. You know what the verdict of Clare was; and I think that I shall carry back the same verdict from America. No! I do not for a moment believe that America will make a shuttlecock of our cause to pass it from party to party (Cries of "We'll make a shuttlecock out of the Democratic Party").

Americans may differ perhaps in their home politics but they are united in the cause of liberty. I come to your grand free land not by any means to make the Irish question a party question in your politics here. It will not become a party question, or if it does only in the sense that both parties

[1] *The Boston Herald*, 'De Valera begins his address in Gaelic', 30 June, 1919, p. 6.

would with each other in a noble emulation to see which could best help Ireland.

I shall not attempt to plead Ireland's cause now. It was sweet to my ears to hear the cause of Ireland pleaded thus by Americans. When I go through this country I hope that I shall continue to hear the cause of Ireland pleaded everywhere by Americans and that I shall only be called upon to represent Ireland by physical presence.

I am going to read this statement to you because of the danger of being misquoted. This danger is made clear to me by the quotation of one of the speakers taken from the press, and widely quoted that after I had been arrested said: Shoot me if you will but spare my men.

I never made such a statement. I would not have insulted my men by asking England to spare them. I said 'arrange for my men'. I was negotiating the surrender at the time.

Advocating the cause that I advocate here in Boston in the very cradle of liberty it requires somewhat of an effort on my part to restrain from making a parallel with those events so closely associated with your city and so nearly parallel to present events in Ireland and the cause for which I am here seeking your support.

I do refrain however, not only because I believe that these parallels are already vividly before your minds and in your consciousness but because I believe that no appeal to your feelings or your sympathies could make your hearts more with us than they are.

Instead of carrying you back a period of 150 years I shall direct your attention to the immediate present moment and its possibilities, a moment which if the American people will it can be made as great a landmark in the history of progress and civilisation as were the events of 1776.

By a curious coincidence on the very day and practically at the same hour that your President was using the words 'America is the hope of the world' in your hall here in Boston, I was using the same words to an American reporter who had sought me out in Dublin to interview me, when the English detectives could not find me.

I gave reasons too, for my opinion. I pointed out to him that considering all the circumstances, America alone of all the powerful nations was in a position to take that calm detached look which was absolutely essential if the world was not to be thrown back once more into the old system of secret diplomacy and intrigue of selfish alliances and balances which have never ceased to breed war and misery and which culminated in the world conflict through which we have been passing.

Now the thought which I expressed on that occasion was the thought of practically every man and woman in Ireland and not merely for the selfish reason that America was the hope of Ireland in particular, but because Irish people are a spiritual people with interests second to none in humanity's future.

I believe there is no nation in the world more keenly alive to the supreme issues for mankind involved in the Paris negotiations. We in Ireland recognise that if the wrong turning be now taken, if violence be re-established in its former supremacy as the final sanction, humanity is faced with a period of misery for which history hitherto has no parallel.

The burdens of taxation due to the debts incurred in the war, the cost of competitive armaments and the old diplomatic intrigues will lead inevitably to the internal social upheavals of states, that is, to anarchy and civil wars – a whole series of irregular wars vastly more terrible than the huge organised conflict now ended.

Peace was nominally signed between the two great combating sides yesterday, I understand. Peace! Peace that gives us twenty new wars instead of the one that it nominally ends. And this is the peace treaty the world has been asked to look forward to as the treaty that would end wars and establish a stable, lasting peace.

Does it not seem already a mockery – and a mockery it will remain unless America takes up the responsibility for the moral headship of the world to which her consistent traditions no less than the aims she set herself in entering this war entitles her. That headship at this moment is freely offered to her by the common sense and the common consent of mankind.

The present opportunity is never likely to return again. The idea of a community of nations recognising a common law and a common right ending war amongst nations as municipal law has ended private wars amongst individuals is today a possibility if America does what the people of the world – the honest, the plain people your President spoke of – pray and expect America will do. To lose this moment would be a disaster that it will be impossible to repair.

The moral propaganda carried on during the war, the doctrines of right and liberty and justice that were enunciated, even though the motives of some of the spokesmen may have been hypocritical, have still done their work.

APPENDIX D

AUSTRALIAN HIERARCHY LETTER TO *THE TIMES* AUGUST 13 1920[1]

We the members of the Australasian Catholic Hierarchy, who have just completed our official visit to the Holy Father at Rome, hasten to enter our most emphatic protest against the outrage and indignity offered by the British Government to our distinguished and beloved colleague, Dr. Mannix, Archbishop of Melbourne. This insult to him and to the high office he adorns is an indignity to us, his brothers, as well as to the whole Catholic body, both priests and people, of Australia and New Zealand.

One of the offences laid to his charge is that he had been the fearless champion of the principle that underlies the just and permanent settlement of the Irish question – namely, the right of the people of Ireland to choose their own form of government. In the advocacy of this principle he has not only the unanimous support of the whole Episcopacy, but also of the Irish people of Australia and New Zealand, as manifested at the Irish Race Convention recently held in Melbourne. He is an acknowledged leader of democracy in Australia, and as such has won the support not merely of Catholics, but of a vast and increasing body of non-Catholics throughout the Commonwealth and Dominion of New Zealand. Recently, at a public banquet in Sydney, the Attorney-General of New South Wales referred to Dr. Mannix as "Australia's first citizen". No doubt, his advocacy of democracy is imputed to him as a crime by the enemies of the people in Australia and England.

We have seen it stated that Dr. Mannix's recent utterances in America have drawn upon him the condemnation of the Holy See. We are in a position to deny that His Grace has ever received a censure or a rebuke of any kind from the Holy See. On the contrary, knowing as we do the splendid services rendered by His Grace to the Church in Australia, we feel sure that he enjoys the full confidence of his superiors in Rome. We have already assured His Grace that, in the trial through which he is

---

[1] 'Treatment of Dr. Mannix – Australian Prelates' Protest', *The Times*, 13 August, 1920.

passing, he has our fullest confidence and support. We learn with pleasure that already arrangements are being made to hold monster demonstrations of protest throughout Australia.

+ P. Redwood, Archbishop of Wellington, New Zealand.

+ P. J Clune, Archbishop of Perth.

+ R. W. Spence, Archbishop of Adelaide.

+ W. Barry, Coadjutor Archbishop of Hobart.

+ P. J. O'Connor, Bishop of Armidale.

+ J. Shirl, Bishop of Rockhampton.

+ J. Heavey, Bishop of Cooktown.

+ D. Foley, Bishop of Ballrat.

+ J. McCarthy, Bishop of Sandhurst.

+ W. Hayden, Bishop of Wileannin-Forbes.

APPENDIX E

IRISH HIERARCHY LETTER
DURING THE WAR OF INDEPENDENCE[1]

"Ireland is now reduced to a state of anarchy by the forces of the Crown, who have established a reign of frightfulness which, for murdering the innocent and destroying their property, has a parallel only in the horror of Turkish atrocities or in the outrages attributed to the Red Army of Bolshevist Russia...But, as more immediately urgent that anything else, we demand, in the name of civilisation and national justice, a full enquiry into the atrocities now being perpetrated in Ireland, by such a tribunal as will inspire the confidence of all, and with immunity for witnesses from the terrorism which makes it impossible to give evidence with safety to life and property.

The Press is gagged, the right of public meetings interdicted, and inquests are suppressed. There has been brutal treatment of clergymen, and, certainly, to ban a distinguished Archbishop of Irish birth, who is the trusted leader of democracy in Australia, is the most unwise step that purblind and tyrannical oppression could take. And still more cruel, and not less destructive of any prospect of peace is the continued imprisonment of the Lord Mayor of Cork, and the other hunger-strikers, who think nothing of their lives if they can do anything for Ireland in the sad plight to which the stranger has reduced her".

---

[1] Rev. Walter Ebsworth, *Archbishop Mannix* (Armadale, Vic.: H. H. Stephenson, 1977), p. 243.

APPENDIX F

ARCHBISHOP MANNIX HOMECOMING SPEECH AT THE EXHIBITION BUILDING MELBOURNE AUGUST 13TH 1921[1]

His Grace: My Lords. Rev Fathers. and my dear friends – I need scarcely tell you how glad I am to be back amongst you. Nor need I assure you that I am a proud man to find that I hold a place of affection in the hearts, not merely of the people of Melbourne and of Victoria, but of the whole of Australasia. And I am particularly gratified to know that I hold that place not merely in the hearts of the Catholic people, but also that I can count upon the friendship of hundreds of thousands of those who do not worship at our altar. Lest I may forget, I had better, at the very outset, return thanks for the signal compliment paid to me and quite unexpectedly by those who have presented me with this picture which is on view at the Exhibition tonight. I shall probably repay them best by telling them that it will remind me in the days to come of the time when I was better looking. As long as I can I will live up to my artistic presentation. But I am truly overwhelmed with the welcome Australasia has given me.

A Voice: You deserved it

His Grace: In Ireland when people got married they used to have what they called a 'hauling home'. As I came along through the various towns and cities of Australia, it occurred to me that I was not getting a welcome back, but rather that I was experiencing a 'hauling home'. When I landed at Thursday Island to start with, I was met by Catholics and Irishmen, and as I reached Townsville, Brisbane and Sydney the volume grew until finally we reached the climax on Saturday in the streets of Melbourne. I should be wanting in my duty if I did not say a word of thanks, not merely to all those who took part in that unique demonstration, but especially to all those who, at great pains and trouble, who organised that stupendous demonstration, and succeeded in maintaining in the midst of the enthusiastic

---

[1] *The Advocate*, 'The Archbishop's Great Address', 18 August 1921, pp 23-24.

crowds the order that must have struck everybody who was a witness to my progress through the city.
Why did I get this welcome back to Australia?

A Voice: You deserved it.

His Grace: I am going to tell me if you let me. I have not received that welcome as a personal compliment to me. I have no personal attributes that would entitle me to the enthusiastic welcome that has been accorded to me. I have no claim whatever to the outpouring of affection and enthusiasm with which I have been met: but though I have no personal magnetism, still I have endeavoured during my time in Australia to speak the truth and take the consequences. That is not what some people like. In spite of threats, I have always stood for free speech. I have given other people the liberty that I have claim for myself, but I claim for myself the liberty that I give to them. Again, as an Australian I have made it my constant text to remind Australians that their country has come of age. I have reminded them that Australia is a nation, and holds a proud place amongst the nations, and therefore that in the mind of Australians, Australia's interests ought to be dominant, and the Australian flag ought to be at the top of the pole. As an Irishmen I have always been proud of my country and my countrymen. And I was never prouder of them than I am now. As a citizen of the Empire – for I claim to be a citizen of the Empire – I have withstood those, so far as I could, who would degrade the Empire. I have withstood those who would condone the dreadful happenings in Ireland, and I have reminded the people that loyalty to the Empire does not mean that any man should set upon the principle. 'My country right or wrong'. Therefore I say again the civic welcome at all events extended to me has been offered, not on account of personal merit but because the Australians are men of principle, and they like to stand by a man of principle. You are not alone in that. Australia is a great country and the Australians are a great people.

Wherever I have gone I have met with welcome as an Irishman and as an Australian. I fought for principle here, and I found sympathy wherever I went – all round the globe I may say. I have seen many nations and visited many people of different creeds and no creed, and of every hue and colour, but wherever I went I found that Australia and Australians were held in honour. When I was welcomed because I was an Australian I was not ashamed of it, and when I was welcomed as an Irishman I was quite proud of it also. Only once – and I have gone round the world and met as it were all the peoples of the earth – has anybody sought to put an indignity upon me and that was when I went aboard Destroyer D66. As I drove up Collins Street on Saturday last I could not help thinking of the contrast between the lonely ecclesiastical who, at the dead of night, was taken from the Baltic and put aboard a British destroyer with one companion (Fr. Vaughan) and the ecclesiastic who rode up Collins Street in triumph on Saturday last amidst the plaudits of better upholders of the Empire than the British Navy that captured me. I had long ago forgotten that incident, but I am reminded of it tonight. I have forgotten all about it, because the indignity the British Government sought to put upon me has long ago been wiped out by the sympathy of the whole world.

When I was leaving on my long trip to Europe – I spoke from this very platform – I promised two things. First of all, I promised to come back, and though I have been long about it, I have kept my word. I promised the Australian people, especially those who had lost sons or relatives at the war, that during my stay in Europe I would visit the graves of Australian fallen men. That promise I also kept. When I knelt over the graves of these brave Australian men – Catholics many of them, with names of Irish origin – I asked myself, why did these brave men face the dangers of the battlefield, and why was it that their bodies or their ashes were resting in foreign soil? We know why they went. We know they went for lofty motives – for the freedom of little nations. They went, as a returned solider in Sydney told us the other night, to fight for the little nations, and because they thought Ireland was amongst the little nations. This returned solider said that if they did not think that Ireland would be amongst the little nations to get freedom many of thousands of Australians would never have gone to the front. I should probably be prosecuted for saying that, but the statement is by a man who has a right to speak and who lost one of his arms in the battlefields of Europe. The answer to the question I asked over the graves of the Australian soldiers I got in the Sydney Town Hall the other night. I know that many of the Australian soldiers died in order that Ireland and other nations might be free, but Ireland is just where she was when they went to the war ('Shame!') However, I knelt at the graves and prayed for them. Others may have been false to their ideals, but these brave Australian soldiers fought for lofty motives and high ideals. They gave all that men could give, and they deserve all the honour that we can pay them in their graves. When I came back to Australia, what did I find? I found that many of the soldiers who returned - some without arms and maimed in many ways – are still roaming up and down Australia unprovided for ('Shame!') They are unprovided for by those who were very ready to send them away, and apparently who have very little welcome for them now that they have come back. It is the duty of us all to stand by these men, who did their duty as they saw it and who fought for the Empire. Though I am not a wealthy man, still if I can lay my hand upon £1000, I will put it into the loan that is being raised for returned soldiers.

My purpose in going to the other end of the world was not mainly to go to France or even to Ireland. It was my duty to go to Rome and give an account of my own stewardship to the Roman Pontiff. I bring back a message from Benedict XV to Australia. His Holiness is proud of the progress that the Church has made in this new land, and is delighted beyond measure to know of the splendid organisation that the Catholics of Australia at great sacrifice have set up. The Holy Father has hopes of a great future for the Catholic Church in Australia and now and always his benediction will rest upon Australia and upon all Australians.

When I was leaving London to return here I said that when I got back my tongue would be unloosed. Apparently, many people were very unwilling that I should get the opportunity of saying the things that they know well within their hearts need saying. When I made the statement in London I meant what I said. Now that I have come back, I repeat that if the occasion and opportunity arise my tongue will be unloosed, and I will make it my business to let the Australian people know the horrible tragedy through which Ireland passed in the last few years. I am not one of those to enter for any reason into a conspiracy of silence that some people like to set up here. I know a great deal what they do not want you to know, and if the occasion arises I will make it may business, as I think it will be my duty to tell you what I know. For the moment my tongue, instead of being loosed, is tied. We know that negotiations are going on between the representatives of England and Ireland, and we in Australia do not want to prejudice the negotiations by any word or act of ours. We hope for the best, and pray to God to give a happy issue to the negotiations. The truce that has been brought about now has come very late indeed. The Irish people were always ready for peace. We are inclined, perhaps, to forget, the fact that before a blow was struck in Ireland the Irish people were ready for peace, and instead of appealing to the sword or machine-guns, they appealed rather to the arbitration of the Peace Conference in Paris, showing thereby that the Irish people were did not want force, and were ready to state their case before the whole world and take the consequences. You know they got no hearing at the Peace Conference, and they have been driven by aggression and force into resistance of the invader.

You know what has been the result. At the end of last year Archbishop Clune, when in London endeavoured to bring about a truce and that it did not come about was not the fault of the Archbishop. Nor was it the fault of the Irish people. They were ready to enter into negotiations with anybody invested with authority to meet them, but they were told from London that nothing could be done, and they could not get a hearing. It was represented that they would be kept on the run until they laid down their arms: The Irish people by this time are too wise to lay down their arms before the end of the day. Hence it is that valuable Irish lives have been sacrificed. Now after months have passed and blood has been shed, and Archbishop Clune is back in Perth, a truce is brought about. The men who were told to lay down their arms have been brought over to London and taken into the counsels of the Empire. They were not even asked to take the oath of allegiance. De Valera, Michael Collins, Griffith and the rest might go to London to visit the King and his Ministers. I was the only outlaw apparently. I would ask you to remember that the Irish people were long ready for the truce which was brought about their own brave struggle on their native heath.

If the negotiations break down, the men who have struggled for Ireland's freedom are just as ready to do and dare and suffer as at the end of last year. It was very unlikely that they would listen to me in London, but if they had listened to me we might have had peace long ago. We certainly might have had a truce and negotiations If only Englishmen were prepared to do the straight and fair thing, and be consistent with their own principles, which they had enunciated in the war, we would have had peace long ago. I reminded the English people that Ireland was a nation, and that she had every right to self-determination. At the present moment even British politicians do not deny that statement. They admit that Ireland is a nation, with a right to self-determination but in the next breath they offer some strategical reasons, and endeavour to whittle down the freedom to which they admit Ireland is entitled. They would not listen to me, but they have listened to de Valera and the men of Ireland, who have sat at the same table as the representatives of England on a footing of absolute equality.

I told them at the beginning that aggression and force in Ireland would never subdue the Irish people. I repeat that statement tonight. In this evening's paper there is very grave, and perhaps alarming news but the negotiations are not yet broken off. If they are broken off I wish to repeat what I said in London that force will never subdue the Irish people. There may be a further wading through blood, but in the end, whether it be months or years, the English Government will have to negotiate with de

Valera, or whoever stands in his place. Even if force made for pretended peace in Ireland, it would never settle the Irish question. British rule is practically unknown in Ireland. The English Government pretended to be ruling Ireland but they were not even able to take a census of the Irish people. In London I told them that the Irish leaders were not a gang of murderers, and not a band of assassins but they would not listen to me. They said that the gang of murderers and band of assassins should be brought to book and that they would be rounded up before negotiations would be entered into with Ireland. But de Valera, Griffith and the rest of the Irish leaders were asked to confer with Mr. Lloyd George. If the negotiations are broken off, the Irish Leaders who were good enough and respectable enough to sit at the same table with the Prime Minister of England, will again be regarded as a gang of assassins. Instead of being a gang of assassins they are belligerents in the proper sense of the word. That fact will be ignored very soon by the vile daily press, but I feel sure that the Australian people will not forget that the Irish leaders were asked to go to London to negotiate for peace between England and Ireland, and sat with representatives on terms of equal footing.

The English representatives were very unwilling to meet them and explored every avenue but the right one. In different ways they failed, and they met with disastrous failure when they endeavoured to get the Roman Pontiff to take action. I told them they would fail in exploring these avenues, and I told them to get on the high road and meet de Valera and his companions, who are the representatives of the Irish people. We know now that Ireland has not been offered Dominion Home Rule, and we have that from De Valera's statement in the evening paper. De Valera, apparently, has asked that Ireland should not have to take an interest in Imperialistic enterprises and should not be called upon to pay for wars, successful or unsuccessful, that England might wage against the civilised or uncivilised world. The Irish leader makes it clear that Ireland has no Imperialistic ambitions, and wants to walk her own way. We know what the morning papers will say, but we can depend on President de Valera, who is an honest man. If the negotiations fail, Ireland will stood where she did before they began, Ireland stands by de Valera, and she will stand with him when he has parted company with Lloyd George. The Irish people trust de Valera, and have every confidence in him. There is a new spirit in Ireland which has been baptised and regenerated in the blood of 1916. The Irish people have set their hearts upon the self-determination and they will achieve their purpose in time. Ireland, I feel sure, will not be disappointed when she looks to America and Australia and the rest of the world for sympathy.

[His Grace concluded the speech by reading an extract from a letter he had received from de Valera on the eve of his departure for Australia. The Irish leader wrote: - "Please convey to the people of Australasia our appreciation of the sympathy and the aid they gave to us in our struggle for freedom. It will be a bond of friendship between the two nations which time will not destroy and no enemy can sunder".]

APPENDIX G

EAMON DE VALERA LETTER TO ARCHBISHOP MANNIX 6 NOVEMBER 1922[1]

Private

His Grace,
The Most Rev. Dr. Mannix,
Archbishop of Melbourne.

My dear Lord Archbishop:

Since this conflict began, I have often wished but had not the heart to write to you. Long explanations would have been necessary to meet the unrestricted volume of hostile press misrepresentation, and then every explanation would have appeared an excuse or an aspersion on other Irishmen.

I thought it better to risk a possible misunderstanding, and there has been nothing more cheering through all these months that the unerring instinct which enabled Your Grace to appreciate the situation truly, and to read correctly between the lines. I had hoped that Dr. O'Reilly would have shown a similar instinct at Paris, but his judgement there seems to have been warped by the atmosphere in which he suddenly found himself without any personal knowledge of any of us to guide him in sifting the true from the false. I still hope he will yet come to understand how he was misled.

The late Pronouncement of the Hierarchy here is most unfortunate. Never was charity of judgement so necessary, and apparently so disastrously absent. Ireland and the Church will, I fear, suffer in consequence. The Pope's recent pronouncement on Italian matters is in very marked contrast indeed.

---

[1] Eamon de Valera letter to Archbishop Daniel Mannix, 6 November, 1922 (UCD Archives: Eamon de Valera Papers, P150-2909).

Mr. Barton sent you some time ago, I am told, documents relating to the Peace Delegation. If you have received them, you are in possession of the circumstances prior to, and attending the signing of the Articles of Agreement and the presenting to us of the fait accompli. The tactics subsequently resorted to were still more unworthy and made inevitable the existing situation which, once the document was signed, could have been averted only by the most delicate tact and rigorous straight dealing.

I am convinced that the Free State Agreement must go. It has brought nothing but disaster so far, and promises nothing but disorder and chaos. It gives no hope whatever of ordered stable government. Human nature must be recast before those Irishmen and Irishwomen, who believe in the national right and the national destiny as in a religion, will consent to acquiesce in the selling of the national birthright for an ignoble mess of pottage, as they regard it. Think then of the prospects of a Government which can only exist by outlawing the most unselfishly patriotic citizens of the State. As Dr. O'Dwyer said, as long as grass grows or water runs, men and women will be found ready to dare and give their lives in the cause of Irish freedom, and will deem the sacrifice virtue and not sin. All these the Free State must now banish, or execute, or murder.

Party feeling is running rather too high now for calm dispassionate thinking, or for real statesmanship to have any opportunity. Still, despite the press which has invariably encouraged the coups that have been attempted, and with the I.R.B. most responsible for the present situation, the people everywhere, young and old, are beginning to realise that the only salvation for the nation now is a return to the old Sinn Féin principle of cleaving to their own institutions, whilst ignoring the authority and the institutions which the foreigner has tried to impose.

Before this reaches Your Grace many things will have happened to determine the future. I cannot but think of the hopes of this time a year ago – the almost certain prospect of a settlement which all could have accepted, or at least acquiesced in, leaving us a united nation with a future to be freely moulded under God by ourselves. It is sad, but chastening to realise how rudely they were all blasted within a month.

I crave Your Grace's blessing, and I assure you of the affection and esteem of all who are striving now that the way may not be closed for those who may be destined to complete the work towards which the hopes of the nation have been set definitely since Easter 1916.

I am,
My dear Lord Archbishop,
Very sincerely yours,
Eamon de Valera

P.S. I enclose you a letter from Mr. Barton to a friend, which will give you an idea of the plight of the prisoners.

APPENDIX H

WILLIAM T. COSGRAVE LETTER TO ARCHBISHOP MANNIX 17ᵀᴴ DECEMBER 1923[1]

My lord Archbishop,

I have hesitated to answer Your Grace's cablegrams addressed to me and supplied to the Press in Ireland and abroad regarding those persons whom the Irish Government have found it necessary in the interest of the public safety to detain in custody. I have also refrained from addressing Your Grace in regard to certain statements which have been attributed to you by the Australian Press and quoted in the papers here. In this I have been actuated by a desire to avoid the appearance of a controversy which might, in the then existing conditions of prison revolt here, have been calculated to embitter rather than to assuage feeling in the country. I had also cherished the hope that with the passage of time Your Grace would come into possession of more accurate information as to events in Ireland than the propagandist falsehoods which have been acciduously circulated by a group of malcontents and mischief-makers.

I have, however, decided that it is due to Your Grace as well as to the Government and the people of SaorStat Éireann that I should correct certain misapprehensions which appear to have influenced Your Grace's view upon current events in Ireland, and I will at the same time endeavour to indicate in general terms the Government policy in regard to those persons still in custody.

In order to prevent misunderstanding it may be well to review briefly the circumstances in which it became necessary for the Government to imprison upwards of 13,000 persons. Following the acceptance of the Treaty by Dáil Éireann in January 1922, a number of men holding officer rank in the Army with the connivance and the instigation of the minority representatives engaged in a conspiracy to prevent the majority decision

---

[1] William T. Cosgrave letter to Archbishop Daniel Mannix, 17 December 1923 (National Archives of Ireland/NAI, D/Taoiseach, S1369-13).

from being carried into effect. They organised mutiny in every locality in the country. They armed themselves in various methods. They acquired a large supply of munitions from the State by undertakings treacherously given at a time when their intentions were not manifest to be treacherously broken as soon as they thought they could do so with impunity. By collusion with the departing British armed forces they possessed themselves of further large quantities of arms and munitions with which to wage war upon their own people. They utilised funds subscribed by Irishmen abroad for humanitarian purposes to purchase weapons of offence, and they secured by various ruses and deceptions possession of barracks and strongholds in different parts of the country.

It was only the forbearance of the Government that prevented an outbreak of hostilities on several occasions during the period March to June 1922. Every possible step that could be taken to prevent recourse to arms was taken by the Government, but they were met by the steady determination that there would be no accommodation, that the people of Ireland would be compelled to swallow the view of the minority or else take the consequences. Every day brought its crop of robberies, murders, burnings, seizures of land and property, until the country was fast becoming a byword for outrage and crime.

The Government thus found itself compelled to take stern measures and demanded that the Four Courts, which had been seized and was being used as rebel headquarters, should be evacuated. This demand was refused and there was no option but to deal quickly and effectively with the situation thus created. It affords me no pleasure to recall at this period the number of men in arms against the Government exceeded 10,000, the vast majority of whom were far from being in evidence in the national struggle from which we had just emerged.

Your Grace will, doubtless, be aware that as soon as the National Army had succeeded in defeating these forces, their scattered remnants formed themselves into small bands and proceeded to burn the homes of peaceful citizens, to assassinate public representatives, to rob banks and post offices, to destroy roads and railways and generally to strike terror into the unarmed populace. Gradually these armed bands were rounded up by the troops and the list of crimes and outrages grew smaller. Many of the men at present in custody are known to have been guilty of arson or robbery – a number of them have indeed been tried and sentenced and some executed for their part in such outrages, but in the majority of cases, owing to the circumstances in which the crimes were committed and the general state of disorder, if would be difficult, if not impossible, to bring the guilt home to the actual culprit. The fact, however, remains that the crimes were committed, and to this the recent graves and ruined homes scattered throughout the country bear sad and silent testimony. The complicity of the prisoners in these crimes is clearly established by copies of reports and orders captured from time to time, many of which have been published.

The Government were at no time desirous of detaining in custody any prisoner against whom there was no definite charge, provided his release would not imperil the safety of the State. From the outset, any prisoner who was prepared to state that if released he would not take arms against the people's Government, and whose undertaking could be relied upon, was set at liberty. Numbers thus released violated their undertakings, and a few, who were subsequently recaptured under arms, suffered the death penalty.

When conditions began to revert to normal, the Government instituted a searching investigation into the cases of all the prisoners still in custody, with a view to the release of every prisoner who could with safety be allowed freedom. The result was that when the general hunger-strike was embarked upon the number of prisoners had been reduced to about 8,000 and the number of releases was increasing from day to day. The revolt of 7,600 prisoners, who refused to take food, had the effect of stopping all releases for a period of about three weeks, but notwithstanding this the number detained in custody will have been reduced to about 1,200 before the end of the present week.

The remainder, apart from the criminals against whom charges are pending, will be released as soon as considerations of public safety will admit, and in this connection the Government will be bound to keep continuously before their minds the state of order in different areas of the country. Any recrudescence of crime in areas to which large numbers of prisoners have returned will necessarily involve prolongation of the detention of the remainder, because the Government have no intention of allowing their people to be subjected to a renewal of the sufferings and destruction of the past eighteen months.

I should perhaps be omitting a very important and relevant fact in connection with the detention of prisoners, if I failed to inform Your Grace that the Government have over and over again offered to release the prisoners provided the arms and explosives which they and their associates without having secreted were handed over to the State. No response has been received to these offers.

I have observed with very sincere regret that on a few recent occasions Your Grace has been induced by misleading and inaccurate information to give publicity to statements which are calculated to produce an impression entirely contrary to fact. The "Irish Independent" of 23rd October last, quoting from the "Catholic Press" of Australia, attributes to Your Grace the following statement: -

> "If they took these 63 men who have been returned to support the Free State and put opposite them all those on the opposite side, they would find 90 in that camp against 63 to support the Free State Government".

Your Grace will perhaps permit me to say that the implication contained in this statement that the 15 Farmer deputies, the 14 Labour deputies and the 14 Independents returned at the Election were associated with the 44 soi-distant Republicans in their hostility to the Free State is one which is an absolute perversion of fact and which will be very strongly resented by the gentlemen in question. So far from this being the case, there are very few, if indeed there is a single one, of those deputies who, in their Election Addresses and in their speeches, have not definitely and repeatedly declared their adherence to the Treaty and their very definite disapproval and reprobation of the tactics of the irregulars. The best possible proof of their sincerity in this regard may be found in the fact that the Government have met the Parliament of the country in Session and continues to enjoy its confidence.

My attention has also been drawn to a further utterance by Your Grace quoted in the "Irish Independent" of 6th December, again on the authority of the "Catholic Press". It runs as follows:-

> "Not long ago a Bill in regard to the Mercantile Marine had been prepared by the Free State Cabinet, who, before submitting it to the Irish Parliament, sent it privately and surreptitiously for the approval or otherwise of certain people in London. A reply was received that the proposal was not in accordance with the customs of any other part of the Empire, and that there was no reason for its adoption. No the matter was quietly dropped without giving the Irish Parliament an opportunity to decide whether its provisions were in the best interests of Ireland."

I take it that Your Grace's remarks are based upon a bogus Despatch which was printed in an Irregular sheet called "Éire" early in August 1923 and quoted in the "Belfast Newsletter" of August 10. The facts are that no such projected measure of legislation was ever drafted, that it could not therefore have been submitted for the approval of certain people in London either surreptitiously or otherwise, and that naturally no such reply was received. It is unfortunate that while the original lie was brought to Your Grace's notice, the categorical and detailed repudiation issued by the Government on 14th August did not meet Your Grace's eye. If it had it would have prevented the publication on Your Grace's authority of a statement which is absolutely without foundation and which is calculated to mislead those of our friends and people abroad who, in the absence of reliable information, may be led by the high authority on which, unwittingly no doubt, the falsehood is propagated, to accept it without further enquiry as a correct exposition of the measure of Ireland's present status.

The source from which this falsehood emanated is exactly the same source which produced the heart-rending description of the conditions under which Irish prisoners were being detained by the Irish Government, and these descriptions contained just as much truth and just as much falsehood as the references to the bogus despatch. Fortunately, the statements regarding the prison conditions were subjected to examination by an independent investigator detailed by the International Committee of the Red Cross and his report upon his visit to the camps and prisons is available to all who desire to obtain accurate information in the matter. He expressed himself satisfied that the treatment accorded to these prisoners so far from contravening international humanitarian conventions was very much better that that usually accorded to prisoners of war.

I have written to Your Grace at great length, and if I have appeared unduly severe upon those who have spent their energies from March of last year in directing a campaign of destruction against their own people, I pray Your Grace to believe that I do so only because it is clear from Your Grace's utterances that the truth regarding events in Ireland has not yet covered the seven thousand miles which lie between us.

Neither my colleagues nor myself desire, or have at any time to desired, to do or say anything which could tend to prevent those of our misguided fellow countrymen who have attempted to set themselves up as the dictators of the Irish nation from renouncing their destructive policy and undertaking the duties and responsibilities of citizenship. May I venture to express the hope that our task will not be rendered more difficult by injudicious and inaccurate pronouncements, however, well-intentioned, circulated amongst those of our far-flung race whose distance from their native land makes it impossible for them to receive correct impressions of the day to day happenings here.

I remain,

Your Grace's obedient servant,

W. T. Cosgrave

APPENDIX I

KILLARNEY URBAN DISTRICT COUNCIL ADDRESS TO HIS GRACE THE MOST REV. DANIEL MANNIX D.D ARCHBISHOP OF MELBOURNE ON THE OCCASION OF HIS VISIT TO KILLARNEY, 1ST JULY 1925[1]

May it please Your Grace.

We, the Urban District Council of Killarney extend our heartiest welcome to your Grace and to your fellow pilgrims on your visit to Killarney.

We trust that you and they will fully enjoy the beautiful scenery with which God has so bountifully endowed our district.

We avail of this occasion to express to your Grace our feelings of warm affection and profound respect, and our pride that in you our Race has found so worthy a representative amongst the peoples of the Australian Commonwealth, a community small as yet in numbers, but destined to become in God's Providence, with the progress of the years, a mighty power amongst the Nations of the world. In the growth of that community in all the Arts that refine and elevate humanity the influence of our Irish race is bound to play a great and beneficial part.

What a happiness to us at home to know that the development of that influence will be safely and surely guided in its proper course by the wisdom, the prudence and the courage that have from the earliest years of your public life marked and characterised your whole career.

The promise of Maynooth is being brilliantly fulfilled in the larger sphere of Melbourne. The vast extension of great public institutions, religious, educational and social, since you assumed the governance of that great archdiocese are a proof of the vivifying impulse of your personality.

---

[1] Killarney Urban District Council, *To His Grace The Most Rev. Daniel Mannix D.D Archbishop of Melbourne on the occasion of his visit to Killarney 1st July 1925* (Killarney, 1925).

We in Ireland who know what alien and class oppression have been to ourselves watched with high gratification and approval your unyielding and successful attitude in vindication of the rights of labour and of the citizen against hostile and powerful interests. We wish your Grace a happy visit to your native land, and on your return many years of continued fruitful service to the cause of humanity and of God.

Signed on behalf of the Council.

Eugene O'Sullivan – Chairman

John Langford – Acting Clerk

BIBLIOGRAPHY

Primary Sources

Private and Unpublished Papers

Archbishop William Walsh Papers, Dublin Diocesan Archives
Éamon de Valera Papers, University College Dublin
Leonard Collection, Glucksman Library, University of Limerick
Limerick City Museum, Archbishop Mannix files
Maynooth College Archives, St Patrick's College Maynooth
Msgr. John Hagan Papers, Irish College Rome

Government Papers

Houses of the Oireachtas
    Dáil Éireann Debates
Killarney Urban District Council
    Council Minutes
National Archives of Ireland
    Department of Foreign Affairs
    Department of the Taoiseach
National Archives of the UK
    CommonWealth Office Records

Oral Histories

Interview with Mrs Patricia Wallis – McCombe (8 March, 2010).

Audio Histories

Macardle, Gerry, Turbulent Priest, (RTÉ drama documentary, 1989).
'The Riddle of Father Hackett', *Late Night Live,* 10 Sept. 2009 (ABC Australia).

Visual Histories

Archbishop Daniel Mannix in an interview with Gerald Lyons (29 Dec. 1961, ABC Archives)
George Morrison, 'Mise Éire' (Gael Linn, 1959).

Newspapers and Periodicals

Irish Independent
The Advocate
The Boston Herald
The Corkman
The Irish Times
The Irish World and American Industrial Liberator and Gaelic American
The Kerry News
The Monitor New Jersey
The New York Times
The Standard Newspaper
The Times
The West Australian
Western Australian Record

Published autobiographies and memoirs

De Valera, Terry, *A Memoir* (Dublin: Currach Press, 2004).
Fr E. J McCarthy Regional Director of Columban Fathers USA Memoirs
Healy, T. M, *Letters and Leaders of My Day* (London: T. Butterworth, 1928).
O'Leary, John, *Recollections of Fenians and Fenianism Volume I* (Shannon: Irish University Press, 1968).
Santamaria, B. A., *Santamaria: A Memoir* (Melbourne: Oxford University Press, 1997)

Other contemporary sources

Coates, Tim, *The Irish Uprising, 1914-1921: papers from the British Parliamentary Archive* (London: Tim Coates, 2000).
Collins English dictionary 3rd edition, (Glasgow: HarperCollins Ltd., 1991). © (1991).
Daniel Mannix – a grandson of Croom' in *Crom Abú*, (5) 1984, pp 12-13.

Griffin, James, 'Revisionism or Reality? Daniel Mannix in ADB 10', in *Irish-Australian Studies: Papers delivered at the Eighth Irish-Australian Conference Hobart* (Sydney: Crossing Press, 1995), pp 133-145.

President Mary Robinson address to Joint Sitting of the Houses of the Oireachtas, 2 February 1995. (http://www.oireachtas.ie/viewdoc.asp?fn=/documents/addresses/2Feb 1995.htm)

Report by Commission of Investigation into Catholic Archdiocese of Dublin (http://www.justice.ie/en/JELR/Pages/PB09000504).

T. P Boland, *The Ascent of Tabor: Writing the Life of Archbishop Duhig* (Queensland, 1986) Aquanius Memorial Lecture, pp 2-17.

Secondary Sources

Books and journal articles

Aan de Wiel, Jerome, *The Catholic Church in Ireland 1914-1918: War and Politics* (Dublin: Irish Academic Press, 2003).

Adams, Rebecca G. and Graham Allan, 'Contextualising friendship' in Adams & Allan (eds.) *Placing Friendship in Context* (Cambridge: Cambridge University Press, 1998), pp 1-17.

Akenson, Donald Harman, *The Irish Diaspora: A Primer* (Belfast: The Institute of Irish Studies, 1994).

Allan, Graham, 'Friendship and the private sphere' in Adams & Allan (eds.) *Placing Friendship in Context* (Cambridge: Cambridge University Press, 1998), pp 71-91.

—. *Friendship: Developing A Sociological Perspective* (Hemel Hempstead: Westview Press, 1989)

Biletz, Frank A., 'The Irish Peasant and the Conflict between Irish Ireland and the Catholic Bishops 1903-1910' in Stewart J. Brown & David W. Miller (eds.) *Piety and Power in Ireland, 1760-1960 : essays in honour of Emmet Larkin* (Belfast: University of Notre Dame Press, 2000), pp 108-129.

Boland, T. P., *James Duhig* (Saint Lucia: University of Queensland Press, 1986).

Boyce, D George & Alan O'Day, '"Revisionism and the "revisionist controversy"' in D. George Boyce and Alan O'Day *The Making of Modern Irish History.* (London: Routledge, 1996) pp 1-14.

Brennan, Niall, *Dr. Mannix* (Adelaide: Rigby, 1964).

Broderick, Joe, 'De Valera and Archbishop Daniel Mannix', in *History Ireland*, 2 (3) 1994, pp 37-42.

Buckley, Vincent, *Cutting the Green Hay - friendships, movements and cultural conflict in Australia's great decades* (Victoria: Penguin Books, 1983).

Byran, Cyril, *Archbishop Mannix: Champion of Australian Democracy* (Melbourne: The Advocate Press, 1918).

Campion, Edmund, *Australian Catholics: The Contribution of Catholics to the Development of Australian Society* (Ringwood: Penguin Books Australia, 1988).

Canetti, Elias, *Crowds and Power* (Hamburg: Classen, 1960).

Chavasse, Moirin, *Terence MacSwiney* (Dublin: Clonmore & Reynolds; Burns & Oates, 1961).

Clear, Caitriona, *Social Change and Everyday life in Ireland, 1850-1922* (Manchester: Manchester University Press, 2007).

Collins, Kevin, *Catholic Churchmen and the Celtic Revival in Ireland 1848-1916* (Dublin: Four Courts Press, 2002).

Coogan, Tim Pat, *De Valera: Long Fellow: Long Shadow* (London: Hutchinson, 1993).

Cooney, John, *John Charles McQuaid: Ruler of Catholic Ireland* (Dublin: O'Brien Press Ltd., 1999).

—. *The Crozier & The Dáil: Church & State 1922-86* (Dublin: The Mercier Press Ltd., 1986).

Corish, Patrick, *The Irish Catholic Experience: A Historical Survey* (Dublin: Gill & Macmillan, 1985).

Corkery, Daniel, *Synge and Anglo-Irish Literature: A Study* (Cork: Cork University Press, 1931).

Davis, Graham, 'The Historiography of the Irish Famine' in Patrick O'Sullivan (ed.) *The Irish World Wide: History, Heritage, Identity, Volume Six: The Meaning of the Famine* (Leicester: Leicester University Press, 1997), pp 15-39.

Donnelly Jr., James S., 'The Land Question in Nationalist Politics' in Thomas E. Hachey and Lawrence J. McCaffrey (eds.) *Perspectives on Irish Nationalism* (Kentucky: University Press of Kentucky, 1989), pp 79-98.

Duck, Steve, *Human Relationships* (London: Sage Publications, 1998).

Duncan, Bruce, *Crusade or Conspiracy? Catholics and the anti-communist struggle in Australia* (Sydney: University of New South Wales Press, 2001).

—. *The Church's Social Teaching: From Rerum Novarum to 1931* (Melbourne: CollinsDove, 1991).

Dwyer, T. Ryle, *Eamon de Valera: The Man & The Myths* (Dublin: Paperview/Irish Independent, 2006).

—. *Eamon de Valera (Gill's Irish Lives)* (Dublin: Gill & Macmillan, 1980).

Ebsworth, Rev. Walter, *Archbishop Mannix* (Armadale, Vic.: H. H. Stephenson, 1977).

Edwards, Ruth Dudley, *Patrick Pearse: The Triumph of Failure* (Dublin: Irish Academic Press Ltd., 2006).

Evans, Richard J., *In Defence of History* (London: Granta Books, 1997).

Fallon, Charlotte, 'Civil War Hungerstrikes: Women and Men' in *Éire-Ireland*, 22 (3), pp 75-92.

Fanning, Ronan, 'Patrick Corish's "Maynooth"' in *The Furrow* 46 (12), pp 703-707.

Ferriter, Diarmuid, *Judging Dev* (Dublin: Royal Irish Academy, 2007).

—. *The Transformation of Ireland 1900-2000* (London: Profile Books, 2005).

Fitzgibbon, Constantine & George Morrison, *The Life and Times of Eamon de Valera* (Dublin: Gill & Macmillan, 1973).

Fitzpatrick, David, 'The Settlers: Immigration from Ireland in the Nineteenth Century' in Colm Kiernan (ed.) *Ireland and Australia* (Cork: The Mercier Press Ltd., 1984), pp 23-33.

Foster, R. F. *Modern Ireland 1600-1972* (London: Allen Lane, 1989 c1988).

Fleischmann, Ruth, *Catholic Nationalism in the Irish Revival: A Study of Canon Sheehan, 1852-1913* (New York: St Martin's Press, 1997).

Gallagher, Tom, 'Fianna Fáil and Partition 1926-1984' in *Éire-Ireland*, 20 (1) 1985, pp 28-56.

Gannon, P. J. 'The Ethical Aspect of the Hunger Strike' in *Studies: An Irish Quarterly Review*, 9 (35) 1920, pp 448-454.

Gilchrist, Michael, *Daniel Mannix: Wit and Wisdom* (Melbourne: IHS Press, 2nd ed., 2005).

Griffin, James, 'Archbishop Daniel Mannix' in *The Old Limerick Journal*, 27 (1990), pp 27-34.

—. 'Daniel Mannix and the Cult of Personality' in O. MacDonagh and W. Mandle (eds.) *Ireland and Irish-Australia: Studies in Cultural and Political History* (London: Croom Helm, 1986), pp 95-118.

Hachey, Thomas E., 'The Quarantine of Archbishop Mannix: A British Preventive Policy during the Anglo-Irish Troubles' in *Irish University Review*, 1 (1) 1990, pp 111-130.

Hannigan, Dave, *De Valera in America: The Rebel President's 1919 Campaign* (Dublin: O'Brien Press Ltd., 2008).

Hook, Sidney, *The Hero in History: A Study in Limitation and Possibility* (New York: Transaction Publishers, 1943).

Hopkinson, M., *The War of Independence* (Dublin: Gill & Macmillan, 2002).

Jordan, Anthony J., *Seán MacBride: A Biography* (Dublin: Blackwater Press, 1993).

Keogh, Dermot, *Ireland and the Vatican: The Politics and Diplomacy of Church-State Relations, 1922-1960* (Cork: Cork University Press, 1995)

—. 'Mannix, De Valera and Irish Nationalism', in John B. O'Brien and Pauric Travers (eds.) *The Irish Emigrant Experience in Australia* (Dublin: Poolbeg, 1991), pp 196-225.

—. 'The catholic church and the Irish Free State 1923-1932' in *History Ireland*, 2 (1) 1994, pp 47-51.

—. *The Vatican, the Bishops and Irish Politics 1919-1939* (Cambridge: Cambridge University Press, 1986).

—. *Twentieth Century Ireland: Nation and State* (New York: St. Martin's Press, 1995).

Kiberd, Declan, *Inventing Ireland: The Literature of the Modern Nation* (London: Jonathan Cape, 1995).

—. 'The Elephant of Revolutionary Forgetfulness' in Máirín Ní Dhonnchadha and Theo Dorgan (eds.) *Revising the Rising.* (Derry: Field Day, 1991), pp 1-21.

Kiernan Colm, 'Appréciation Archbishop Daniel Mannix of Melbourne, 1864-1963' in *Éire-Ireland*, 19 (3) 1984, pp 121-130.

—. *Daniel Mannix and Ireland* (Morwell, Victoria: Alella Books, 1984).

Lanier, S. C., 'It is New-Strung and Shan't be Heard': Nationalism and Memory in the Irish Harp Tradition' in *British Journal of Ethnomusicology*, 8 (1) 1999, pp 1-26.

Lee, Joseph, *The Modernisation of Irish Society 1848-1918* (Dublin: Gill & Macmillan, 2008).

Lee, J. J., *Ireland 1912-1985 Politics and Society* (Cambridge: Cambridge University Press, 1989).

MacDonagh, Oliver, 'The Irish in Australia: A General View' in Oliver MacDonagh and W.F. Mandle (eds.) *Ireland and Irish-Australia: Studies in Cultural and Political History* (London: Croom Helm, 1986), pp 155-174.

MacLysaht, Edward, *The Surnames of Ireland* (Dublin: Irish Academic Press Ltd., 1973).

MacNeill, Major General Hugh, 'Na Fianna Éireann: Senior Corps of the Old Army' in Terence O'Reilly (ed.) *Our Struggle for Independence*:

Lessons from the pages of 'An Cosantóir' (Cork: The Mercier Press Ltd., 2009), pp 172-185.

McBride, Ian, 'Memory and identity in modern Ireland' in Ian McBride (ed.) *History and Memory in Modern Ireland*. (Cambridge: Cambridge University Press, 2001), pp 1-42.

McCaffrey, Lawrence J., 'Components of Irish Nationalism' in Thomas E. Hachey and Lawrence J. McCaffrey (eds.) *Perspectives on Irish Nationalism* (Kentucky: University Press of Kentucky, 1989), pp 1-19.

McCartney, Dr. Donal, 'From Parnell to Pearse (1891-1921)' in F. X. Martin & T. W. Moody (eds.), *The Course of Irish History* (Cork: The Mercier Press Ltd., 1984), pp 294-312.

McCartney, Donal, 'De Valera's Mission to the United States 1919-20', in Art Cosgrave and D. McCartney (eds.), *Studies in Irish History* (Naas: : Leinster Leader, 1979), pp 304-323.

McDonald, Walter, *Reminiscences of a Maynooth Professor* (Cork: The Mercier Press Ltd., 1967).

McGovern, J. J. & P. J. O'Farrell, 'Australia' in P. J. Cornish (ed.), *A History of Irish Catholicism* (Dublin, Gill & Macmillan, 1971), vol. 6, part 6, pp 1-76.

McInerney, Michael, 'Eamon De Valera: 1882-1975: Controversial giant of modern Ireland' in Peter O'Mahoney (ed.), *Eamon De Valera: A Survey in text and pictures by the Irish Times of the Life and Influence of a Famous Leader* (Dublin: The Irish Times, 1976), pp 5-24.

Mannix, Dr. Daniel, *Speeches of His Grace Most Rev. Dr. Mannix, Archbishop of Melbourne in the Rotunda, Dublin, October 22nd and 29th, 1925* (Dublin: Mellifont Press, 1925]).

Miller, David W., *Church, State and Nation in Ireland, 1898-1921* (Dublin: Gill & Macmillan, 1973).

Mitchell Joan Towey, 'Yeats, Pearse and Cuchulain' in *Éire-Ireland*, 11 (4) 1976, pp 51-65.

Moody, T. W. & F.X. Martin (eds.), *The Course of Irish History* (Cork: The Mercier Press Ltd., 1967).

Murray, Patrick, 'Obsessive historian: Eamon de Valera and the policing of his reputation' in *Proceedings of the Royal Irish Academy,* section c, 101:2 (2001) pp 37-65.

—. *Oracles of God: The Roman Catholic Church and Irish Politics, 1922-37* (Dublin: Dublin University Press, 2000).

Murphy, Daniel J., *A History of Irish Emigrant and Missionary Education* (Dublin: Four Courts Press, 2000).

Murphy, Frank, 'A great Irish Archbishop' in *The Capuchin Annual* (1965), pp 90-107.

—. *Daniel Mannix: Archbishop of Melbourne 1917-1963* (Melbourne: Advocate Press, 1948).

—. *Daniel Mannix: Archbishop of Melbourne 1917-1963* (2nd ed., Melbourne: The Polding Press, 1972).

Murphy, John A., *Ireland in the Twentieth Century* (Dublin: Gill & Macmillan, 1975).

—. 'Priests and People in Modern Irish History' in *Christus Rex: Journal of Sociology*, 23 (1969), pp 235-259.

—. 'The Achievement of de Valera' in *De Valera and His Times* by J. P O'Carroll & John A. Murphy (eds.) (Cork: Cork University Press, 1983), pp 1-16.

Murtagh, James G., *Australia: The Catholic Chapter* (New York: Sheed and Ward, 1946).

Newman, Jeremiah, *Maynooth and Victorian Ireland* (Galway: Kenny's Books, 1983).

Newsinger, John, "I Bring Not Peace but a Sword": 'The Religious Motif in the Irish War of Independence' in *Journal of Contemporary History*, 13 (3) 1978, pp 609-628.

Niall Brenda, *The Riddle of Father Hackett – A life in Ireland and Australia* (Canberra: National Library of Australia, 2009).

Nunan, Seán, 'President Éamon de Valera's Mission to the United States of America 1919-1920' in *The Capuchin Annual* (1970), pp 236-249. (© Capuchin Provincial Archive, Dublin, Ireland).

O'Briain, Cearbhall, *Dr. Mannix in Australia: the brief story of seven strenuous years under the Southern Cross* (Dublin, 191-?).

O'Brien, John B., *Daniel Mannix: Builder of the Australian Church* (Dublin: Vertias, 1988).

—. 'The British Government and Archbishop Daniel Mannix' in *Journal of the Cork Historical & Archaeological Society*, 93 (1988), pp 55-58.

Ó Broin, Leon, 'The Gaelic League and the Chair of Irish in Maynooth' in *Studies: An Irish Quarterly Review*, 52 (208) 1963, pp 348-362.

O'Farrell, Patrick, 'De Valera in Australia: 1948' in *The Old Limerick Journal*, 23 (1988), pp 180-183.

—. ©O'Farrell, Patrick, *The Irish in Australia* (Kensington NSW: New South Wales University Press, 1987).

—. *The Irish in Australia: 1788 to the present* (Cork: Cork University Press, 2001)

Ó Fiaich, Tomás, 'The Catholic Clergy and the Independence Movement' in *The Capuchin Annual* (1970), pp 480-502.

Ó Lúing, Seán, *John Devoy* (Báile Átha Cliath: Cló Morainn, 1961).

O'Riordan, Ted, 'Great men we have given to history' in *Charleville and district Historical Journal*, 2 (1987), pp 54-83.

O'Sheehan, John, *Archbishop Mannix: A Sketch of His Life and Work* (Dublin: Emton Press, n-d.).

O'Sullivan, Michael, *Mary Robinson: the life and times of an Irish Liberal* (Dublin: Blackwater Press, 1993).

Pahl, Ray, *On Friendship* (Cambridge: Polity Books, 2000).

Pakenham, Frank Earl of Longford & Thomas P. O'Neill, *Eamon de Valera* (London: Hutchinson, 1970).

Paseta, Senia, *Before the Revolution: nationalism, social change and Ireland's Catholic elite, 1879-1922* (Cork: Cork University Press, 1999).

Rafferty, Oliver J., 'The Catholic Bishops and Revolutionary Ireland: Some 19th and 20th Century Comparisons' in *Studies: An Irish Quarterly Review*, 83 (329) 1994, pp 30-42.

Santamaria, B. A., *Archbishop Mannix: His Contribution to the Art of Public Leadership in Australia* (Melbourne: Melbourne University Publishing, 1978).

—. *Daniel Mannix: A Biography* (Melbourne: Melbourne University Publishing, 1984).

Sullivan, Dennis M., 'Éamon de Valera and the Forces of Opposition in America, 1919-1920' in *Éire-Ireland* 19 (2) 1984, pp 99-115.

Sweeney, George, 'Irish Hunger Strikes and the Cult of Self-Sacrifice', in *Journal of Contemporary History*, 28 (1993), pp 421-437.

Sweetman, Rory, *Bishop in the Dock: The Sedition Trial of James Liston* (Auckland: Auckland University Press, 1997)

Tanner, Marcus, *Irelands Holy Wars: The Struggle for a Nation's Soul 1500-2000* (New Haven, London: Yale University Press, 2003).

Tierney, Mark, *Ireland Since 1870* (Dublin: CJ Fallon, 1998).

Turi, John J., *England's Greatest Spy – Eamon de Valera* (London: Stacey International, 2009).

Vaughan, Fr. Arthur, 'The Vaughan Letter' in *Footprints: Quarterly Journal of the Melbourne Historical Commission*, 1 (8) 1972, pp 13-24.

Walker, Graham, 'Propaganda and Conservative Nationalism during the Irish Civil War, 1922-1923' in *Éire-Ireland*, 22 (4) 1987, pp 93-117.

Whyte, J. H., *Church & State in Modern Ireland 1923-1970* (Dublin: Gill & Macmillan, 1971).

Whyte, J. H., 'The Influence of the Catholic Clergy on Elections in Nineteenth Century Ireland' in *The English Historical Review*, 75 (295) 1960, pp 239-259.

Unpublished theses

Murray, Patrick, 'Voices of De Valera,' unpublished M. Litt. Thesis, Trinity College Dublin, 1995).

—. 'The Political Involvement of the Roman Catholic Clergy in Ireland 1922-37,' unpublished PhD. Thesis, Trinity College Dublin, 1998).

INDEX